THE

Pope

MEETS THE

Ayatollah

AN INTRODUCTION TO
SHI`A ISLAM

Hassan al-Hakeem & Jalal Moughania

THE
MAINSTAY
FOUNDATION

Title: The Pope Meets the Ayatollah: An Introduction to Shi'a Islam

Authors: Hassan al-Hakeem & Jalal Moughania

© 2021 The Mainstay Foundation

ISBN: 978-1943393121 (paperback); 978-1943393138 (hardcover)

"For they are of two kinds, either your brother in faith
or your equal in creation."

Imam Ali

CONTENTS

NOTE ON USAGE AND SPELLING

We have chosen to standardize usage and spelling in a manner that should be accessible to most readers.

Words that are commonly used in the English language or are defined in a standard English dictionary are used in their common spelling (e.g. Mecca, not Makkah). This applies to some commonly used given names (e.g. Ali, not ʿAli). This is also specifically applied to the word Shiʿa (not Shiʿah).

Diacritical marks have been omitted, except for the *hamza* (ʾ) and the *ʿayn* (ʿ). We have used the IJMES transliteration system, with some notable deviations. For the ninth Arabic letter *thal*, we have opted to use th (like the th in *that*). The Arabic *ta marbutah* is rendered *ah* if it is not in the Arabic *idafah* construction. If it is in an *idafah* construction, it is rendered *at* except where it is part of a given name.

All words are rendered in their *marfuʿ* state where possible (e.g. Ali ibn Abu Talib, not Ali ibn Abi Talib).

Elision are rendered only if the elided letter is preceded by a *harf ʿillah* (e.g. Thuʾl-Hijjah). A notable exception is found in all given names beginning in *ʿAbd*, which are always elided with the succeeding name (i.e. ʿAbdulmalik, not ʿAbd al-Malik).

The reader should note that the supplication of *salawat* (may God send his peace and blessings upon Muhammad and the household of Muhammad) and salutations (peace be upon them) are usually recited at the mention of the Holy Prophet and his family. This is normally marked in elaborate calligraphy in Arabic text, or with (s), (a), or a similar mark in English text. Such marks do not appear in this book so as not to disturb the flow of the reader. At times, we have also dropped the title of some important religious and historical figures. For example, we refer sometimes to Ali rather than Imam Ali. Again, the intent in these instances is to maintain the flow of the book. These decisions in no way are meant to disregard the status and reverence of these individuals.

Finally, we relied on the translation of Ali Quli Qara'i when citing to the verses of the Holy Quran throughout this book, with minor adaptations that allowed us to weave the verses more properly with the rest of the work.

FOREWORD

In the Name of God, the All-beneficent, the All-merciful.

Peace and blessings on the Holy Prophet Muhammad and his pure family.

The scholarly value of this book – which The Mainstay Foundation has worked diligently to accomplish –is evident in its discussion of the foundational pillars of the structure of the Jaʿfari school of thought (Shiʿism). Their approach is academic and keeps pace with contemporary scientific methods. These foundational pillars are:

First, the philosophy of religion in its three axes:

(a) The purpose of religion.

(b) The interactive relationship between knowledge and faith. This relationship allows for building mankind and developing our role in utilizing the universe and its energies in order to construct a just cosmic civilization. This is expressed by the Holy Quran, which states that God created man to be His vicegerent.

(c) The need for religion at the level of the psychological structure of the person, the regularity of social life, and the achievement of a link between the physical and metaphysical realms.

Second, the practical manifestations of the organic hierarchical relationship between faith's foundational and vital concepts – namely, *tawhid*, *nubuwwah*, and *Imamah*. These three concepts cannot be separated. Nor can we imagine that the objectives of monotheism, prophethood, and divine leadership (in its knowledge and infallibility), can be rooted in a society without a proper understanding of their interdependence. They are the root to building a civilization built on justice, dignity, and brotherhood. This is a heavenly objective visible in Abrahamic, Pentateuchal, Biblical, and Quranic traditions.

Third, the importance of ethical values and the highest human ideals that were evident in the personalities of the Imams from the household of the Holy Prophet. They are the only starting point for developing an integrated and coherent system for meaningful community relations within the four spheres of identity. The right approach must achieve balance between relationships and protect each type from devolving, thus protecting the peculiarities that serve the preservation of full and true faith. The first and smallest sphere is the brotherhood of faith based on Alid devotion and Husayni spirit. The second sphere is the brotherhood of Islam, which is comprehensive of the various sects and based on the principle of one nation calling unto good and adopting reform through enjoining virtue. The third sphere encompasses all religions which rely on devotion to the divine and bearing the responsibility of the heavenly message in this world. The last and largest circle is that of humanity, which cannot achieve a stable life without the ideals of the Quran, Holy Prophet, and Imam Ali (encompassed in the wisdoms of Imam Ali and the Treatise on Rights). They comprise the principles of dignity, social peace, and good citizenship based on integration and coexistence in societies and countries. They impart the spirit of dialogue, social stability, and generosity which support the harmony of people and strengthen the cohesion of the human civilization.

Fourth, explaining the role of the immaculate Imams in spreading and protecting Prophet Muhammad's message. They guard the faith against distortion and root it in the community of the faithful. They do so through the following roles:

(a) The foundational role concerned with the interpretation of the Quran and explanation of the Prophet's hadith, as well as their preservation and maintenance. This includes the development of an integrated epistemic system in the fields of theology, legislation, ethics, and universal and general human knowledge.

(b) The spiritual role that aims to refine the human spirit, satisfy its basic needs, and address the root sources of its imbalance. They do so with an approach that is charming, delicate, and transparent that creates harmony and balance – between the soul's relationship with the physical and metaphysical worlds, and between reason and desire. This is evident in the overwhelming amount of devotional heritage, supplications, and prayers (such as those found in the prayerbooks of Imam al-Sajjad, Imam al-Sadiq, and Imam al-Rida), as well as their spiritual directives, and their embodiment of an impeccable ethic.

(c) The inspirational role most evident in their encouragement of Husayni rituals, rites of worship, and the affirmation of the brotherhood of faith through gatherings and commemorations, as well as through construction, visitation, and gathering at the holy shrines.

(d) The political role represented in their maintaining relations with legislative entities and defining positions on public matter. They diagnose the objective conditions of their time, which may require silence, divulgence, or demonstration of the rightful guardianship of the immaculate Imam or his representative.

(e) The custodial role exemplified in the long-term planning of the immaculates. They sought to preserve the community of believers in the era of their presence as well as the era of their occultation. They strived to connect their followers with scholars that can be trusted to safeguard the commands and prohibitions of God in the spheres of jurisprudence, society, and rites and rituals.

Fifth, the importance of the Promised Day of al-Mahdi's leadership. The necessity of this is seen from several angles:

(a) The necessity of accomplishing the divine mandate of establishing a cosmic civilization that relies on justice, dignity, and brotherhood.

(b) The necessity for divine messages to be implemented in their shared and celebrated similarities, such as establishing and fostering faith in human society.

(c) The importance of exemplifying the wisdom of Islamic teachings, especially those which circumstances have not allowed for their exemplification.

(d) The necessity of the rule of law and the prevalence of love. All nations must come to live in harmony. Injustice, poverty, and ignorance must be erased from all societies. This can only be achieved through true leadership which is rooted in knowledge and immaculacy, thus ensuring the continuity of civilization in prosperity and justice.

Sixth, the importance of the position of marjiʿiyyah, which embodies the message of the Holy Prophet and his pure household, through its intellectual weight and wise foresight. This can be seen in the chronology of Shiʿa leadership and its legitimate transfer through the ages. During the minor occultation, this was through the Imam's appointment of his representative. In this era, the time of the major occultation, this is seen in the procession of marjiʿiyyah from the time of al-Mufid, to al-Murtada, al-Tusi, al-Muhaqqiq al-Hilli, al-ʿAllamah al-Hilli, Sahib al-Jawahir, al-Murtada al-Ansari, al-Mujaddid al-Shirazi, al-Yazdi, al-Asfahani, al-Hakeem, and al-Burujurdi. This brings us to our contemporary times, where we clearly see the integrity of the marjiʿiyyah and its distance from material temptations and false titles. This history's great heritage and scientific accomplishments can be observed in the multitude of seminaries throughout the globe. These institutions have protected the message of divine legislation by its adamant emphasis that the role of fatwa is reserved to those highest in knowledge and piety. They have preserved the heritage of the Ahl al-Bayt through books and schools, as well as their constant struggle in support of Muslim communities and oppressed minorities everywhere. The marji'iyyah has served as the protector of Islam and all that it holds sacred through its famous fatwas, as well as its emphasis on global peace in its stances and statements. It has spread the message of harmony amongst nations, respect and coexistence amongst faiths, and rejection of sectarian conflicts. It has stood side by side with other sects and faith in the most pivotal of circumstances.

For all this and more, this is a valuable book that deserves the reader's keen attention.

And praise be to God, Lord of the realms.

Sayyid Muneer al-Khabbaz*

February 26, 2021

---

* Ayatollah Sayyid Muneer al-Khabbaz, is a scholar, thinker, author, and professor of Islamic sciences. At the age of 14, he traveled to the Holy City of Najaf to begin his training in the Islamic seminary. He studied under renowned scholars such as Grand Ayatollah Sayyid Abulqasim al-Khoei, Grand Ayatollah Sheikh Murtada al-Borujurdi, Grand Ayatollah Mirza Jawad Tabrizi, Grand Ayatollah Wahid Khorasani, and Grand Ayatollah Sayyid Ali al-Sistani. Under the tutelage of Grand Ayatollah Sistani, he benefited greatly in the study of Usul, or principles of jurisprudence, as well as an extensive examination of modern sciences and their correlation with Islamic sciences. The Ayatollah has authored numerous publications, two of which have been translated in English: 1) *The Mahdi: Understanding the Awaited One*, and 2) *Begin with Praise: Inspirations from Du'a al-Iftitah*.

PREFACE

The lives of those who do not fight you are sacred, especially the weak among the elderly, the children, and the women, even if they were the families of those who fight you.

Grand Ayatollah Sistani

March 5-8th, 2021 will go down in history as the first visit of the Roman Catholic Church to the Republic of Iraq. While the Christian community in Iraq is considered as one of the oldest in the world, their numbers have dwindled over the years from a sizable 1.5 million believers to about 500 thousand after the advent of terrorist groups such Al-Qaeda and ISIS. Though Pope Francis, the 84-year-old Bishop of Rome, will be entering Iraq for pilgrimage to the religiously significant city of Ur in the southern Dhi Qar province, that is not the only objective of his trip.

In addition to meetings with representatives of the Catholic Church in Iraq, as well as Iraq's Prime Minister and President in Baghdad, the Pontiff will travel to the Holy City of Najaf. There, the Bishop of Rome will privately meet with the leading religious authority of nearly over 300 million Shiʿa Muslims worldwide – Grand Ayatollah Ali Al-Sistani, the 90-year-old scholar and descendant of the Holy Prophet Muhammad.

After the fall of Mosul to ISIS in 2014, Ayatollah Al-Sistani issued a *fatwa*, or religious decree, obligating every able-bodied Iraqi to take arms and defend their homeland by joining the national guard to fight against ISIS.

Hundreds of thousands of young Iraqi men immediately responded and joined the Iraqi army. The Ayatollah's fatwa was arguably the single most important turn of events in the battle against ISIS. Without the Ayatollah, experts argue, the whole of Iraq would have fallen to the emerging terrorist group.

But even before 2014, Ayatollah Sistani played a quintessential role in deescalating sectarian tensions and promoting national unity between Iraq's factions. One of those incidents was the 2006 'Askari Shrine bombing that caused a huge uproar within the Shi'a community. Ayatollah Sistani urged the Shi'a community to remain calm, forbade reprisals and bloodshed of Sunni counterparts, and promoted national unity in a time of tragedy and anguish.[1] He has been that voice of reason and wisdom that time and time again has pulled Iraq from the brink of chaos and destruction. The Ayatollah is noteworthy in his pursuit to protect the rights of all citizens, regardless of religion, creed, or background.

When he was elected to be Pope in 2013, Pope Francis chose his new name "Francis" after Saint Francis Assissi – a man who embodied love and service to others. That is what he vowed to focus his leadership on. In his tenure as the Bishop of Rome, Pope Francis has been an advocate of ecumenism, as well as interfaith relations and dialogue.[2] * Even before he became Pope, he was known and applauded for his concerted efforts with the Muslim community in his home country of Argentina. The Pope has hosted numerous conferences and meetings, and has time and time again emphasized universal values of love, tolerance, and kindness between Christians, and non-Christians alike.[3]

But why did the Vatican request to meet with the Grand Ayatollah, and why now? Is this merely a "courtesy visit" among the many other meetings planned in the Pope's visit to the Republic of Iraq? Or is there a deeper

---

* Ecumenism is the concept and principle in which Christians belonging to different Christian denominations work together to develop closer relationships among their churches and promote Christian unity.

interest in the Ayatollah and the faith group that he represents? Between the followers of these two giants, there are over 1.5 billion people watching. Catholicism is deeply rooted in the western psyche and the Roman Catholic Church is perhaps the most formidable and longest standing religious institution in the western world. Shi'ism and the spiritual leadership of Shi'a Muslims, however, still remain obscure to most of the West.

This book aims to provide insight into the significance of Shi'a Islam's Marji'iyyah, led today by Grand Ayatollah Sayyid Ali Sistani, as a voice of peace, tolerance, and moderation in today's world. Moreover, this original work provides a comprehensive background to this historic visit and an insider's introduction to Shi'a Islam and its worldview.

The discussion of Shi'a Islam and Shi'a Muslims, whether it be in the West or the Near East, is contemporary, relevant, and essential for anyone interested in the study of Islam or the region of its birth. Shi'a Muslims have existed since the inception of Islam, not merely after the death of Islam's Prophet Muhammad in 632 AD, as some argue. As opposed to what has been maintained by some scholars analyzing Shi'a history and doctrine, in that the Shi'a have historically been a revolutionary lot attempting to gain power back from a Sunni majority, this book clarifies the intentions and core objectives of Shi'a leadership and their followers.

The reader will find that Shi'a tradition has been more concerned with maintaining the sanctity of Islam and the integrity of the Prophet Muhammad's message – one based on the universal principles of peace, moderation, and coexistence – rather than the power assumed at the helm. This is evidenced by both the actions and religious focus of the Twelve Imams of the Shi'a, as well as the institution building of the scholars that inherited this school of thought over the past millennium through the body of the Islamic seminary and the Marji'iyyah.

In today's context, how do Shi'a Muslims view their responsibility? In addition to spiritual rituals, there is a consistent concern for how they can individually, and collectively, contribute to the growth and development of their community and humanity at-large. This is especially true during the era of the occultation in which Shiʿa Muslims await the return of the Mahdi and Jesus Christ.* This question is foundational for the Shiʿi worldview, as it sets the tone for one's pursuit in education, employment, marriage, civic and civil society, migration, and affiliation with social and political movements and organizations.

To understand this Shiʿi perspective, the authors closely examined some of the works of the scholars of the Islamic seminary, especially those produced in the post-modern era of which have the most contemporary relevance to today's Shiʿi community. One of such works was *Dawr Ahl al-Bayt Fi Binaaʾ al-Jamaʿat al-Salihah* (The Role of Ahl al-Bayt in Building the Virtuous Community). This book was written by the Late Ayatollah Sayyid Muhammad Baqir al-Hakeem, the grandfather of the co-author Hassan al-Hakeem.

A theme that is found in the late Ayatollah's book, was a continued emphasis on people's inalienable rights. Those rights are coupled with responsibilities to one's nation and society. Muslim or not, Shiʿa or not, human beings are all created equal and must be honored and respected as such. This inspiration and worldview, philosophically and theologically, is derived from the movement and life of the Ahl al-Bayt themselves, the Prophet's disciple descendants. The other contemporary seminal works that were essential in this study included: *The Mahdi: Understanding the Awaited One*, by Sayyid Muneer al-Khabbaz; *al-Imam al-Mahdi waʾl-Dawahir al-Qurʾaniyyah* (Imam al-Mahdi in the Holy Quran) by Ayatollah Sheikh Muhammad al-Sanad; and *The Marjaeya: A Candid Conversation* by Grand Ayatollah Sayyid Muhammad Saʿid al-Hakeem.

The book before the reader serves to fill a gap in understanding Shiʿa identity and worldview, written with the western reader in mind and keeping

---

* The occultation, to be discussed more thoroughly throughout the book, refers to the disappearance or hiding of the Twelfth Imam in Shiʿa Islam. His hiding took place as a measure to save his life from the threat of the Abbasid rulers who wanted him dead. His followers continue to wait for his reappearance over a thousand years later.

in view contemporary context – both in a religious and political sense. It is no more an 'Islam and the West' issue, but has to be seen through the prism of 'Islam in the West' framework. Through this discussion the authors aim to answer questions on Shiʿism and its position with the rest of the world. By studying this book, the reader will be able to gain insight into questions like: is Shiʿism compatible with modern society? How does Shiʿa doctrine tell Muslims to see themselves and the world around them? What is the Shiʿa narrative of history and what is their vision of the future?

To answer these questions and more, the book is divided into three parts. (Part 1: Chapters 1 – 2; Part 2: Chapters 3 – 7; and Part 3: Chapters 8 – 12).

Part 1 provides a comprehensive background to the historic meeting between Pope Francis and Grand Ayatollah Sistani in the Holy City of Najaf taking place in March 2021. Part 2 is primarily theological based explaining some of the most fundamental tenets of Shiʿa Islam and the institutions that have preserved its school of thought. Finally, Part 3 focuses on contemporary questions of identity, assimilation and isolationism, people's practical impact on the occultation. The chapters are outlined below.

Chapters 1 give the reader insight into who is the Grand Ayatollah Sistani and background on the institution of Marjiʿiyyah, or religious authority, in Shiʿa Islam. It equips the reader with an overview of the role of the Grand Ayatollah and why he has been so important to Iraq, the region, and Muslims around the world. Chapter 2 delves into the questions regarding the historic meeting. Is there a history of Shiʿa-Catholic engagement? Why is the meeting taking place and what should the reader expect from the meeting?

Chapter 3 begins the introduction on Shiʿa Islam and starts from the very beginning, at God's decision to create a "caliph" or viceroy on Earth. A conversation is had between God and his closest angels about this plan and the future that lies ahead. The chapter continues to discuss the responsibility of God's viceroys and how Shiʿa Muslims theologically see the roles of prophets, messengers, and Imams. Chapter 4 focuses on introducing the disciples of the Prophet Muhammad, with a focus on the last disciple – Imam Muhammad al-Mahdi – who is believed to be the living and awaited savior for Shiʿa Muslims. It further discusses the primary principles that characterized the movement of the twelve disciples, from the passing of the Prophet Muhammad to the advent of the occultation of the Mahdi.

Chapter 5 distinguishes the difference between *Iman*, or faith, and *Islam*, and the fundamental practices and rituals that make up the Shiʿa school of thought. The discussion continues in Chapter 6 with the highly significant theme of education brought forward by the Prophet's disciples and their companions through the system of narration, supplications and psalms, as well as the wills and letters shared from disciple to disciple. Chapter 7 outlines the significant institutions such as the *Hawzah*, mosques and *hussayniyyat*, and the Marjiʿiyyah, that have historically preserved and protected the Shiʿa community, and what the Shiʿa argue has gone to protect the overall body of Islam.

Part 3 begins with Chapter 8's discussion on Shiʿa identity. A particular focus is given to the "Four Spheres of Identity", a framework that outlines how Shiʿa see themselves in spheres of commonalities within their socio-religious communities, greater society, and the rest of the world. Chapter 9 takes a more introspective look into the significance and meaning of "community," the principles that make up that community, and the observance of the rights of others. The discussion continues in Chapter 10 with an analysis of social engagement options by minority groups on the spectrum of assimilation and isolation. Focus is given to the doctrines of coexistence and citizenship, as well as a discussion on *hifz al-nizam* or maintaining public order, as understood in Shiʿa tradition.

Finally, Chapters 11 and 12 delve into a deep discussion on the subject of *occultation* in prophetic tradition as interpreted by Shiʿism, with references to the biblical and Quranic stories of Joseph, Moses, Jesus, the "Virtuous Servant", and the "Companions of the Cave". The discussion concludes with inferences to the practical impact that post-modern society has on the occultation of the day, as Muslims and Christians await the return of the Mahdi and Jesus Christ, together believed as the saviors to mankind in Shiʿi doctrine.

The authors will note that the arguments and perspectives presented in this book are not meant to ignore or neglect other positions within the study and scholarship of Shiʿa Islam. The authors do not assume to speak for the of Shiʿism or the Shiʿa community; instead, they present positions and perspectives that have been understood as the mainstream approach and school of thought within the long history of intellectual scholarship in the Islamic Seminary. Moreover, the authors are greatly indebted to the many individuals all over the world who contributed with their valuable insights as well as the team members that selflessly helped deliver this work forward. To you all we are forever grateful.

Through this timely work on the Pope's meeting with Grand Ayatollah Sistani, the reader will gain a greater appreciation for the international dialogue in furtherance of coexistence, moderation, and peace. Furthermore, with this introductory and candid discourse on Shiʿa Islam, the reader will gain a deeper understanding of the faith that the Ayatollah represents. Moreover, the reader will gain a greater appreciation for the universality of Shiʿa thought, and perhaps see in the Shiʿa community a partner and an ally in working towards coexistence, tolerance, and peace around the world.

Sincerely,

Hassan al-Hakeem (Holy City of Najaf, Iraq)

Jalal Moughania (Dearborn, Michigan, USA)

February 28, 2021

PART 1:
THE POPE & THE AYATOLLAH

CHAPTER 1

SAVING THE CRADLE OF CIVILIZATION

Never inflict harm on non-Muslims, regardless of their religion and sect. The non-Muslims are under the protection of the Muslims in their lands. Whoever attacks non-Muslims is a betrayer and traitor. Let no one think that there is a solution in oppression which cannot be gained by justice.

Grand Ayatollah Sistani

IRAQ'S SAVING GRACE

"Welcome! *Hella bikum!*" the armed ISIS gunmen called out to the young Iraqi cadets. The untrained recruits, now wearing civilian clothing, gazed back at the gunmen worriedly. They had changed out of their military uniforms that morning after they realized all their commanding officers had left the base. They thought they may be able to leave too, but it was too late. "Don't be afraid, we are just here to escort you to the presidential palace," they told them. "There you will simply give formal notice of leaving the Iraqi Armed Forces. After that you are free to go home to your families. Okay?" With none of their supervising officers in sight, the young cadets just nodded their heads.

The unarmed cadets were made to walk in a single file line on the main road. The onlookers watched. They did not know what was going to happen to these men, but they knew it would be unsightly. They had no choice but to look away and carried on.

They were round up in groups and thrown in the back of pickup trucks down the road. Every truck had three gunmen, one in the front with the driver and two in the back watching the cadets every move. The trucks did not take them back to their families or the presidential palace. The young cadets were piled on top of one another. They could not move. They could not breathe. They knew something was wrong. Then the trucks stopped. Some stopped at open fields while others went to a nearby riverbank.

The young men were dragged out of the trucks, some of them having passed out. The ISIS gunmen battered them as they lined up before them. Hands tied behind their backs, the cadets were ordered to sit on their knees and look at the open fields. And then the firing began. One by one, the men were shot in the head, execution style. The young Iraqi cadets, and soon to be martyrs, from all walks of life had their lives flash before their eyes as they watched each other die. Thrown to the rivers and the open fields, hundreds of young men were slaughtered. The fields of Tikrit were stained red with their blood.

The Massacre at Camp Speicher on June 12, 2014 was one of the deadliest acts of terrorism in history. After the fall of Mosul and the massacre in Tikrit, the world thought that Iraq was doomed. Within hours, they came with their black flags, kidnapped the women and children, and killed the men of villages in the north. Baghdad would soon fall to ISIS and the terrorist group would take over the rest of Iraq. So they thought.

The very next day on June 13, 2014, Grand Ayatollah Sistani issued a fatwa calling all Iraqis to arms and join the Iraqi military in the fight against ISIS. "We are calling upon all civilians who are able to carry a weapon to fight these terrorists, to defend their country, their people and their holy sites…" Within hours, thousands of men across Iraq from different faiths and ethnicities heeded the call of the Grand Ayatollah. Iraq would regain hope and the black flags of ISIS would fly over the sons and daughters of Iraq no more. With a single statement, the Grand Ayatollah pulled Iraq from the brink of utter collapse and destruction.

Mesopotamia, in modern-day Iraq, is known as the cradle of civilization or the site of mankind's earliest developments in agriculture and settlement dating back to 10,000 BC.[1] As the birthplace of Prophet Abraham, the Father of the Monotheistic faiths, some also call it the cradle of religion. This cradle has seen turmoil, war, and bloodshed for decades. It continues to suffer an array of challenges such as corruption, stagnation, and COVID-19. But the Pope is not visiting Iraq to save it. In fact, it is safe enough that the Pope is traveling to all different parts of the country for official meetings, prayer gatherings, and pilgrimages. But if the Pope is not saving the Cradle of Civilization, who is? That would be Grand Ayatollah Sayyid Ali Sistani, whom the Pope is meeting on March 6th, 2021 at his home in the Holy City of Najaf.

Though the world has been plagued by hate, terrorism, and extremism; it is also filled with individuals that are working for peace, justice, and coexistence for all on the highest levels of leadership. Pope Francis is certainly recognized as one of those leaders. Hence, his meeting with Ayatollah Sistani is no accident. The historic meeting of March 6, 2021 will certainly be a meeting of the minds working for the salvation of humanity's soul. The Pope may wish to have the Grand Ayatollah as a partner and an ally. The Champion of Christian and minority rights in Iraq, Ayatollah Sistani has stopped at nothing short of calling his own followers to put the needs of these minorities before their own. The Shiʿa school of thought, which the Grand Ayatollah represents, manifests the principles of coexistence, tolerance, and the sovereignty of people – principles advocated for by the Pope and the Vatican.

The Grand Ayatollah, and his school of thought, are being recognized on the world stage as strategic partners in the continuous struggle for human rights, the sovereignty of nations, and peace. If this relationship is invested in more seriously, which the Pope's visit is a step in that positive direction, then the future of the region is that much brighter.

The people of Iraq say that the Grand Ayatollah represents the light in the darkness that has covered their country for decades. Like his predecessors, Ayatollah Sistani is seen to be a humble ascetic man that has always avoided the limelight. He lives humbly in a bare home that is rented in the old city of Najaf, located in southern Iraq and 181 km from Baghdad. He rarely leaves his home, but his doors are open daily for visitors. The entire focus of the Grand Ayatollah has been on education, the service of others, and protecting the rights of all people. A true man of the people, he has put the needs of others before his own. He refuses to live beyond the means of the humblest of citizens. Some of his closest aides report that the Ayatollah has repeatedly instructed them, "Whatever extra money from my personal income remains, it is to be handed over to the orphans."

The people see Ayatollah Sistani as a graceful continuation of the line of Ayatollahs that have come before him since the onset of the Mahdi's occultation. In Shi'a Islam, the occultation refers to the period in which the Mahdi, the twelfth descendant disciple of the Holy Prophet Muhammad, had disappeared and will one day appear to fill the world with justice and peace. It is reported that in his last letter the Mahdi had written, "As for current affairs, go back to the narrators of our traditions. They are my proof on you and I am the proof of God."

Shi'a Muslims have heeded to this directive of their living Imam for over a thousand years since his occultation began in 941 AD. Since then, the Shi'a have followed the Grand Ayatollahs as spiritual guides to navigate the challenges of the day. Accordingly, the Imams gave the following instructions, "If there is a scholar amongst you who has self-control, who is preservative of his religious beliefs, who goes against his whims, is obedient to the rulings of his Lord, then follow him."

BRIEF OVERVIEW OF THE MARJI'IYYAH

Marji'iyyah is the institution of religious authority that forms the spiritual and religious leadership for Shi'a Muslims, particularly in the era of occultation since 941 AD. Shi'a Muslims adhere to the system of taqlid, emulating a *marji'*, a religious scholar in matters of Islamic law.

In Shi'a doctrine, the *marji'* is fallible. Thus, there is an emphasis within the understanding of the instructions of the Imam to refer to the "narrators of our tradition" that there exists a multiplicity of religious authorities (*maraji'*) within the Shi'a milieu. The one *marji'* that is followed by the majority of the Shi'a community is sometimes referred to as *al-Marji' al-A'la*, or the Supreme Religious Authority.

Al-Marji'iyyah al-'Ulya has been represented by the likes of Shaykh al-Mufid, Sayyid al-Murtada, Shaykh al-Tusi, and 'Allamah al-Hilli since the late 10th century AD. While the seminary and the Marji'iyyah has been focused in numerous cities across the centuries, such as Isfahan, Qum, Hilla, Karbala and others, for the last two centuries, the hub of this religious authority has primarily been the Holy City of Najaf. The Shi'a seminaries have characteristically been humble institutions, autonomous and self-sustained by the religious dues of the adherents of the faith.

Shaykh al-Jawahiri (1771 – 1845 AD) was the supreme religious authority at his time. He had authored the famous seminarian book, *Jawahir al-Kalam fi Shara'i' al-Islam*, which is arguably one of the greatest books of fiqh, jurisprudence, until today. After the passing of al-Jawihiri, Shaykh Murtada al-Ansari (1793 – 1860 AD) also known as Shaykh al-A'zam "the Great", would become the leading Marji' of the Shi'a milieu. The seminaries of the Shi'a world still study his books as part of the primary curriculum in jurisprudence. Those two primary books are *al-Makasib* (Gains in Transactions) and *al-Rasai'l* (Letters in Principles). A student in the seminary cannot reach the level of *ijtihad*, and become a *mujtahid*, without mastering these two books.

After the death of Shaykh al-Ansari, the leading jurist became Sayyid Muhammad Kazim al-Yazdi (1826 – 1916 AD). He was famous for his seminal work called *al-'Urwah al-Wuthqa*. Sayyid al-Yazdi's contemporary Shaykh al-Akhund al-Khurasani was a pillar of his own. Having published the famous book *al-Kifayah*, which is the primary book in the study of *usool*, or principles of jurisprudence. A student of the seminary cannot go on in his upper-level studies without mastering this book. After both of these scholars passed, the Marjiʿiyyah was taken up by leading jurists like Sayyid Abul-Hasan al-Isfahani, Shaykh Ahmed Kashif al-Ghitaʾ, Shaykh Muhammad Taqi al-Shirazi, and Shaykh Muhammad Husayn al-Naʾini. Many of the known Marajeʾ of the modern era were students of al-Naʾini including the likes of Sayyid Abulqasim al-Khoei, Sayyid Muhsin al-Hakeem, and Shaykh Hussein al-Hilli.

The Marjiʿiyyah of Grand Ayatollah Sayyid Mushin al-Hakeem (1885 – 1970 AD) spread substantially across the Shiʿa Muslim world. He established dozens of institutions in numerous cities and regions across the Middle East and beyond. Academically, he is known for his book *al-Mustamsak*, a meticulous work of Islamic jurisprudence. His tenure as al-Marjiʿ al-Aʿla was characterized by a definitive sense of leadership. His predecessors, Shaykh Muhammad Taqi al-Shirazi and Shaykh Muhammad Husayn Kashif al-Ghitaʾ, were indeed grand religious scholars who upheld their responsibilities in delivering jurisprudential guidance to the Shiʿa milieu. What set Ayatollah al-Hakeem apart from those before him, however, was his leadership and charisma.

The institution and influence of the Marjiʿiyyah was tremendous under the leadership of Ayatollah al-Hakeem. His opinion on communism, deeming it synonymous with atheism, proved to be instrumental in bringing an end to the spread of communism in Iraq. His influence and legacy continue today in the institutions he built. The old city of Najaf is known for its vast libraries. Ayatollah al-Hakeem established one of those main libraries, which still serves the students of the seminary today. The library boasts over 100,000 books and has one of the largest number of original manuscripts in the Shiʿa Muslim world.

After the death of Ayatollah al-Hakeem in 1970, the Marjiʿiyyah would be led by Grand Ayatollah Abulqasim al-Khoei (1899 – 1992 AD). Though there were other leading jurists contemporary to Ayatollah al-Khoei, such as Ayatollah Sayyid Mahmud al-Shahrudi and Ayatollah Ruhollah Khomeini, Ayatollah al-Khoei was looked to as Marji' al-A'la by the seminary and the majority of Shi'a Muslims worldwide. Even though Grand Ayatollah al-Khoei had faced a tremendous deal of difficulty under the oppressive Baathist regime of Saddam Hussein, he still managed to be the source of religious and spiritual guidance for millions of Muslims around the world. When he died in 1992, the Marji'iyyah was assumed by Grand Ayatollah Sayyid Abdula'la al-Sabzawari for one year before he too passed away. After Sayyid al-Sabzawari was buried in the Holy City of Najaf, the mantle of the Marji'iyyah was assumed by Grand Ayatollah Sayyid Ali Sistani.

Observers of modern Shi'a history, note that through all the difficult periods the Marji'iyyah faced, be it under the Ottoman empire, colonial mandate, or the despotic Baathist regime, the Grand Ayatollahs always remained steadfast in their role as beacons of enlightenment and inspiration within the seminaries and for the rest of the world. The hub for this power has long been Holy City of Najaf. The experience and significance of the leading jurists in the seminaries of Qum, Mashhad, Karbala, Hilla, Jabal 'Amil, Damascus, and the many others, cannot be ignored or denied. They are all rooted in the same foundation, and that is Imam Ali ibn Abu Talib whose body rests in the Holy City of Najaf. The holy city, and consequently its 1000-year-old seminary, was built around his shrine.

WHO IS GRAND AYATOLLAH SISTANI?

Today, the Marji'iyyah and consequently most of the Shi'a Muslim world is led by Grand Ayatollah Sayyid Ali Sistani. Ayatollah Sistani was born in the holy city of Mashhad, Iran in August of 1930. He was named Ali after his grandfather. Ayatollah Sistani was brought up in a distinguished scholarly family, renowned for its educational background and heritage. Sayyid Sistani began to study reading, writing, and the Holy Quran at the age of five. At the age of eleven, he began to study the Islamic sciences. When he was about 16 years old, he moved to the holy city of Qum. There he was able to learn directly from the leading jurist, Grand Ayatollah Sayyid Husayn al-Burujurdi.[2]

Ayatollah Sistani had moved to Najaf to continue his studies in 1952. He became a mujtahid, one who independently deduces the religious rulings, at the age of 31, a rare feat in Islamic seminary studies. It was his teacher, Grand Ayatollah al-Khoei, who gave him written testimony for certifying his ijtihad; something he had done for only a handful of students in his long life.

Ayatollah Sistani was one of the closest students to Ayatollah al-Khoei during his lifetime. He was near and dear to him and his fellow colleagues. Ayatollah al-Khoei is still seen today as al-Ustath al-Akbar, the Great Teacher, as most of the Grand Ayatollahs today were all students of his. For his numerous merits in knowledge and character, Ayatollah al-Khoei designated Ayatollah Sistani to lead prayers at al-Khoei's mosque, al-Khadrah, in 1987. Ayatollah Sistani continued leading prayers there until it was closed in 1993. Ayatollah al-Khoei also selected Ayatollah Sistani to lead an important network of schools and institutions in Najaf, as well as take on several other high-level responsibilities within the Marji'iyyah and seminary establishment. Ayatollah Sistani took on this work at a sensitive time, under the watchful eye of the Baathist authorities and intelligence apparatus, which tried to infiltrate all levels of Shi'a society.

When Ayatollah al-Khoei passed away, it was Ayatollah Sistani that led the ritual prayer over his body. While his teacher was alive, Ayatollah Sistani refused to assume the leadership of Marji'iyyah. Though he was a jurist of the highest caliber, he refused to print his *Risalat 'Amaliyyah* – a Marji's book showcasing his religious rulings to his followers. The Risalah is symbolic to a jurist's acceptance of the role of Marji' for himself and invitation for people to follow him if they so choose. Ayatollah Sistani did not want to appear in the limelight or become the focus of public attention. He was a deeply pious and ascetic man. Nonetheless, duty called, and Ayatollah Sistani was the most qualified to lead the mantle of Marjiʿiyyah.

Throughout the 1990s, Grand Ayatollah Sistani quietly led the millions of Shiʿa Muslims that looked to him for spiritual guidance around the world. From his small humble home in the old city of Najaf, he continued to be an inspiration for people in and outside of Iraq. He did so under the Baathists' watchful eyes, remaining under house arrest until their fall in 2003.

After the collapse of the Baathist regime in 2003, Iraq was administered under the US-led occupation. Grand Ayatollah Sistani played a critical role in this transition. He issued a fatwa stating that the framers of Iraq's Constitution had to be elected, not appointed. He also required that the United Nations be involved in overseeing the elections, while stressing that all Iraqis take part in the elections and vote.

In mid-2004, Ayatollah Sistani commented on the new government formed, emphasizing the importance and legitimacy of the electoral process. He further stressed that all segments of Iraqi society must be represented and accounted for. From day one, Ayatollah Sistani signified that all citizens must be respected, and their rights safeguarded and protected under the law.

While most discourse on political systems and governance in the Middle East has been reduced to an Islamic or religious state (*al-dawlat al-diniyyah*) versus a secular state (*al-dawlat al-ʿilmaniyyah*), Grand Ayatollah Sistani has advocated for an alternative of the two for Iraq, that could arguably be a model for other nations. The Grand Ayatollah has called for *al-dawlat al-madaniyyah* – the civil state. The idea of the civil state is the basis of citizenship by which all Iraqi countrymen experience the equal protection of the law. Religious confession does not play a role in the status or rights of the Iraqi citizen, as all citizens of the civil state are equal. Minority rights are not to be neglected or considered second to a ruling majority. The moral duty goes beyond "majority rules and minority rights." The majority must fight for the rights of the state's minorities before the minorities ask for them themselves. In the same light, all religious groups are respected and honored to practice their faith free from persecution or intimidation of other groups. The civil state is embedded with the fundamental principle of the will and power of the people. Hence, the Grand Ayatollah has urged for this direction of democratic representation of the people through fair and free elections, accountability, and transparency of government institutions, and has not endorsed political candidates or parties as a way to empower the people's choice.

In August 2004, The Holy City of Najaf would be embattled by skirmishes between "The Mahdi Army" and the US-led coalition forces. Fighting engulfed Najaf for weeks. Ayatollah Sistani had traveled to London on August 6, 2004 for immediate treatment due to heart complications. After treatment, Ayatollah Sistani returned to Najaf and a ceasefire was negotiated between the coalition forces and "the Mahdi Army." An agreement was reached, and the violence was put to an end in the holy city on August 26, 2004.

In 2005, tensions were severe and political dispute continued to grow leading to a volatile sectarian civil war. Tensions were at an all-time high with the terrorist bombing of the ʿAskari Shrine in Samarra. Grand Ayatollah Sistani publicly condemned sectarian violence and division repeatedly. He specifically urged the Shiʿa community to remain calm, forbade reprisals and bloodshed of Sunni counterparts, and promoted national unity in a time of tragedy and anguish.[3] He voiced his immediate concerns to the people of Iraq. He wished to unite the people under one humanitarian and nondenominational banner. The public showed unity behind Ayatollah Sistani, which was a major step in overcoming the deadlock reaction of violence sweeping the country.

Iraq has been in a state of instability and insecurity for decades. Many observers contribute the insecurity and instability to not only corruption and weak government institutions, but to the conflicts of regional and world powers as well. The scholars of the seminary especially faced difficulty in

Iraq, whereby their mere expression for religious freedom was suppressed by the despot authorities of the Baathists. Such suppression of the scholars took place because of the significant role that the scholars played in the lives of the Iraqi people. The position of the Marjiʿiyyah has always been one of peace, coexistence, and defending the sovereignty of one's nation.

Generally, in the political arena, the Marjiʿiyyah traditionally plays the role of an advisor. Its style of leadership and the extent of its involvement in community affairs is unique. The Marjiʿiyyah is not seen to interfere in the intricacies of politics. They do not get involved with the details of the administration or its ministries. The Marjiʿiyyah does not micromanage the affairs and details of the religious endowments such as the Shrines of Najaf and Karbala either. To interfere and be involved in such details would mean that the Marjiʿiyyah wished to dictate a particular mindset for people. The Marjiʿiyyah has never wanted that, nor does it want people to follow it in a way where the people do not have their own agency to live, work, and lead their own lives. The Marjiʿiyyah sees itself in the role of empowering and equipping the people with what they need in guidance to live fulfilling and successful lives.

While groups such as Christians, Yazidis, and other non-Muslims continued to be victims of terrorism; Grand Ayatollah Sistani released a statement in July 2006 condemning the perpetrators of violence against non-Muslims in Iraq.

> I say to those perpetrators of violence against their fellow non-Muslim citizens, be them Christians, Sabeans, or of other faiths, have you not heard the saying of the Commander of the Faithful, Imam Ali, peace be upon him? When he was told of a non-Muslim woman being harassed and assaulted for her jewelry by some so-called "Muslims", Imam Ali said, 'If any Muslim dies of grief after all this he is not to be blamed, but rather there is justification for him before me.' So why do you harm your brothers in humanity and your partners in the homeland? Dear Iraqis, exiting the dilemma that Iraq is going through in the current circumstances

requires a decision from all parties to care for the sanctity of Iraqi blood, [all Iraqi blood]. It requires a commitment to stopping violence in all its forms, so that the scenes of car bombs and random executions in the streets will be forever gone, God willing. Campaigns of forced displacement and other tragic images are being replaced - in cooperation with the elected national government - with scenes of constructive dialogue to resolve the outstanding crises and disputes. This is all on the bases of justice and equality between all citizens, sharing the same rights and duties to one another and to the nation.

After 2006, the Marjiʿiyyah began utilizing the platform of Friday sermons from the Holy Shrine of Imam Husayn in Karbala to deliver advice and guidance to the Iraqi people. The sermons would be read by either one of the Ayatollah's two representatives – Shaykh Abdulmahdi al-Karbala'i or Sayyid Ahmad al-Safi.

The Grand Ayatollah consistently called for unity across Iraq and the region. His efforts and message of moderation, coexistence, and unity saved thousands of lives from the backlash of internal strife and enmity. In 2007, during the infighting between Muslim groups, Ayatollah Sistani declared in a landmark message:

> Our call has always been for unity. I have said before and I will repeat: Do not simply refer to Sunnis as your brethren, but rather refer to them as your own souls. It is incumbent upon the Shiʿa to fight for the social and political rights of the Sunnis before the Sunnis even fight for their own rights. I am the servant of all Iraqis – Sunnis and Shiʿa, Muslim and non-Muslim. I love everyone and this religion is a religion of love.[4]

Ahead of the upcoming provincial elections in 2013, Grand Ayatollah Sistani repeated his encouragement for all Iraqis to vote. He stated that he would not be endorsing any candidates, which was a policy established by the Grand Ayatollah early on. As he urged all Iraqi citizens to vote, he empowered them with the agency to elect the politicians they wished to be represented by. The will of the people was a principle that the Grand Ayatollah continued to emphasize. He was not pleased if only the majority was represented and empowered. All citizens must have a voice and all citizens must have their rights protected by a country they call a homeland – *al-watan*.

On March 19, 2013, Iraq's capital of Baghdad, along with other cities in the center and north of Iraq, were rocked by a series of car bombings that took the lives of nearly 100 civilians and injured 250 more. The attacks were carried out by the terrorist organization ISI ("Islamic State of Iraq"). Amidst rising tensions, Grand Ayatollah Sistani issue a clear statement prohibiting bloodshed and violence against all Iraqis and especially Sunnis.

Grand Ayatollah Sistani would issue his most famous fatwa after the collapse of Mosul at the hands of ISIS in June of 2014. This call urged the collective responsibility to defend and uphold the safety and security of Iraq's religious and historical sites, regardless of religion or sect. In addition, it called to protect and defend the lives of all Iraqis, regardless of faith or creed.

> Due to the dangers facing our country and its people, in this time
> of oppression, it is a must to defend our country and its citizens.
> Therefore, this fight is an obligation upon all of our people. We are
> calling upon all civilians who are able to carry a weapon to fight
> these terrorists, to defend their country, their people and their holy
> sites. They are called to join the Iraqi military forces and help
> achieve this sacred purpose.

The Grand Ayatollah's call to action led to thousands of men to join the volunteer brigades of the Iraqi military in what became known as the Popular Mobilization Forces, or *al-Hashd al-Sha'bi*, to defend Iraq. The Marji'iyyah continued to provide direction to Iraq and the Iraqis through its weekly sermons to promote the values it wished to see manifested in the battle against ISIS. Though the terrorists would stop at nothing to achieve their aim, the Marjiʿiyyah was steadfast in advising the young fighters to maintain humanitarian ethics and ideals.

If it were not for the Ayatollah's verdict, and the 30,000 young men who gave their lives to defend Iraq's sovereignty, perhaps the Pope would not be able to visit Mosul and Baghdad today. Since 2003, the Grand Ayatollah and the institution he represents have played a quintessential role in safe-guarding human rights and the sovereignty of Iraq for all its people.

In February 2015, Ayatollah Sistani issued a statement of advice to the fighters on the frontlines which included twenty important guidelines, the most notable of which was included from a tradition from the Holy Prophet Muhammad.

> Do not indulge in acts of extremism
> Do not disrespect dead corpses
> Do not resort to deceit
> Do not kill an elder
> Do not kill a child
> Do not kill a woman
> And do not cut down trees unless necessity dictates otherwise.[5]

His guidelines further urged the fighters to protect innocent lives.

> By the majesty of God! The lives of those who do not fight you are sacred, especially the weak among the elderly, the children, and the women, even if they were the families of those who fight you.[6]

The Grand Ayatollah's statement also called for the protection for Muslims and non-Muslims alike. The Marjiʿiyyah made its verdict clear. Violence of any kind against any people – Yazidis, Christians, Jews, and Muslims alike – is strictly forbidden. "It is the responsibility of all Iraqis to fight and stop these terrorists. This call does not apply to one sect or one side only."

> Never inflict harm on non-Muslims, regardless of their religion and sect. The non-Muslims [who live in predominantly Muslim lands] are under the protection of the Muslims in those lands.

Whoever attacks non-Muslims is a betrayer and traitor. Let no one [among you] think that there is a solution in oppression which cannot be gained by justice.[7]

The Grand Ayatollah told his aides and representatives to know that, "The nation which loses its willpower is unable to defend itself." This *fatwa* was aimed at bringing back willpower and confidence to the people, empowering their sovereignty.

Like his predecessors, Grand Ayatollah Sistani has protected Iraq with his wisdom and persistence for progress, prosperity, and above all equality amongst all people. The Grand Ayatollah does not distinguish between people by faith or background, rather he is a leader working for a society which neither discriminates nor differentiates.[8]

CHAPTER 2

THE HISTORIC MEETING OF THE POPE AND THE AYATOLLAH

I think constantly of Iraq – where I want to go next year – in the hope that it can face the future through the peaceful and shared pursuit of the common good....

Pope Francis

POPE FRANCIS: THE BISHOP OF ROME

Pope Francis was born Jorge Mario Bergoglio in Buenos Aires, Argentina on December 17, 1936. He grew up with his mother, father, and four younger siblings. He went to a technical secondary school where he earned a degree in chemistry. At the age of 21, he was inspired by a local priest and decided to pursue seminarian studies thereby earning a doctorate in theology years later.[1] After training in a Jesuit seminary, he became an ordained catholic priest in 1969.

Bergoglio became Archbishop of Buenos Aires in 1998 and continued in that role until 2013. He was known for his frequent visits to the slums of Buenos Aires to work firsthand with the poor and less fortunate. When he was Archbishop, he used to ride public transportation and lived a very modest lifestyle. This continued to translate into his life as the Pope.

When Pope Benedict XVI resigned on February 28, 2013, the papal conclave was convened to elect a new pope. In the Catholic Church, popes are elected by their fellow cardinals through a ceremonial convening in the Vatican. Exactly 115 cardinals gathered to form the papal conclave on March 12, 2013 to elect the new pope. The following day, Bergoglio was named the 266th Pope of the Roman Catholic Church at the age of 76. Bergoglio became the first Jesuit Pope, the first from a non-European country since the 8th century, and the first from the New World.

Bergoglio took on the pontifical name "Francis" in honor of Saint Francis of Assisi, one of the most revered saints in Catholicism.[2] Bergoglio later described his own admiration for Saint Francis in saying, "He brought to Christianity an idea of poverty against the luxury, pride, vanity of the civil and ecclesiastical powers of the time. He changed history."[3] It is reported that a fellow cardinal in the conclave had embraced Bergoglio and whispered, "Don't forget the poor."[4] It was at that moment that he chose the name Francis, the spirit of which embodied the style of his papacy.

Pope Francis does not live in the papal palace, nor does he ride in a fancy motorcade. He notably wears very simple clothing and walks in old shoes. The Pope has been observed to make immediate changes to papal tradition and norms through his own conduct of humility. He did not receive the congratulations of his peers sitting down on the papal throne, instead he received the cardinals and greeted them while standing. Instead of wearing the gold cross of his predecessors, Pope Francis continued to wear the same iron cross he wore around his neck as the Archbishop of Buenos Aires.[5]

On his first Holy Thursday, Pope Francis washed the feet of ten male and two female prisoners held in the papal detention facility. This was a ritual done by the Pope as a symbolic gesture to show that he was at the service of the people. "The Church should not be self-referential," Pope Francis has notably said, emphasizing his worldview of the Church as one that needs to share its message of peace, giving, and reconciliation with the world.[6]

Pope Francis is the spiritual leader of nearly 1.2 Billion Catholics worldwide. They look to him not only as the holy representative of their Church, but as a leader for humanity. He is now headed for a pilgrimage to the biblical land of Abraham and the cradle of civilization.

WHY IS THIS MEETING HAPPENING?

The Cardinal Patriarch of Iraq, Louis Raphaël I Sako, called for Pope Francis to visit the Middle Eastern nation as early as 2013.[7] The Patriarch has been a long-time advocate of the Pope's visit to Iraq, as well as his meeting with Grand Ayatollah Sistani. This invitation to the Vatican was formally extended by Iraq's President Barham Salih in July 2019.

On July 12, 2020, Director of the Holy See Press Office Matteo Bruni made the following declaration.

> Pope Francis, accepting the invitation of the Republic of Iraq and of the local Catholic Church, will make an Apostolic Journey to the aforementioned Country on 5-8 March 2021. He will visit Baghdad, the plain of Ur, linked to the memory of Abraham, the city of Erbil, as well as Mosul and Qaraqosh in the plain of Nineveh. The programme of the Journey will be made known in due course, and will take into consideration the evolution of the worldwide health emergency.[8]

For the first papal visit outside of the Vatican since the COVID-19 pandemic began, Pope Francis broke his 15-month hiatus from international travel and has chosen Iraq as his destination. In 2020, the Pope expressed his long-time desire of visiting the cradle of civilization saying, "I think constantly of Iraq – where I want to go next year – in the hope that it can face the future through the peaceful and shared pursuit of the common good on the part of all elements of society, including the religious, and not fall back into hostilities sparked by the simmering conflicts of the regional powers."[9]

Though the visit of Pope Francis "will come as the realization of a dream of his predecessor, Pope St. John Paul II,"[10] his pilgrimage has dimensions that have greater implications than a mere visit of a spiritual leader to an old land. In finalizing the schedule of the Pope's visit to Iraq, the Vatican formally requested a meeting with Najaf's Grand Ayatollah Sistani. The Grand Ayatollah's office accepted the Vatican's request, making it the very first time in history that the heads of the Catholic Church and the Shiʿa Seminary ever meet. The historic meeting was set to take place in the Grand Ayatollah's humble home, nestled in the neighborhood of the Shrine of Imam Ali, the most revered figure in Islam after its Prophet Muhammad.

Pope Francis's visit to Grand Ayatollah Sistani in the Holy City of Najaf signals the importance the Vatican has placed on dialogue with the major centers of the Muslim world and its spiritual leadership. The Holy City of Najaf, and its seminary, is certainly one of those hubs. The leadership of the Najaf Seminary is especially recognized and highlighted because of its exemplary emphasis on peace, dialogue, coexistence, and tolerance through its role in Iraq, the region, and the world.

The Najaf Seminary is celebrating the beginning of its second millennium since its founding by Shaykh al-Tusi in the early part of the 11th century AD. Even with all the challenges that this seminary, and its school of thought, has faced throughout history – especially in the recent decades of war, violence, and terrorism in the Middle East – the seminary has not wavered from its firm commitment to its universal ideals. The Vatican's overture to meet with the Grand Ayatollah is a symbol of recognition to the establishment that he represents and its long history of noble stances for minorities' rights, moderation, and peace for all.

The Grand Ayatollah's many positions, covered in the previous chapter, showcasing his will to protect all people and promote an accepting and tolerant society, comes from the teachings and heritage of this school of thought. Grand Ayatollah Sistani's leadership has been successful in defending the sovereignty of Iraq in the region, empowering the Iraqi people through agency, and consistently reminding the world of Iraq's presence as a bridge of civilizations, cultures, and faiths.

Within the "civil state" that the Grand Ayatollah has supported, by which the political system is neither a religious state that imposes its faith on others nor a secular state that disregards religion, he has graciously recognized and advocated for the inclusion and empowerment of all of Iraq's groups, especially minorities such as Yazidis and Christians.* Because of his genuine commitment to the cause of minority rights, the sovereignty of Iraq, and a staunch opposition to violence and extremism of all kinds, the Grand Ayatollah has gained the trust of all Iraqis. Thus, it is not only the Christians of Iraq that welcome this visit and meeting but rather all Iraqis do, in the spirit of pursuing dialogue and peace.

Nonetheless, the Grand Ayatollah's positions have not been limited to Iraq alone. He has been a strong supporter of social justice, peace and stability, and a champion in the fight against terrorism and violence across the region and the world. Looking carefully at the Iraqi experience, it is arguably becoming a model for coexistence and tolerance amid some of the most extenuating challenges and circumstances. The Grand Ayatollah's calls to restraint and nonviolence during Iraq's civil strife, as well as his bold call to arms that saved Iraq from the grip of ISIS in 2014, brought Iraqis together in defending their sovereignty against the terrorist menace.

In recent years, the Vatican has taken a keen interest in Muslim schools of thought that exhibit emphasis on moderation and coexistence within their societies. On February 4, 2019, Pope Francis and the Grand Imam of al-Azhar University Shaykh Ahmed el-Tayeb met in Abu Dhabi. They signed "Document on Human Fraternity for World Peace and Living Together", also known as the Abu Dhabi Declaration.[11] The Pope emphasized that this "was no mere diplomatic gesture, but a reflection born of dialogue and common commitment."[12] Al-Azhar University in Cairo and the Islamic Seminary of Najaf, both of which were founded near the late 10th and early 11th century AD, are deemed to be within the more moderate schools of thought in the Islamic world today.

Though Najaf and al-Azhar may be seen in that similar light of moderation, Najaf stands unique in its autonomy, independence, and being closer to the

---

* Dr. Ibrahim Bahr al-Ulloum, Iraqi parliamentarian and former Minister of Oil, provided comprehensive insight in the history and development of this concept of the "civil state" amongst other valuable insights on Iraq, Najaf, and the Grand Ayatollah.

pulse of its own people. Nonetheless, the Vatican's focus on building a relationship and meeting with the heads of these two schools within the Islamic world today, arguably sends a message: the Vatican sees Najaf and al-
Azhar as their representatives of choice in on behalf of the major Islamic
schools of thought within for future dialogue and cooperation.

This visit is a step in a positive direction for further dialogue between the
world's major religions. The Vatican's request for this meeting, and Najaf's
acceptance, is a huge accomplishment in the space of dialogue and understanding. Even if the meeting did not take place as planned, the fact that
mutual assent for this meeting was expressed and announced to the world,
sends a very strong message for world peace and stability in the region.

HISTORY OF SHI ʿA-CATHOLIC RELATIONS

Ahead of the historic visit of Pope Francis to Grand Ayatollah Sistani at his
home in the Holy City of Najaf, it is important to acknowledge the history
of interfaith dialogue that has taken place between their faith groups. To
those who have been involved in this work, it was not a big surprise that
this meeting would take place. Without a doubt, it is acknowledged that
this meeting is of the highest caliber and a great achievement in it of itself.
Still, there is a history of interfaith dialogue between the two institutions
that built a path for such a first-time historic meeting to now take place in
2021.

The history of Shiʿa-Catholic relations, within the context of Muslim-
Christian dialogue, goes back decades. Scholars of the Islamic Seminary of
the Holy City of Najaf have been strong proponents and advocates for this
dialogue. Several mutual-exchange visits for education and cultural-en-
richment purposes have been underway for many years. Within Iraq, the
seminary has hosted Christian priests in the Holy City of Najaf and welcomed them within their establishments. At the same time, Muslim clergymen have visited churches in Baghdad and other cities across the north.

The past several years have been instrumental in building up interfaith dialogue between these major faith groups. In 2015, the first international Shi'a-Catholic meeting took place in Rome in partnership with the Community of Sant 'Egidio. In 2016, another meeting took place between Catholic priests from the Vatican and Shi'a clergymen from Najaf. The conference was held at the Catholic University in Paris. Two years later, in 2018, a delegation from the Catholic University visited the Islamic Seminary in the Holy City of Najaf as a continuation of the progress made in Paris in 2016. They were hosted by al-Balaghi Academy of al-Khoei Institute. Some of the scholars of Najaf working on these efforts have expressed their deep belief in interfaith dialogue.[*]

Interfaith dialogue plays a crucial role in shaping the future of Iraq and the whole region. It is seen as one of the only viable options for positive change, and such a principle applies across the world. The Middle East is not unique in the history of societies to be plagued with violence and sectarian conflict. Europe endured decades, if not centuries, of its own bloody wars and conflicts.[13] Asia, Africa, and the Americas are no different. It is not a problem with a specific religion or faith tradition, or religions in general for that matter, that contributes to conflict. Instead, conflict is experienced as a natural course of human condition and societal experience in the struggle for contradicting interests. Conflicts take place. Peace also takes place. Interfaith, intercultural, and other forms of dialogue that bring different groups together are essential. The first step in understanding is listening. The more groups listen and seek to understand one another, the greater likelihood they have in getting their own message across and understood.

In the spirit of interfaith coexistence, the Grand Ayatollah has consistently expressed the interdependence of the citizens of Iraq in terms of

---

[*] Sayyid Jawad al-Khoei, Secretary General of the al-Khoei Institute in Iraq, has expressed this sentiment with numerous news outlets in Italy during his own travels and work on interfaith dialogue in Rome and in Najaf. He has also shared his valuable insights and positive outlook on the planned visit between Pope Francis and the Grand Ayatollah.

maintaining security and stability. One group cannot be safe or secure at the expense of the next. It is incumbent upon the Shiʿa to fight for the social and political rights of the Sunnis before the Sunnis even fight for their own rights. I am the servant of all Iraqis – Sunnis and Shiʿa, Muslim and non-Muslim."[14]

That was the call of the Grand Ayatollah urging his own followers to fight for the rights of others before their own. Thus, the security and stability for the different factions of the country naturally depend on one another. Shiʿa communities are not stable without the security of their Sunni brethren. Muslim society cannot be at peace if their Christian neighbors are facing plight.

Grand Ayatollah Sistani's 2014 fatwa was perhaps the greatest instrument in protecting minorities, especially Christians, against the persecution and tyranny of ISIS. Over thirty-thousand young men from central and southern Iraq gave their lives to defend the lands of the north for their fellow Iraqis from different ethnic and religious backgrounds. In answering the call to arms by the Grand Ayatollah, they made it possible for these minorities to return to their homes safely after they quelled the spread of ISIS.

In Mosul, alone, the statistics of Christian and Yazidi students are very telling of the great impact this fatwa had on these minority communities. Before 2014, the number of students in Mosul were allegedly 800 Christian students. In 2021, there are reportedly 3,000 Christian students. The number of Yazidi students were approximately 100 in 2014. Now, they are 700 students.[15] Of course, there is still much to be done rebuild and develop after the carnage caused by ISIS in Mosul and other parts of Iraq. Nevertheless, the Iraqi people see hope at the end of the tunnel.

WHAT IS TO COME FROM THE MEETING?

Iraqi President Barham Salih has welcomed the meeting between Pope Francis and Grand Ayatollah Sistani emphasizing its great importance for Iraq and the world. "The meeting between the Pope and Ayatollah Sistani would represent a very, very profound statement about moderation in religion... These terrorists, these extremists, these bigots cannot invoke the name of God and the name of Abraham, our forefather of prophets as we say in Arabic, they cannot speak for that," Salih said.[16]

Here are the following things to expect and understand from the historic meeting between Pope Francis and Grand Ayatollah Sistani.

The meeting will not include the signing of a declaration.

The meeting will most likely not be prefaced with a commitment to signing any documents or declarations between the two spiritual leaders. That should not come as a disappointment, however. As people around the world discuss the possibilities of this meeting, one thing is for sure. The very fact that this meeting has been announced is a historical feat. That alone is of merit and deserves acknowledgement and recognition. For the advocates of dialogue, peace, and tolerance this is a huge milestone. The meeting itself is a declaration in the continued fight against violence and the equal protection of all people, be it in Iraq, the region, or around the globe.

Pope Francis is committed to his mission for peace, service, and the upliftment of the less fortunate. Grand Ayatollah Sistani has saved Iraq, and the region, from the grip of terrorist fanatics and continues to push for the equal protection of all people. These leaders will continue doing their work. The fact that they will meet, shake hands, and drink Iraqi chai (tea) in the Grand Ayatollah's humble home is the greatest reflection for their common commitment to regional stability, protection of human rights, and world peace.*

It is worthy to note that while the meeting is taking place amid the COVID-19 pandemic, the counterparts' commitments to make this meeting happen

---

* Sayyid Ali al-Hakeem, professor of the Islamic Seminary and Secretary-General of al-Hakim Foundation based in Beirut, provided valuable insights and expressed a positive outlook towards the meeting between the Pope and the Grand Ayatollah. He emphasizes that the Seminary and the Vatican share in the common vision of serving humanity.

is admirable and should be recognized on all sides. Both men have committed themselves to a life of humility and service of their fellow man. They care deeply for the orphans, the marginalized, and for the equal protection of all people's rights. Even if the meeting were not to take place at this time for whatever security or health reason, the fact that the meeting was scheduled and announced is arguable enough in this common cause.

Religion does not stand in the way of peace and coexistence.

This historic meeting between Pope Francis and the Grand Ayatollah also communicates a clear message to people all over the world. As religious leaders to collectively over 1.5 billion people, these two men are displaying their commitment once again to dialogue and coexistence. Religion does not stand in the way of world peace and neither do the religious institutions. This meeting is a testament to the divine doctrine of diversity and dialogue.

> O mankind! Indeed, We created you from a male and a female, and made you nations and tribes that you may identify yourselves with one another. Indeed, the noblest of you in the sight of God is the most Godwary among you. Indeed, God is all-knowing, all-aware.[17]

The meeting with Grand Ayatollah Sistani manifests the reality of religion, as one that rejects violence and the subjugation of any people, regardless of creed or background. Religion continues to be relevant to the everyday lives of people around the world. It is a force of good and the religious leaders representing their respective faiths have a tremendous role in promoting tolerance, coexistence, and dialogue. The meeting between these two towering figures speaks volumes to not only their followers but is a testament to all people of the world.

Iraq is a partner to the Vatican in protecting Christian minorities.

The Pope's visit to Iraq brings recognition to the Republic as a likely geo-strategic partner for the Vatican in its mission of building peace and tolerance, unity between faith groups, and protection for Christian minorities in the Middle East. The major player that has helped Iraq get to that level has been Grand Ayatollah Sistani. The Grand Ayatollah's consistent and effective platform in defending the rights of all people, let alone all Iraqis, especially minorities such as Christians and Yazidis, should not go unnoticed by the Papacy.

The personality and leadership of Grand Ayatollah Sistani has embodied and practically manifested the divine commandment in the Holy Quran.

> Hold fast, all together, to God's cord, and do not be divided [into sects]. Remember God's blessing upon you when you were enemies, then He brought your hearts together, so you became brothers with His blessing. And you were on the brink of a pit of Fire, whereat He saved you from it. Thus, does God clarify His signs for you so that you may be guided.[18]

Though Iraq has been historically ignored or judged a merely a nation plagued by violence and bloodshed, the visit of the Pope to Iraq and his meeting with the Grand Ayatollah, cements the transformation of Iraq and its deserved recognition as a real model for the power and will of a people.

Iraq is open to the world.

One of the underlying takeaways from the Pope's visit is significant to Iraq as a nation on the world stage. The visit tells that Iraq is sufficiently stable and secure to become a global destination for visitors from different religions, backgrounds, and interests. The Pope's pilgrimage to Ur, at this time, tells the millions of Christians around the world that it is safe for them to embark on this pilgrimage themselves. This will contribute significantly to further outside Christian engagement with Iraq as a tourist destination. The ancient city of Ur is located in Iraq's deep south in the Dhi Qar province. To get there, visitors would need to fly into Baghdad International Airport or one of the other airports in the south like Basra or Najaf. The Pope's visit to Iraq generally, and Najaf specifically, sends a message of Iraq's openness to the world. Visitors will certainly enjoy the tea.

Moreover, the Pope's visit to Iraq simply could not be complete without visiting the Grand Ayatollah. The arrangement for this meeting has been made for all the reasons mentioned above and possibly more. As the reader watches this meeting take place in the Holy City of Najaf, the authors invite the reader to take a deeper look into the school of thought that the Grand Ayatollah represents. Thus, the authors have presented the next chapters in this book as an introduction to Shi'a Islam as a means to educate the reader on the faith and its worldview. In understanding Shi'a Islam, the reader will develop a greater appreciation and knowledge base for the leadership of Grand Ayatollah Sistani and his universal calls for tolerance, co-existence, and human rights.

PART 2:
Shiʿa Islam

CHAPTER 3

THE VICEGERENTS OF GOD AND HUMAN PURPOSE

And We did not send you [O' Muhammad] except as a mercy to all the nations.

The Holy Quran, 21:107.

A CONVERSATION WITH GOD

In the second chapter of Islam's holy book of scripture, the Quran, it describes God's conversation with the angels of Heaven. God tells the angels of his plan to set a *khalifah*, or vicegerent, of His on Earth. The angels immediately express their wonder as to why God would do such a thing, given the negative experience with the creation that had already been on earth.[1] They conjectured what could come from a creation that would shed blood and wreak havoc in the world. They asked and God replied: "Indeed I know what you do not know." [2]

In this and the following verses, God demonstrates the purpose of creating the vicegerent. The classical definition of vicegerent is a person who is exercising delegated authority on behalf of a sovereign. In this theological context, it is a person designated as an earthly representative of God. It is important to realize the unique relationship involved between the sovereign and the vicegerent, as understood in Shi'a doctrinal framework of necessitating *reason* for the fundamentals of their creed.

Shi'ism argues that the sovereign would only reasonably choose the best fit individual to represent the sovereign, so that their interests and pursuits could be manifested as they wished. In such a role of delegated authority and representation, the vicegerent would necessarily carry the ideas, thoughts and decision making of the sovereign he represents. For example, if a principal were to send an agent on their behalf to represent them in a negotiation, they would ensure that their agent was completely on the same page as to what the principal wanted accomplished from the negotiation. The principal would want to make sure that the agent was fully aware of the principal's thoughts, ideas, and objectives in the matter perfectly.

Thus, the principal would probably choose someone who knows them very well and would be confident in their ability to represent the principal in a way that would properly manifest their presence in their absence. Now apply this to the vicegerent of God on earth. The individual here that would represent God as His vicegerent on Earth would need to be one who knows God so well and consistently manifests the attributes of God through his presence on Earth.

The angels were bewildered by the introduction of a vicegerent on earth. They assumed that nothing, but havoc and bloodshed, would be the result. Shiʿa scholars maintain that the angels are infallible, created only with God's light and the faculty of intellect. Thus, they are not objecting to God's wish to create or set the vicegerent. They are merely questioning the idea based on the limited knowledge they have regarding the situation.

The story in the second chapter continues, illustrating that God, "taught Adam the Names, all of them; then presented them to the angels and said, 'Tell me the names of these, if you are truthful.'" [3] Baffled and having no knowledge of the "names", the angels simply replied "Immaculate are You! We have no knowledge except what You have taught us…"[4] Shiʿa teachings assert that the angels' questioning did not come out of disobedience, or ʿisyan, but simply as a yearning to learn. The notion of yearning or striving, also understood as saʿi, to learn is encouraged in the Shiʿa school of thought. Thus, the questioning and criticism of ideas, within circles of learning and scholarship, are not only tolerated but welcomed.

God then turned to Adam and said, "O Adam, inform them of their names." Adam would recite the names taught to him by God beautifully. The angels would stare in awe. "Did I not tell you that I know the Unseen of the heavens and the earth, and that I know whatever you disclose and whatever you conceal?" God told his angels. They bowed before his grace and prostrated to Adam by His divine command.[5]

God created both the power of intellect and the power of desire in Adam and his descendants. He had created creatures with these two faculties before, yet some creatures rebelled against the will of their Lord and caused havoc on earth. The Angels thus assumed that any creature would act similarly given these two qualities. By replying that He knows what they do not, God is conveying the potential of excellence that lies in humanity through the combination of these faculties. Thus, humanity would have the potential to be the greatest creation of God and to perfectly manifest God's attributes on earth.

He illustrated this through the excellence shown by Adam in reciting the names taught by God, names that the angels had never heard before until Adam's immaculate recitation. It was God's will that Adam would know these names, as He taught them to him. And thus, it was God's will that Adam would be His vicegerent and a manifestation of God's excellence on earth.

Nonetheless, the potential of excellence in humanity is not automatically triggered – it is contingent upon the will and choices of the creation. Shi'a theosophy maintains the order of human free will, or *ikhtiyar*, people have the power of choice and their decisions are not dictated by predestination as argued by other schools of thought. Humanity can choose excellence and have it or elect wretchedness and fall to it. "We certainly created man in the best of forms; then We relegated him to the lowest of the low, except those who have faith and do virtuous deeds. There will be an everlasting reward for them."[6]

There is a direct relationship between the potential of humanity and its deeds. At the end, it is the choice of the individual to reap the fruit of that potential or to send himself or herself downward into desolation. So how does each person reach that potential they are destined for?

In order to answer that question, Shi'ism teaches the importance of understanding the very purpose of humanity's creation.

RISING THROUGH SUBMISSION

In the words of the Holy Quran, God says, "I did not create the *jinn*˙ and the humans except that they may worship Me."[7]

To reach the potential of excellence that is manifested in being a vicegerent of God, humanity is to strive in the practice of the essential purpose that God created it for – worship. This may be misunderstood by some to mean that God created beings to submit to Him and end it at that.

However, there is a much deeper meaning to the word "worship" in this context. Islam establishes that humanity's God-given purpose is to reach *yaqin*, or certainty. The path to yaqin, Islamic scholars explain, is worship. To worship God is to submit to His will. To worship Him is to heed to His advice and command. To worship Him is to rely on Him and Him alone. It is to realize that even with all the faculties and power human beings may have, mankind would not be and could not be without Him. Through worship, mankind is able to realize its potential and actually bring it to life. Imagine what it means to connect oneself to the One that has no need, no dependency, and no weakness. One that gives life to everything else. One that sustains everything else. One that was before and will be after everything else. One that cannot be compared to anything else.

˙ Like humans and angels, jinn are a creation of God according to Islamic belief. They are mentioned about 30 times in the Holy Quran. Robert Lebling, *Legends of the Fire Spirits*, 21. Also, according to Islamic doctrine, the Prophet Muhammad was sent as a messenger of God to both mankind and jinn; whereby the jinn are judged for their deeds and called for reckoning on the Day of Judgement as humans are. Al-Tabari, *Tuhfat al-Ghara'ib*, 1:68; al-Razi, *Rawh al-Jinan*, 193, 341.

Ali ibn Abu Talib describes God in his own words in saying, "He is One (*wahid*), not in terms of number (*'adad*); Everlasting (*da'im*), without duration (*amad*); Standing (*qa'im*), without supports (*'umud*). He is not of a kind (*jins*) that (other) kinds should be on a par with Him, nor an object that objects should be similar to Him, nor like things that attributes should apply to Him. Powers of reason go astray in the waves of the current of perceiving Him, imaginations are bewildered at encompassing the mention of His beginninglessness, understandings are held back from becoming conscious of the description of His power, and minds are drowned in the depths of the heavens of His kingdom (*malakut*)."[8]

Worshipping God is the innate disposition of the human being and a natural result of his simple reflection. As seen in other monotheistic faith traditions, Shi'ism holds that the worship of God is the ultimate power source and guiding compass for the truth seeker. Through it, the pious is able to see his or her destiny and realize their potential. As the faithful direct themselves completely to God, they tap into a source that is far greater than themselves. That source, God, is the source of existence and the essence of being. Shi'a piety holds that it is through this submission that mankind can unlock the keys to its definitive success.

The term in the Arabic language that describes this relationship of worship is the word *'ubudiyyah* – servitude. All Muslims realize their role as the servants of God as the basic tenet of their faith. This servitude was manifested in the first and best Muslim, Muhammad, whom Muslims follow as the messenger and greatest servant of God. The role of Muhammad as both messenger and servant is emphasized through the *shahada*, or declaration of faith – one that is made by any person who decides to convert to the faith. *Ashhadu an la ilaha illa Allah, wa ashhadu anna Muhammadan 'abduhu wa rasuluh* – "I bear witness that there is no deity by God, and Muhammad is His servant and messenger."

Muslims believe that it is through their submission, to God and God alone, that they rise in station both in this life and the next. The notion is held and believed by Muslims, forming a foundation for worldview of piety, that the most honorable way to achieve one's purpose and attain excellence is by submitting completely to the One who created that very purpose and potential.

God promises the faithful that if they trust and follow Him, He will guide them into the light. This notion of guidance, or *huda*, is mentioned 316 times in 268 verses of the Holy Quran. Muslims ask for guidance at least ten different times throughout their five daily prayers. "Guide us on the straight path,"[9] Muslims supplicate to their Lord. It is a constant theme that is embedded in a Muslim's daily conversation with God.

A history of divine guidance, and the prophets as conduits of such guidance, can be summarized in the following Quranic verses. "Mankind was a single community; then God sent the prophets as bearers of good news and warners, and He sent down with them the Book with the truth, that it may judge between the people concerning that about which they differed, and none differed in it except those who had been given it, after the manifest proofs had come to them, out of envy among themselves. Then God guided those who had faith to the truth of what they differed in, by His will, and God guides whomever He wishes to a straight path."[10]

The concept of guidance is seen throughout the Holy Quran. For example, in chapter 6 of the Holy Quran, God talks to us about true guidance. "Say, 'Shall we invoke besides God that which can neither benefit us nor harm us, and turn back on our heels after God has guided us, like someone seduced by the devils and bewildered on the earth, who has companions that invite him to guidance, [saying,] "Come to us!"?' Say, 'Indeed it is the guidance of God which is [true] guidance. And we have been commanded to submit to the Lord of all the worlds...'"[11]

In chapter 33 of the Holy Quran, God emphasizes that He is the one who guides mankind to the right path and that He speaks the truth for people to realize and be guided through it. "God has not put two hearts within any man, nor has He made your wives whom you repudiate by *zihar* your mothers, nor has he made your adopted sons your [actual] sons. These are mere utterances of your mouths. But God speaks the truth and He guides to the [right] way."[12] Muslims believe that God promises guidance, and there is no better promise than the divine. This divine guidance has been manifested in three primary roles which hold a great deal of responsibility: the prophet, the messenger, and the Imam.*

THE PROPHET: RECEIVING THE MESSAGE

As guidance is established from the divine, an essential question would arise in early Muslim discourse. How does humanity actually receive the guidance spoken so extensively in Muslim text? Does God share His guidance directly to the pious and impious alike? Can each individual receive it and comprehend it independently? Are ordinary fallible persons capable of fully comprehending such guidance if they are to receive it?

Some scholars ascertain that there are several forms of *hidayah* (guidance). *Hidayah 'ammah* (general) is divided into two: *tawkiniyyah* (creational) is given to every creation from the moment of its inception, and *tashri'iyyah* (legislative) which is delivered through revelation. Scholars also discuss the idea of *hidaya khassah*, a special form of guidance.[13] For the purposes of this discussion, the use of the term "guidance" will be in reference to revelation, the *tashri'i* or legislative form.

Shi'a theology and philosophy holds that ordinary individuals cannot independently retrieve that guidance promised by God. Some scholars have argued to the contrary, however, citing the verse in the Quran that states, "Call upon me, I will answer."[14] God has not created any barriers between Himself and His creation. He sends humanity His guidance and blessings constantly. The dominant Shi'a rebuttal to this reasonable argument is:

---

* Imam, with a capitalized "i", in the Twelver Shi'i context, is a title given to the twelve disciples from the descendants of the Prophet Muhammad.

True, but human beings have created the barriers to receive and comprehend divine guidance as an effect of their choices and misdeeds.

God is providing the guidance; yet, because of the fallible person's own deeds he is veiled from realizing that divine grace. Thus, it is argued that every individual has the theoretical potential of receiving divine guidance. Practically, however, the vast majority of human beings simply do not because of their fallibility – which is believed to be a choice rather than divine mandate in the makeup of one's creation.

Shi'a theology ascertains that those who received and delivered divine guidance to humanity – prophets, messengers, imams – were not angels or non-humans. They were human beings that enjoyed the status that they were born with and did not deviate from it – 'ismah – *immaculateness*. Thus, these individuals were not *infallible* in the sense that they could not make a mistake, like the angels who only had the faculty of intellect and thus could not functionally commit sin. Instead, these individuals were *ma'sum*, immaculate, in that they chose not to sin even though they had the capability to do so otherwise.

From Adam, the Father of Man, to Prophet Muhammad, God's guidance to mankind was delivered through human beings. Shi'a teachings establish that the construct of every human being has the potential of receiving divine inspiration and guidance. Thus, every human being is born *ma'sum*, or immaculate. Though the potential was there, not every being realized it in order to receive the guidance directly, however. Those individuals, then, must follow and utilize God's messengers – those who chose not to create a barrier with God and maintained their immaculate purity.

To better understand the idea discussed above, consider the example of Global System for Mobile Communications, or GSM for short. GSM signals govern the communication between people's cellular devices. When a person gets a phone call, there is a GSM signal at play. How does a person know that someone is trying to call them without their actual cell phone nearby to receive the signal and ring or vibrate? Could a person intercept the signal using only their physical body without any external devices? Could a person tune in to a conversation between two other individuals talking on their own cell phones without having some sort of device for such interception? Not that we humanly know of. Indeed, people need a device that can receive the sound waves and interpret the signals for them.

Some schools of thought within Islam have asserted that so long as the Book of God is amongst people, it is sufficient in guidance. In fact, one of the early companions said something profound, in the Prophet's last days, that would echo with some future sects. On his deathbed, the Prophet requested from the company in his midst to hand him a pen and something to write on. He said that he wanted to give them some final words of advice and instruction to keep them on the straight path. One of those present replied, "The man is hallucinating, the Book of God is sufficient for us."[15]

Shi'a doctrine asserts that the Book of God is not sufficient if the Holy Prophet is absent in the equation of divine guidance. For one, Muslims would not have received the verses of revelation without Muhammad's immaculate personality. And without the Prophet and his Household, the Muslims would not have seen the manifestation, deliverance, or implementation of God's will. God gave mankind, personalities from amongst the people to guide the people. These individuals chose to fulfill their greatest potential and manifested the attributes of God. They were capable of receiving guidance because of their choice and some of them were able to deliver that message of guidance as well. They took on the role of being the means to God, and God reinforced them with divine inspiration, wisdom, and insight for this purpose.

"But why them?" bystanders have begged this question in the context of prophetic envoys. Whether it be Jesus Christ's contemporaries who doubted and rejected him, or some of the early Muslims that refused to follow Ali even with the decree of the Prophet Muhammad, some people have simply objected to divine wisdom.

"When a sign comes to them, they say, 'We will not believe until we are given the like of what was given to God's apostles.' God knows best where to place His apostleship! Soon the guilty will be visited by a degradation and severe punishment from God because of the plots they used to devise."[16]

Such people could not accept that God appointed individuals other than themselves as messengers, out of sheer envy and conceit. If they were capable of receiving revelation, as did the apostles of God, then they would have received it. But they were not. It is not that God's guidance cannot reach them; it is rather that they cannot receive it due to their ineptitude. Some may have the misunderstanding or misguided belief that God's selection of prophets and vicegerents is random; that the people he chooses are generally good people, but not necessarily anything special, and God makes them special through selecting them as representatives. This is an essential understanding in Shi'a doctrine that preludes the significance of the individuals chosen by God as prophets, messengers, and leaders to mankind.

Shi'ism holds al-'adl, or divine justice, as one of the five fundamental principles of faith.* Divine justice dictates that God's selection of prophets and vicegerents is with the absolute best choice and is the greatest proof upon his creation. Only the most pristine of His creation is chosen to represent Him. Still, that divine choice comes by and with the creation's choosing, as God-ordained freewill – ikhtiyar – is an integral part of the design of mankind's universe.†

Islam teaches that the divine guidance will not leave His faithful servants, but that they are to be distinguished from those who are not. In chapter three of the Holy Quran, God says, "God will not leave the faithful in your

---

* The five principles of faith, or Usul al-Din, are sometimes referred to as the roots of religion. In the Shi'a Islam, they are as follows: 1. Tawhid (the oneness of God), 2. 'Adl (divine justice), 3. Nubuwwah (prophethood), 4. Imamah (divine leadership), 5. Ma'ad (resurrection).

† This does not mean that freewill is in the absolute sense assuming independence from the will of God (tafwid). In God's attribute, al-Qayyum, it is ascertained that God is the Independent and upon Him everything relies. See: al-Sabzawari, Sharh al-Asmaa', 363.

present state, until He has separated the bad ones from the good. God will not acquaint you with the Unseen, but God chooses whomever He wishes from His apostles. So have faith in God and His apostles; and if you are faithful and Godwary, there shall be a great reward for you."[17]

These individuals reached a level of purity such that they were capable of receiving revelation. The individual that is at that caliber of receiving divine guidance, is a *nabi*, or prophet.* Prophets are immaculate individuals, with the ability to receive communication from God. Examples of prophets include Adam, Jacob, Joseph, Ishmael, and Aaron.†

THE MESSENGER: DELIVERING THE MESSAGE

While a prophet receives revelation and may call people to guidance, he is not necessarily tasked with delivering and teaching a specific message (for example, a scripture). The one who is tasked with delivering the message of guidance is a *rasul* or messenger.[18] Like prophets, messengers are pristine and able to receive divine guidance. Their purity is of a level that allows them not only to receive revelation, but also to be designated by God to deliver divine guidance to others – be it a select group, community, or all of humanity. Shi'a creed argues, by way of *hadith* reports as well as *dala'il 'aqliyyah* or rational proofs, that the characteristics of purity from sin and immaculate character are prerequisites for those fulfilling these roles. A prophet, and especially a messenger, must be immaculate.

The value of the message does not rest in the words of revelation alone, but rather it manifests itself in the conduct and character of the messengers

---

* There are individuals that have reached this state of purity and are not necessarily prophets, such as the saintly figures the Holy Prophet's daughter, Lady Fatimah, and the mother of Moses, Lady Asiyah. However, in order for an individual to be a prophet, which is a stepping stone to being a messenger of God, they must have the level of purity alluded to above.

† Twelver Shi'ism establishes that the prophets have been granted a 'blessing such that they have no occasion to disobey a command or commit a sin, despite their ability to do so.' See: al-Hili, *al-Bab al-Hadi 'Ashar*. They are not, as some may assume, incapable of sinning. They have the ability and opportunity to sin, but they choose not to.

who represent the message itself. Contrast this with the mail carrier or delivery service such as FedEx. As a person awaits their package in the mail, they are not concerned with the personality of the individual delivering the much-anticipated package. Instead, the person cares only about what is inside the box, not necessarily who the carrier is.

However, if the same person went to a business negotiation later that day and the terms of the anticipated agreement were being discussed by in-house counsel of the CEO of the opposing party, the dynamic would definitely be different. Counsel here has full authority to negotiate on behalf of the company and to come to a final agreement. Knowing his position, authority, and agency would make all the difference in the legitimacy of his representation. What if he had no authority at all, no delegated power to negotiate or agree to a contract? The person's time would be wasted, and they would not be able to move forward with pursuing your interests or ambitions for your company.

Shiʿa creed would argue that the role played by a messenger of God is definitely more similar to the in-house counsel than to the mail carrier or courier. He does not just deliver a message, he represents it and has the delegated authority from the one who sent him. Thus, he would need to have the aptitude, the moral character, and the consistency to properly represent the one who has delegated him with authority. If this did not exist, it would contradict the fundamental belief of divine justice. Some schools of thought in Islam do not necessitate divine justice as a fundamental tenet of the faith. Thus, they do not necessarily believe that the prophets and messengers must be immaculate. The Shiʿa, however, emphasize the logical necessity for the messengers and vicegerents of God to be immaculate as a manifestation of God's justice.

A messenger of God is proof that it is possible to implement the message and live by it each and every day of your life. Without the example, the message would merely be theory. Moreover, if the example was not an immaculate one, humanity would have the legitimate excuse of being given an incomplete or imperfect message because the one delivering it could not deliver it properly. That reasoning could go on to doubt the very authenticity of the message. If the messenger was not immaculate, there would be no proof to people that the message being delivered is actually from God – the Immaculate.

THE IMAM: IMPLEMENTING THE MESSAGE

Shi'a doctrine presents a third responsibility that falls upon the representatives of God, and that is to lead people on the basis of the message delivered. The immaculate individual, a vicegerent of God, fulfills this necessary role of actively leading people to guidance and developing their community based on divine teachings. Through that leadership and guidance, people are able to reach and fulfill their potential in life. Shi'a history and belief maintains that this role is not theoretical or abstract, and is implemented considering the circumstances and context in which the vicegerent lives. Their role is that of pragmatic and practical implementation developed through a thorough understanding of the hurdles that prevent humanity from taking God's guidance and reaching their potential.

The Quran states, "It is He who sent to the unlettered [people] an apostle from among themselves, to recite to them His signs, to purify them, and to teach them the Book and wisdom, and earlier they had indeed been in manifest error."[19] Delivering the message, as referred to in this verse, is just the first step. Leadership in this context also includes educating people, encouraging active practice, and developing the whole community. This is the role of the divinely appointed leader, or *Imam*, one of the distinguishing roles held in Shi'a Islam.

As mentioned earlier, Shi'a belief maintains that it is people's own misdeeds that prevent them from receiving divine guidance. It is only the few that choose to stay true to their immaculate nature that receive it. Knowing the tendency of His creation, God did not choose to deliver the final manifest message to humanity from day one. Instead, He gave his prophets and messengers the revelation in stages, in correlation to the readiness of humanity to implement the guidance He gave. Divine instruction came in correlation to humanity's maturity. "God does not burden a soul beyond what it can bear."[20]

Islam teaches that after thousands of prophets and a series of books and revelations, humanity finally reached a level of maturity in the 7th century to receive the final Message of God through the Seal of Messengers – Muhammad.* Note that the Final Message was sent to humanity as a whole, not just one group of people or region – as a completion to the works of the previous messages which were continuous and completed one another. After the messages of Abraham, Noah, Moses, and Jesus, the message of Islam was sent to humanity. "And We did not send you [O' Muhammad] except as a mercy to all the nations."[21]

Shi'a scholars emphasize that it was not until the end of the Holy Prophet's life that this final message was completely delivered to the people. In his final year, the following verse was revealed where God said, "Today I have perfected your religion for you, and I have completed My blessing upon you, and I have approved Islam as your religion…"[22] †

The delivery of the message of God, Islam, was completed. The Holy Prophet had fulfilled his roles as a prophet and a messenger. The Holy Prophet, however, did have a third role as a divine representative of the Almighty. He was the immaculate leader of the people. He was the Imam. Shi'a belief maintains that God designated the most pristine of his prophets

---

* It is widely held in Islamic tradition that there were thousands of prophets, numbering up to 124,000, and that every nation from the dawn of time was not void of divine guidance through the presence of prophets. See: Al-Majlisi, *Bihar al-Anwar*, 11:32.

† Shi'a tradition holds that this verse is connected to the Day of Ghadir, in which the Prophet Muhammad openly declared to an audience of 100,000 Muslims that his cousin and son-in-law Ali ibn Abu Talib was his heir and successor. Both religious guidance and state leadership was to continue in his personality.

and messengers as imams as well, to lead their people and implement the advancement and development that was meant for their communities.

The Prophet had the three responsibilities of guidance as prophet, messenger and Imam. The first and second were most definitely fulfilled and completed. By the time of the Prophet's passing, we acknowledge without a doubt that the final message of God was completely received and delivered. Thus, he was the Seal of the Messengers. However, the third responsibility was not absolutely implemented in his person. There were numerous areas and regions around Arabia that had not realized the most basic development of their communities or their potential as individuals. Thus, implementing the third responsibility, which is dependent on the readiness of the people, was not completed in the person of the Holy Prophet. And thus, he was not the final Imam.*

It is because of this that the verse mentioned above was delivered. According to the Shi'a scholars and historians noting the time of delivery for the verse, this piece of revelation referring to the completion of faith coincides with the Prophet's historic declaration at Ghadir Khum. The proclamation came upon the Prophet's return from Mecca, after his *farewell pilgrimage,†* in which nearly a hundred thousand Muslims joined him in his final year of life in 632 AD. At Ghadir, the Prophet famously proclaimed that leadership and guidance will be safeguarded through his successor – Imam Ali. We will discuss these events in more detail in the coming chapters. Nevertheless, it is in this vein that *Imamah*, or divine leadership, continued after the Prophet Muhammad. Twelver Shi'ism, as opposed to other sects within broader Shi'ism such as the Ismaili and Zaydi, teaches that there are twelve

---

* Some of the prophets and messengers before Prophet Muhammad were also considered to be Imams in Muslim tradition. An example of such a prophet was the father of monotheistic faiths, Prophet Abraham. This is evidenced in the Quranic verse, "And when his Lord tried Abraham with commands, he fulfilled them. He said: Surely, I will make you an Imam for mankind. [Abraham] said: And of my offspring [will there be leaders]? He said, my covenant does not include the unjust." The Holy Quran, 2:124.

† The "Farewell Pilgrimage" was coined as the Prophet's last pilgrimage with his people before he passed away. As divine inspiration showed him that his end was near, he let his people know that this would be his last pilgrimage to Mecca.

divinely appointed leaders after Prophet Muhammad.* The first imam being Imam Ali ibn Abu Talib, and the last of them being the living and awaited Imam Muhammad al-Mahdi.

At the Prophet's time, humanity was mature enough to receive and accept the message from God's messenger, but it was not mature enough to implement the message. In reading *Du'a' al-Nudbah*,† a central supplication in Shi'a piety and spiritual tradition related to the awaited Imam al-Mahdi, the Twelver narrative of history can be observed. The supplication speaks of the betrayal experienced by the Prophet and his family. People abandoned the principles they had once accepted as their new faith in Islam, and sought out their carnal desires as opposed to their higher calling. The supplication shows how people were not yet ready to implement the message itself. Thus, the Shi'a lament and weep for the appearance of their awaited Imam al-Mahdi to bring forth the implementation of the faith through justice and equity for all.

A DESIRE FOR EXCELLENCE

When God created human beings with so much potential, He embedded in them a desire for fulfillment, greatness and excellence. Islam teaches that this is embedded in humanity's *fitrah*, or innate nature. In every decision that a person makes, he or she has a natural inclination to choose what they think is best for them. From choosing flavors at an ice cream parlor to career paths on the way through college, people's decisions are guided by the inclination to do what they feel or think is best.

---

* Ismailis, sometimes known as seveners, stop at the sixth imam, Ja'far al-Sadiq, within the Twelver tradition. Historically they elected to follow Ismail, the elder son of Imam al-Sadiq, instead of Imam Musa al-Kazim – the seventh imam in Twelver tradition. Zaydis, another Shi'i sect, adopt the first three Twelver imams (Ali ibn Abu Talib, Hasan ibn Ali, and Husayn ibn Ali). Their fourth imam was the son of Imam Hasan, Hasan II. Their fifth imam, the namesake of their school of thought, was Zayd ibn Ali. Zayd was the son of the fourth Twelver imam Ali ibn Husayn, the only son of Imam Husayn ibn Ali that survived the Battle of Karbala in 680 AD.

† Du'a' al-Nudbah, the Supplication of the Weeping, is recited by Shi'a in honor of their awaited twelfth Imam on major holidays such as 'Id al-Fitr and 'Id al-Adha, as well as on Friday mornings. See: al-Majlisi, *Bihar al-Anwar*, 99:104; Ibn Tawus, *Misbah al-Za'ir*, 446; Ibn al-Mashhadi, *al-Mazar*, 573-584.

These decisions are based on people's belief or conception of what is the best, most perfect, most excellent option for them. In this, the reader can observe that human beings have a natural attraction to all things that are perfect, complete or excellent. People are attracted to beauty because of their love for excellence. People are moved by expressions of art and poetry, captivated by the architecture of man, and enchanted by the landscapes of nature, because of a deep innate love for excellence and a yearning for completeness and fulfillment.

That desire for excellence makes human beings that much more receptive to the guidance of God delivered by and through God's representatives – the prophets, messengers, and Imams. When humanity taps into that innate longing for excellence, it becomes closer to accepting and implementing the guidance of divine leadership.

The Holy Quran states, "The faithless say, 'Why has not some sign been sent down to him from his Lord?' You are only a warner, and there is a guide for every people."[23] Islam teaches that each and every messenger is a prophet. The messenger must receive the message in order to deliver it. From Adam to Muhammad, God sent guidance to humanity.*

After the series of divinely ordained prophets, the seal of them being Prophet Muhammad, Shi'ism focuses on the life and legacy of the twelve Imams. To understand their *Imamah* and the legacy of their leadership, it is encouraged to look at them collectively as one unit. The Imams are essentially one team that worked together on one project and continued each other's work. The Shi'a believe that this "project" is the implementation of the true religion of Islam – the final message of God. The final product of this project is *dawlat al-Imam*, or the reign of Imam al-Mahdi, which will usher an era of peace, justice, and equity for all of mankind.

---

* Note that the reference here to humanity is not a reference to every single living human being. It is a reference to humanity at large and its potential to reach all collectively.

The Prophet was responsible for receiving the message and delivering it to the people. He fulfilled that role. In addition, he implemented the faith in his role as Imam as well. He knew, however, that his own lifetime would not suffice for the complete implementation of the message. Thus, he made sure that the responsibility would be carried on after his death, and he made that clear to his followers. That the implementation of the message will continue until completion, and guidance shall remain for his people.

THE ROLES OF AHL AL-BAYT

Taking a closer look at the lives of the Ahl al-Bayt, the Household of Islam's Prophet,* Shi'ism reflects on the role they played and continue to play in the world. What were their primary functions and what were the responsibilities divinely assigned to them as understood in Shi'ism?

This is an essential question for the Shi'a paradigm and its worldview. The widely believed, but incomplete answer to the question, is that the Imams are the spiritual and political successors of the Prophet Muhammad, and they are the authoritative source of religion and knowledge for Muslims after him.† Some scholars argue that if the answer is reserved to these two primary positions mentioned, then it would attribute a lack of fulfillment on the Imams' part. In both scenarios, the Imams did not completely realize those roles due to the circumstances of their time. With the exception of Imam Ali who ruled for less than five years before he was assassinated as he led prayers in the Grand Mosque of Kufa,[24] and Imam Hasan who assumed the caliphate for only about seven months before abdicating to his

---

* Shi'ism maintains that the Household of the Prophet Muhammad, Ahl al-Bayt, refers to his daughter Lady Fatimah, son-in-law Imam Ali, and grandsons Hasan and Husayn, as well as their descendants. The twelve Imams – Imam Ali and the eleven Imams that descend from his marriage to Lady Fatimah – are collectively referred to as Ahl al-Bayt. Other descendants and honorable figures from the family, such as Imam Ali's son Abu al-Fadl al-'Abbas (martyred in the Battle of Karbala alongside his half-brother Imam Husayn) and Imam Ali's daughter Lady Zaynab (who survived the Battle of Karbala to tell its tale and carry on her brother Husayn's movement) are also included when referring to the Prophet's Household, or Ahl al-Bayt.

† Adherents to Twelver Shi'ism also maintain a set of beliefs about the Imams' metaphysicality in their ability to perform miracles as the prophets before them and manifest divine graces by the authority and inspiration given to them by God.

adversary Muʿawiyah in 661 AD to achieve a peace accord and avoid bloodshed,[25] none of the Imams ruled over the *ummah*, or nation, as caliph or statesman. Nor were all the Imams recognized as the main religious authorities of their times.

It is a fundamental belief in Shiʿa theology that lack of fulfillment cannot be attributed to the immaculate disciples of the Prophet. So what is their true role and responsibility, according to Shiʿa teachings?

Indeed, they do possess temporal and religious authority as the vicegerents of God. Such authority exists even if the people of their time did not recognize them as such. More importantly, they carry out the following roles and divine responsibilities.

Firstly, they are the *hujjah*, the proof of God's grace, upon the people. With the presence of prophets, messengers, and Imams amongst creation, it cannot be claimed that humanity did not know and have the ample opportunity to fulfill their responsibility before God in one's time on Earth. This proof of God upon creation is a necessity that exists in every era. This is a fundamental belief in Shiʿi *ʿaqidah*, or creed, in that the Imams are manifestations "of divine grace, and the earth cannot be without an Imam at any time."[26] It flows from the principle of God's justice and His perfect delivery of truth to humanity.

Secondly, the Imams serve as the divine successors of the Prophet Muhammad. In this capacity, they carry his torch and continue the enactment or operation that he started. His role of leadership continued to be fulfilled with their presence. They possess all the qualities and characteristics that he possessed, with the exception of prophethood. Shiʿa piety often cites narrations from the Holy Prophet, recorded in both Shiʿa and Sunni traditions, venerating the position of Ali. Prophet Muhammad said, "Ali, you are to me as Aaron was to Moses, except that there shall be no prophet after me."[27]

The Prophet made Imam Ali's position clear to his companions and the Muslim community at large, especially with his declaration at Ghadir

Khum. In front of nearly one hundred thousand onlookers he proclaimed, "Whoever takes me as master, Ali is his master!"[28]

Thirdly, the Imams played the extremely significant positions as the true role models and ultimate example of human potential. They are the manifestation of the highest potential that can be reached as human beings – intellectually, ethically, and spiritually.

Moreover, in these roles the Imams were tasked with the guardianship of the faith. They set the example for guidance, manifest it through their leadership, and protect it from being adulterated. Guidance is preserved in two primary vessels: the faith and the faithful. These two vessels have been under the protection of the Imams from day one and continue to be the objective of preservation for the Shiʿa today.

The Imams protected and ensured the continued existence of the community of faithful. By their actions, they devised the strategy to protect the faith and the faithful. During their lives, seeing that people were not mature enough to accept and implement the prophetic message with the Imams, they knew they had to plan ahead. With the vision of doing God's work on Earth, Ahl al-Bayt created a strategy for the message to be implemented by humanity. Regardless of how long it will take, the day will come for that implementation. As each one of the Imams were martyred one after the other, the mantle was finally passed to twelfth Imam, al-Mahdi, who has been in his state of *al-ghaybat al-kubra*, or major occultation, since 941 AD.[29]

Hence, Shiʿa Muslims believe that the major responsibilities that are expected of them, as the community of the occultation, as they await the public reappearance of their awaited Imam follow suit with the same objectives of the Ahl al-Bayt – to protect the faith and the faithful. Shiʿa history and heritage has focused on the preservation of its faith and the existence of its community of faithful. A commitment to protecting oneself and community from banishment, exile, slaughter and harm, while preserving one's faith and religion, is central to the Shiʿa experience and psyche. The Imams trained their companions and followers to carry these responsibilities during the time of occultation with their divine goal in mind; the true implementation of God's message, which will only be fulfilled with the *zuhur*, or reappearance, of the Imam.* Thus, a third responsibility arises: preparing for the reappearance of the Imam.

In the next chapters, the authors will discuss how the Shi'a believe they are expected to fulfill these three major responsibilities as they continue to live in the era of the occultation. The following questions will be explored. How do the Shi'a maintain and preserve their faith and its principles? How did the Imams work with their followers and their companions, who were intended to be that virtuous group to carry on these responsibilities?

How do the Shi'a protect and preserve their communities and humanity as a whole? How did the Imams direct their communities in a way to deal with the challenges of their time? How do the Shi'a actually prepare for the *zuhur* of their awaited Imam and what is their understanding of his occultation?

---

* The companions of Imam al-Mahdi who represented him in his *al-ghaybat al-sughra*, or minor occultation, were 'Uthman ibn Sa'id al-Asadi, Abu Ja'far Muhammad ibn 'Uthman, Abu al-Qasim Husayn ibn Ruh al-Nawbakhti, and Abu al-Hasan Ali ibn Muhammad al-Samari. They were companions of his father Imam Hasan al-'Askari.

CHAPTER 4

THE SOURCES OF DIVINE GUIDANCE

O' Apostle! Deliver what has been sent down to you from your Lord; and if you do not do so, you have not delivered His message.

The Holy Quran, 5:67.

THE BEGINNING OF AN OCCULTATION

The final disciple and vicegerent of the Prophet Muhammad is known as Imam Muhammad al-Mahdi, according to Twelver Shiʿism. He is the Prophet Muhammad's descendent, the twelfth prince of Banu Hashim* and son of the eleventh imam, Imam Hasan al-ʿAskari. He was born in 869 AD, on the 15ᵗʰ of Shaʿban† 255 AH, in Samarra, Iraq during the reign of the Abbasid caliph al-Muʿtamid. Due to the turbulent political situation of the time and being the last disciple of the holy household, his birth was concealed from the Abbasid authorities. For years, the very existence of the Imam continued to be hidden from outsiders except for a handful of close confidants. At the death of his father, poisoned by agents of the ruling authorities, the young Imam was about five years old. Despite people's bewilderment, he presented himself at his father's burial to lead the funeral

---

* Banu Hashim was the clan of the Prophet Muhammad, one of the clans of Quraysh tribe.See: Al-Mubarakpuri, *The Sealed Nectar*, 30.

† Shaʿban is the eighth month of the Islamic lunar calendar. It is the month before the holy month of Ramadan. The Islamic calendar's months are as follows: Muharram; Safar; Rabiʿ al-Awwal; Rabiʿ al-Thani; Jumada al-Awwal; Jumada al-Thani; Rajab; Shaʿban; Ramadan; Shawwal; Thu'l-Qiʿdah; Thu'l-Hijjah.

prayer. He would then immediately enter what has become known as "the minor occultation" thereafter.

For over sixty years, the Imam communicated to his followers through designated ambassadors, who were close companions of his father Imam al-ʿAskari. The companions were ʿUthman ibn Saʿid al-Asadi, Abu Jaʿfar Muhammad ibn ʿUthman, Abu al-Qasim Husayn ibn Ruh al-Nawbakhti, and Abu al-Hasan Ali ibn Muhammad al-Samari.

In 941 AD, the Imam made it known to his followers that the last ambassador would soon die and the door of deputyship would close. A few days later, al-Samari indeed passed away and hence the major occultation began. Over a thousand years have passed and his followers continue to await his return.

During this era, those who await the return of the Imam are naturally inclined to seek a deeper understanding of their relationship with the one they wait for. As the last disciple of the Prophet and the final vicegerent of God on Earth, he embodies the hope for humanity and a lasting peace that will come when the world is ready for it. The relationship between the one who waits and the Awaited One is intrinsic to one's connection to God and the universe. To reiterate the verse mentioned at the beginning of the first chapter; God said, "I am going to set a vicegerent on the earth…"[1] Adam was the first in this regard and Imam al-Mahdi is the last. The very purpose of his occultation is to preserve this representation of God on Earth until humanity is ready to accept the divine leadership that will implement God's will and allow for the fruition of true justice and equality for all. But until that time comes, what do the faithful do? What is their role and what are they responsible for? Shiʿa scholars, studying the revelation and the traditions of the Prophet and his family, indicate that there are three primary responsibilities to be assumed during the occultation.[2] They are as follows:

1. Preserving the religion of Islam
2. Protecting and preserving the community of faithful and humanity as a whole

3. Preparing for the return

It is not enough to have a general vague acknowledgement, as each responsibility ties directly to a person's relationship to the awaited Imam, their relationship to their community, and ultimately their relationship with God. That is essentially what most of Shi'a discourse will return to – that intrinsic relationship with the Divine that bellows from the depths of the soul. A relationship that cannot be denied or assumed by anyone else, because everything else flows from it. Shi'a piety focuses on this reminder through its heritage of supplications and the work of its scholars, reminding that the central focus of its faith is bringing oneself closer to God Almighty. That is the pursuit of the Imam, and that should be the pursuit of every believing man and woman.

This chapter, and the chapters that follow, will begin to detail the three responsibilities starting with preserving and protecting the religion and message of God. To delve into this subject, the authors will be giving particular focus to a discourse on the sources of religion and divine guidance in Shi'a doctrine. This is significant to establish early on, as it provides the reader a foundation and framework of the Shi'i worldview.

TO PRESERVE AND PROTECT

The Prophet and his family made sure to raise a group of followers and companions to preserve the message of the faith and protect the believers. God says in the Holy Quran, "Indeed We have sent down the Reminder, and indeed We will preserve it."[3]

God gave a promise to the world. His promise was the excellence of man – an existence destined for greatness in this life and the next. He revealed the message of Islam as the complete message purposed in giving humanity a path to reach that excellence and meet its full potential, through the Prophet Muhammad and his Household. The revelation came in the form of the Holy Quran, which was delivered and exemplified through the person of Prophet Muhammad. There is a key relationship between the one who delivers the message of God, the message itself, and those who receive it. All of those ultimately tie back to the relationship with God Almighty and one's position before Him. The prophet is that perfect vessel that holds the message and delivers it. God ensures that the delivery is perfect because nothing but perfection comes from Him.

Because of that perfect conveyance, Shi'a teachings maintain that every person should aim to fulfill that excellent potential they were created for. When questioned for one's life choices on the Day of Reckoning, no blame can be attributed to others for one's own actions. "There is enough light for those who wish to see," said Imam Ali.[4] The Holy Quran highlights this reality, between God's prophets or apostles, the message, and mankind, in the following verse. "Apostles, as bearers of good news and warners, so that mankind may not have any argument against God, after the [sending of the] apostles; and God is all-mighty, all-wise."[5]

The bearers of good news, the representatives of God, set the foundation. They manifested His will and delivered the guidance to mankind it needed to carry on towards its excellence. Given that, inadequacy cannot be argued on the part of the messenger or the One who sent him, nor can human beings blame any shortcomings on anyone but on their own selves. This principle of accountability and responsibility for one's own actions is central to Shi'i ethics.

With that established, the reader should now direct their attention to the central focus of this chapter – sources of religious guidance. What are the primary sources of the message and religion of Islam that Shi'ism claims to protect and preserve? Where does religious guidance come from? For Shi'a Muslims to activate their role in preserving the religion, they must answer that essential question.

The first fundamental source of religion is the Holy Quran; the undisputed Book of God by all Muslims. Any individual who testifies that there is no god but God and Muhammad is His messenger adheres to the Quran as the unadulterated revelation sent to humanity through the Holy Prophet. There is no doubt or argument in that.

But beyond the Quran itself, what are the sources of religion? Are there any other primary sources to be relied on? Several Muslims have tried to argue, as early as the final days of the Prophet's life, that all they needed was the Quran. "The Quran is enough for us," those early Muslims proclaimed. Though this may seem comprehensive on its face, given that what is relied on is God's Word, such a position is, in fact, inadequate and misguided. The argument neglects the reality that the Quran does not presume the role of an all-encompassing book of guidance that needs nothing to supplement it. In fact, the Holy Quran tells us that a few its own verses cannot be taken by themselves, but instead must be interpreted by those "firmly grounded in knowledge."[6]

God says in the Holy Quran,

> It is He who has sent down to you the Book. Parts of it are
> definitive verses, which are the mother of the Book, while others
> are metaphorical. As for those in whose hearts is deviance, they
> pursue what is metaphorical in it, courting temptation, and seeking
> its interpretation. But no one knows its interpretation except God
> and those firmly grounded in knowledge; they say, 'We believe in
> it; all of it is from our Lord.' And none takes admonition except
> those who possess intellect.[7]

This verse establishes, along with other verses that indicate a very similar reality, that the Quran should not be taken as the sole end-all source of divine guidance. The individuals of "knowledge" and "intellect" must be the sources taken along with the Book, to provide the necessary guidance in explaining God's word, exemplifying its principles, and clarifying any ambiguity. For the message of guidance to be complete, as is characteristic of God's revelation, those individuals are needed. They provide the true meanings and interpretation of the Holy Quran.

Most of thought in Islam have come forward to argue that there is another primary source, one that is needed in fact to supplement the Holy Quran, being the *sunnah* – the tradition of the Prophet. To refer to the tradition of the Holy Prophet comes with the practical need to detail the duties and obligations obliged in the Holy Quran, but that may not be necessarily detailed for practice.

Take the examples of daily prayers, fasting, pilgrimage, and the different forms of charity. The Quran expands on these practices in some ways but does not necessarily provide for some of the crucial details, like the number of units per prayer or some of the less obvious things that may invalidate a person's fast. Given that the Quran discusses obligations, and commands Muslims to uphold those duties, but does not give all the details in those regards, referring to the way the Prophet himself practiced those commandments would fill in the void.

With the sunnah of the Prophet utilized to supplement the instructions of the Quran, some Muslims argue that this is sufficient for people's complete guidance in faith. Shiʿism maintains that another step is needed in this theological framework.

History documents that soon after the Prophet's passing, much of what was recorded of his tradition was compromised by those who intended to have the Holy Quran be the sole source of religious guidance. The recordings or written narrations of the Holy Prophet's traditions, what became known as *hadith*, were seen by some as an unnecessary or potentially threatening coupling source of religious guidance. A number of historical accounts, agreed on by the vast majority of Muslims across the different schools of thought, showed that the early Caliphs ordered to have all the narrations of the Prophet gathered and burned.[8]

The intent expressed by these early caliphs was that they wanted to make sure there were no other words to conflict or compete with the words of the Holy Quran. The first caliph, Abu Bakr (ruled 632 – d. 634), discouraged those who narrated from the Prophet. He said, "You are reporting narrations that you differ on and people after you will differ even more. So, do not narrate anything. Tell the people that what we differ on will be cared for by the Book of God. What it permits you permit and what it prohibits you prohibit." [9] *

The notion of detesting the recordkeeping of the Prophet's narrations was reflected in ʿAbdullah ibn ʿAmr ibn Al-ʿAs words when he said, "I used to write everything I heard from the Prophet. But Quraysh stopped me from doing that. They told me you write everything you hear from the Prophet. He is a human being. He talks when he is angry and when he is not. So I stopped writing. And I told the Messenger of God. He told me to write, by God that nothing came from me except the truth." [10]

Without delving into the topic further, it showed a deliberate attempt to eradicate the record of the prophetic traditions and practices, in order to keep what was gathered of the Holy Quran as the sole reference for Muslim guidance.

Nonetheless, today most Muslims refer to the Holy Quran and the *sunnah* as the primary sources of the religion though early attempts were made to extinguish the remanence of the latter. Looking at the Holy Quran and the traditions, customs, and lifelong actions of the Prophet Muhammad, a Muslim can delve deeper to see what other sources are primary for religious guidance. In examining the corpus of the *sunnah*, or prophetic tradition, there was a deliberate emphasis on a sister-source to the Holy Quran – one that the Prophet promised would remain with it until the Hereafter.

"THEY WILL NEVER SEPARATE"

In the city of Mecca, the Holy Prophet announced the faith of Islam and his role as Messenger of God in 610 AD when he was 40 years old. Initially,

---

* These same sources reference the second caliph, ʿUmar ibn al-Khattab (ruled 634 – d. 644) ordering that all the written narrations be gathered, and consequently had them burned. It is said that it took a month execute this executive order.

the announcement was not a public one given the anticipated uproar from the chieftains of Quraysh, one of the dominant tribes amongst the Arabs and the tribe the Prophet himself belonged to. The nature of Prophet Muhammad's message would spoil the political and economic status quo because much of Meccan society, especially its economy, was built on the pilgrimage of idol worshippers. So, when the Prophet's message did become public a few years later, he was met with great hostility and opposition from those who benefited from the status quo. The early Muslims were severely persecuted and marginalized.

The Prophet had sent some of his followers to Abyssinia, modern-day Eritrea and northern Ethiopia, to escape persecution. He would also leave Mecca and settle in Yathrib which is now known as the city of Medina. The *hijrah*, or migration, from Mecca to Medina took place in 622 AD – which also marked the beginning of the Islamic calendar.* The Muslims that migrated to Medina would become known as the *Muhajirun*, or migrants, and those who welcomed them in Medina would become known as the *Ansar*, or supporters. In Medina, the faith flourished. The religious, social, political, and economic affairs of the new Muslim community grew dynamically. The Prophet chartered a constitution to unite the tribes of Medina, called the Charter of Medina or the Constitution of Medina, and within a few short years was not only a spiritual leader but a head of state and a commander of a growing army.

The Prophet governed Medina for ten years, before his passing in 632 AD. In the last year before his passing, he invited the Muslim community to join him on his Farewell Pilgrimage. This was the first time that the Muslim community had gathered in such large numbers with their leader. Some historical traditions cite over 100,000 Muslims being in attendance of pilgrimage that year with the Prophet.[11] It was an opportunity for the Muslims to learn the correct and uniform pilgrimage directly from their Prophet.

---

* The Islamic calendar is also known as the hijri calendar. Dates are followed by the A.H. which is an abbreviation for "after hijrah", or after the migration.

But that was not the only significant takeaway from this journey. After completing the pilgrimage and as they left Mecca towards Medina, the Prophet and those with him stopped in a place called *Ghadir Khum*. It was known to be a place of departure and split routes, a place where people gathered from different provinces and parted ways to head back home.[12] It was here that following revelation came to the Prophet, "O Apostle! Deliver what has been sent down to you from your Lord; and if you do not do so, you have not delivered His message (at all); and God will protect you from the people…"[13]

The Prophet knew that there would be apprehension to his announcement. He also knew that there would be those of his followers that would not heed his final message. Thus, as shown in that last sentence of the verse, the Prophet is reassured by God's promise that he has His protection and support.

The Holy Prophet went so far as to send messengers to have those who had traveled ahead to return. The gathered group also waited for those behind them to catch up. Clearly the message was an important one to gather thousands in the desert enduring the heat of the sun. It is narrated that people wrapped whatever extra clothing they had around their feet to alleviate the pain from the blistering sands they stood on. Some sat on rocks but those too suffered from the heat of the sun. In the meantime, he ordered his close companion and confidant Salman al-Farisi to set up a makeshift pulpit for the Prophet to ascend and deliver a sermon to the masses. Salman and those assisting him used large rocks and horse and camel saddles to do so.[14]

Once the pulpit was ready, the Holy Prophet ascended and began speaking to his people. He began in God's glorious name and spoke with divine inspiration. He recited the verses of the Holy Quran and reminded his people of their obligations and to guard against heedlessness. He then turned his attention to a particular matter pertaining to guidance and the future that lies ahead.

The Prophet looked on to the masses before him and said,

> It seems that I have been called [by God to His side] and I [will
> soon] answer. I am leaving for you two weighty things, one of
> which is greater than the other. They are the Book of God and my
> Progeny, my Ahl al-Bayt. Be careful in how you succeed me in
> regards to them. Surely, the two shall never separate until they
> reach me at the Pond [of Paradise].[15]

After this declaration, he followed up with a question to all those present.
He asked, "Do you not bear witness that I have greater authority over any
believer than he does over himself?"

The people cried out in unison, "Indeed, yes!"

At that point, Imam Ali was standing next to the Holy Prophet. The
Prophet grabbed his arm and lifted it high enough for all to see, proclaim-
ing,

> Surely, whoever takes me as his *mawla* (master), Ali is also his
> master! O' God, oppose those who oppose him and support those
> who support him.[16]

The Shi'a narrative and experience has a tremendous focus on this prophetic speech, which culminated with these declarations of allegiance to
Imam Ali as the Prophet's heir. By divine order, the Prophet made it clear
where people's allegiance should lie and most importantly where they were
to receive their guidance after him.

Historically there has been debate amongst differing schools of thought in
Islam as to the intended meaning of the word *mawla* in Prophet Muhammad's declaration at Ghadir Khum. Sunnis generally maintain that the
Prophet's emphasis on Ali being a *mawla*, is in the meaning of friend rather
than master or leader. That people must befriend and love Ali. The argument purports that Ali had made many enemies amongst the Arabs after
being at the forefront of much of Islam's battles; and thus, he had killed
many of the brothers or sons of the Arabs that had later entered Islam.
Therefore, the Prophet arguably wanted to make sure that the Muslims
acknowledged Ali as a friend and clear the air from previous conflicts so to

speak. Surely, Islamic history records Imam Ali as the champion of Islam's early battles, becoming known as *Asadullah al-Ghalib*, the Victorious Lion of God.* He was entrusted by the Prophet as the standard bearer of the Muslim army, challenging the best warrior of the opposing army at the onset of each battle. The valiant warrior he was, he never lost a confrontation.

At the Battle of Khaybar in 628 AD, Ali defeated the infamous warrior Marhab of Khaybar, a fortress town that no army had previously penetrated.[17] The legendary tale tells of Ali's miraculous feat of strength, whereby he single-handedly pried open the Gate of Khaybar and the rest of the Muslim warriors rushed the fort. At the Battle of Badr in 624 AD, Imam Ali led a force of 300 Muslims against nearly a 1000-man force from the pagans of Mecca. Outnumbered 3 to 1, he smiled in the face of such odds. Imam Ali not only slew the commander of the opposing Meccan army, al-Walid ibn 'Utbah, but he also claimed more than half of the total killed enemies.[18]

Though it may be true that people had grown animosity towards Ali after these battles, the Shi'a argue that the same animosity would then be shown to the Prophet himself who led as the commander of these battles that Ali championed. The Shi'a position also rebuts that this sentiment was not such a significant case that it would be the cause for the Prophet to have his people stand under the scorching desert sun for over three hours as an aftermath to his last pilgrimage with them. Moreover, Shi'a scholars maintain that the interpretation of *mawla,* along with its variants, root, and derivatives of *wali and wilayah,* is one that encompasses the meanings of friend, helper, and supporter; but is more broadly based in the connotation of guardianship and leadership.[19]

Given the context, Shi'a doctrine asserts that it is unreasonable to accept the notion asserted here because it lacks substance. The Prophet's actions are guided by divinity. He does not act in vain, nor does his conduct have

---

* Imam Ali had many honorific titles from his victories in battle. "Asad Rasulillah" – the Lion of God's Messenger; "Haydar" – the Lion; "karrar ghayr farrar" – the one who plunges into battle and never retreats; "Sayf al-Islam" – the sword of Islam.

any vein of imprudence. To say that the Prophet ordered to have tens of thousands gathered in the unforgiving desert to hear him say that Ali was his friend is perplexing to adherents of the Shi'a faith. Why would the Prophet build up such a momentous occasion for such an uneventful announcement? He did not. And that is because, "He does not speak out of whim, he is nothing but revelation."[20] *

In furtherance of the argument and belief of the Ahl al-Bayt as the supplemental source of religious guidance with the Holy Quran, Shi'a scholars refer to the following verses in addition to what was already mentioned of verses within a historical context. "This is indeed a noble Quran, in a guarded Book —no one touches it except the pure ones — sent down gradually from the Lord of all the worlds."[21]

Some scholars from other schools of thought have argued that the touching notion here is a merely a reference to a physical touching. More specifically, it is generally established that it is indeed forbidden to touch the words of the Holy Quran if one is in a state of spiritual impurity, according to Islamic jurisprudence. Though this jurisprudential and ethical ruling is widely accepted, it is not the sole takeaway and ultimate explanation of the verse above. Shi'a scholars pay closer attention to this verse and explain that it does not say that no one is *allowed* to touch it except the pure ones. If diction related to prohibition or allowance were utilized, it would be reasonable to deduce such a conclusion. However, the verse says it *will not be touched* except by the pure ones. God is making a promise here. The Quran will not be touched except by the pure. For the mere fact that anyone can physically touch the Quran, whether they are pure or not, would nullify the verse if it spoke to a physical touch. Therefore, the word *yamassuh* here is not referring to a mere physical touch.

---

* This verse is a central piece of revelation to Shi'i dogma on the Prophet Muhammad's standing as an immaculate figure in all respects. While some schools of thought may argue that the Prophet was merely infallible in terms of delivering revelation; the Shi'a argue that he was immaculate in every way, and that he cannot act or speak out of whim – he, himself, is revelation.

Instead, as evidenced by the Shi'i scholar and exegetist Allamah Tabataba'i in his seminal work, *Tafsir al-Mizan*, "touching" here is not a physical one, but an intellectual and spiritual one; a reference to the knowledge and understanding of the Holy Book in its deepest meanings.[22] Thus, only those who are pure may truly understand and embody the Holy Quran in its greatest depth. It is they who can then provide its guidance and show its illuminating light.

In another verse, God speaks of the pure ones and says, "Indeed, God desires to repel all impurity from you, O People of the Household, and purify you with a thorough purification."[23]

The People of the Household, Ahl al-Bayt, was a reference to the Prophet's family – his daughter Lady Fatimah, his son-in-law Imam Ali, and his grandsons Imams Hasan and Husayn. The Prophet would knock on the doors of his family members and announce to people that he came to visit a member of his Household. It was a unique greeting that he gave to each and every one of his family, one that he did not give to anyone else. Even though the Prophet made clear who his household consisted of on numerous occasions, some make it a contested issue in Muslim discourse. However, if you look closely at the narrations and the verses of the Holy Quran it is clear who belonged to the Household. Nonetheless, the Quran defines who the Ahl al-Bayt are in the following verse.

> Should anyone argue with you concerning him, after the
> knowledge that has come to you, say, 'Come! Let us call our sons
> and your sons, our women and your women, our selves and your
> selves, then let us pray earnestly, and call down God's curse upon
> the liars.'[24]

This particular verse was revealed to the Prophet in what became known as the event of *Mubahalah*. The Christians of Najran, a city in southwestern Saudi Arabia near the border with Yemen, engaged in a debate with the Holy Prophet in the 9th year after hijrah, 631 AD. The Prophet had invited the Archbishop of Najran, 'Abdulharis Ibn 'Alqamah, and his people to embrace Islam. Ibn ʿAlqamah was an official representative of the Roman Church in Hijaz, western region in modern-day Saudi Arabia. The written letter turned into in-person dialogue and engagement. As the communication continued between the Prophet and the Christians of Najran, the verse above was revealed.

God ordered the Prophet to tell the Christians to expand the circle of dialogue and bring out the best of each side to engage in discourse. "Our sons and your sons, our women and your women, our selves and your selves…" Following God's command, at this crucial moment, The Prophet selected Imams Hasan and Husayn, his young grandsons who did not exceed the age of seven, his daughter Lady Fatimah, and his closest companion and successor Imam Ali to accompany him. People were in awe of the confidence and presence of this family made of 5 individuals.

Out of all the people in his midst, the Prophet brought two children as his sons – one that he held on his arm and another that held his hand. That was half of his delegation. The other half was his daughter Fatimah and son-in-law Ali, both, of course, highly respected individuals but very young nonetheless. One of the members of the Christian delegation had said previously,

> If he challenges us with his people, we accept the challenge for he is not a prophet; but if he challenges us with his family in particular we don't challenge him, for he is not going to put forward his family unless he is truthful.[25]

ʿAbdulharis Ibn ʿAlqamah was present, leading the Christian delegation. Seeing the Prophet put forth his own flesh and blood in this great debate led him to retreat. He encouraged his fellow Christians to concede the debate and they did.

The aforementioned verses from the Holy Quran are essential references in the corpus of Shiʿa doctrine on immaculateness of the Ahl al-Bayt and their relationship to God's Word.

THE PROPHET'S DISCIPLES

The Prophet Muhammad lauded his heir, Imam Ali, for many reasons. It was not because Ali was his cousin and son-in-law, as some have wrongly presumed. The Prophet had many relatives, some who were his staunchest enemies like his uncles Abu Lahab and Abu Jahl. In Shi'ism's strict adherence to the immaculateness of the Prophet, his moral character was far from any inclination towards nepotism or biases of any sort.

Indeed, Muslims maintain that Prophet Muhammad was surely a man amongst men, with human emotions, feelings, and ambitions. But he was the par excellence of men. His impeccable character and reputation were unmatched. He was trusted and praised by his friends and foes alike. And honored by God as the "mercy to all the nations,"[26] and one who "does not speak out of whim,"[27] and is "nothing but revelation."[28] Thus, Shi'a creed maintains that the Prophet's praise of an individual comes from the individual's merit alone – one that deserves the greatest level of attention and admiration because it is essentially the praise of God himself.

The Holy Prophet describes the proximity between Imam Ali and the Quran itself. He says, "Ali is with the Quran and the Quran is with Ali. They will not separate until they reach me at the Pond [of Paradise].[29] In another narration, the Prophet emphasizes that, "The truth is with Ali and Ali is with the truth. They will not separate until they reach me at the Pond [of Paradise]."[30]

The Shi'a corpus of hadith also maintains several narrations from Imam Ali himself that describes his status with the Prophet and proximity to him. He described to people his relationship with Prophet Muhammad, especially as his student and protégé. However, even his descriptions of the discourse between the teacher par excellence and the student par excellence left the listener bewildered. Imam Ali is famously quoted to have said, "The Messenger of God taught me a thousand gates [of knowledge] and each gate opens a thousand more."[31]

Imam Ali's great grandson, Imam Muhammad al-Baqir – the fifth imam in Twelver tradition, was asked about these thousand doors of knowledge on one occasion. The inquirer, a companion by the name of Kamil Al-Tammar, asked, "Were [these thousand gates of knowledge] revealed to your Shiʿa and devotees?" Al-Baqir replied, "O' Kamil, only a door or two."[32]

Kamil al-Tammar commented on this narration that he remembers Imam Muhammad al-Baqir saying that it was only one gate, not even two – stressing the extent of how vast the knowledge possessed by his great grandfather Imam Ali was.

There is a particular verse in the Holy Quran that scholars of exegesis have agreed to be in reference to the authority of Imam Ali as a vicegerent of God. "Your guardian (*wali*) is only God, His Apostle, and the faithful who maintain the prayer and give the *zakah* while bowing down."[33]

The subject of this verse is *wilayah*, or divine guardianship. Guardians assume authority and protection over those they guard. In the context of divine guardianship, God follows his name with His Apostle – Prophet Muhammad. Following that is the "faithful". The faithful is described therein; those "who maintain the prayer and give the *zakah* [or alms] while bowing down." Both Shiʿa and Sunni scholars say that this verse is a reference to Imam Ali and narrate the following documented story in Muslim history.[34]

The Prophet had settled in Medina after leaving the harsh persecution of the people in Mecca. Though, the community of Muslims grew substantially in Medina, Islam was still very young. One day, as Imam Ali prayed in the mosque, a beggar walked around asking people for help. "Could you spare some change?" he asked. "Please help me," he pleaded. No one paid attention to him. He entered the mosque and continued to ask, but people did not come to his aid. In his rounds of seeking people's sympathy or pity, he neared the area where Imam Ali prayed. In the state of *rukuʿ* – the ritual bow performed in the middle of each unit of prayer – the Imam extended his hand out to the beggar. Upon closer inspection, the beggar saw an open palm offering a precious ring. Elated, the beggar took the ring and was off on his way. The verse mentioned above was revealed to the Holy Prophet after this unique show of piety and worship.[35]

Indeed, the Holy Prophet's praise of his successor Imam Ali was unique. Still, he certainly discussed the authority and position of all the disciples that would follow him – the Twelve Imams. Jabir ibn ʿAbdullah al-Ansari, a prominent *muhaddith*, scholar and narrator of *hadith,* was a companion of the Prophet Muhammad and lived long enough to be a companion of not only Imam Ali, but his sons and grandsons as well. Jabir narrated the following directly from the Prophet himself. Prophet Muhammad said, "I am the Master of the Prophets and Ali is the master of successors and the successors after me are twelve. The first is Ali and the last is *al-Qaʾim al-Mahdi.*"[36] *

ʿAbdullah Ibn ʿAbbas, the Prophet's cousin and companion, also narrated on the very same subject. The Prophet said, "My successors and heirs, and the proof of God over His creations after me, are the twelve Imams. The first of them is Ali and the last is my son al-Mahdi."[37] Ibn ʿAbbas also narrates that the Holy Prophet stated, "I, as well as Ali, Hasan and Husayn, and nine from the progeny of Husayn are purified [by God Almighty] and immaculate."[38]

These hadiths and historical accounts should give the reader an overview of the corpus of Shiʿa hadith and the lens in which the Shiʿa see their Imams and the sources of religious guidance. In summary, the sources of guidance in the Shiʿa school of thought are discerned by the commands of the Holy Prophet – that vicegerent of God who was sent as the flawless mercy to mankind. These sources are referred to as *al-thaqalayn,* the two weighty things – the Book of God and the Prophet's Holy Household. The Shiʿa maintain that these two sources of divine guidance are immaculate and

---

* Al-Qaʾim means the one who stands or rises. It is a title attributed to the Twelfth Imam of the Shiʿa, Imam Muhammad al-Mahdi, and often is short for *qaʾim al Muhammad,* the riser from the family of Muhammad. Al-Mufid, al-Irshad, 2:380-386.

essential for a Muslim's salvation, in remaining committed to the final instructions of the Prophet of Islam.

CHAPTER 5

FAITH & WORKS

I love everyone and this religion is a religion of love.

Grand Ayatollah Sistani

FAITH AFTER ISLAM

Islamic teachings view the Prophet Muhammad as one who emphasized a practical approach to faith, *Iman*, and religion, *Islam*, for his followers. Islam was not an abstract or theoretical system of belief. God did not send a celestial being that had no relationship or root in humanity. He did not send angels to guide mankind through the journey of life. Instead, "He sent to the unlettered [people] an apostle from among themselves, to recite to them His signs, to purify them, and to teach them the Book and wisdom."[1]

The Prophet was a man of his people. He lived amongst them, worked with them, arbitrated for them and helped resolve their disputes. Even before he announced his prophethood at the age of 40, he was known in his community as *al-Sadiq al-Amin*, the Truthful and Trustworthy. This was attributed to his honesty and fair dealings as a trader in Mecca. Thus, when he preached the ideals of justice, fairness, and honesty, the people of his community had already seen him live up to his word.

One of the main elements that the Prophet emphasized in guiding his nation was the integration of practice with concepts. The preservation of any idea or message comes through the establishment of a system that integrates that idea into the daily life of those who adopt it. The Prophet made clear that it was one thing to verbally express an idea, but it was another thing to adopt it and make it part of who you are. This applies to all facets of a Muslim's life. Whether it is a one-time concept or a continuous idea, the quality and value of the idea is contingent on its realization and application.

Take the example of an architectural structure. Imagine that some of the world's greatest architects come together to design a concept for a record-breaking skyscraper. They spend several months working on designs and sketches. After multiple drawings and drafts, it ends up taking much longer than originally expected. They realize this is one of the most important structures any one of them would have ever worked on. They agree the time put in is worthwhile. The architects ultimately come to a consensus on the final design for the new building and it was immaculate. Unfortunately, the investors pull the plug on the project and design was never used. Despite the perfection of the concept design, it did not come to life. Architecture is not admired for the concepts created on paper; it is admired for the real structure erected on land. In the end, an architect wishes for his or her work to be manifested through construction. Ideas are beautiful, but they are that much more beautiful when they are manifested outside in real time and space. This is the same with the message of Islam.

In his book *Usul al-Kafi*, Shaykh al-Kulayni has a narration from Imam Muhammad al-Baqir distinguishing *Iman*, faith, from *Islam*, the religion. Imam al-Baqir states, "Faith is to accept and to work, or practice. Islam is [simply] to accept without the work."[2]

To be a *Muslim*, a person must accept the religion and its tenets. It starts by declaring *la ilaha illa Allah, Muhammadun rasul Allah* – there is no god but God, and Muhammad is his prophet. With that declaration, a person has become Muslim. However, for one to become *Mu'min*, a believer, they must *practice* the ideas, beliefs, and concepts that they have accepted. They must put in the work beyond merely declaring faith.

Shaykh al-Hur al-'Amili, a notable Shi'a traditionist and scholar of the 17th century, compiled the widely regarded book of hadith, *Wasa'il al-Shi'a*. He includes an insightful narration by Imam Ali al-Rida, the eighth Shi'i Imam, on the relationship between faith and practice.

> Whoever loves someone who disobeys us, he himself is in disobedience. Whoever loves someone who obeys us, he himself is in obedience. Whoever helps an oppressor is himself an oppressor. Whoever abandons an oppressor is just. Indeed, there is no kinship between God and any [of His creations]. Indeed, [affiliation with us] is attained only through obedience [to God].[3]

The word "obedience" in the last sentence of the narration is a clear reference to practice – acting on the belief that one holds. What human beings do reflects their state of mind and the beliefs they have in their hearts. Imam al-Rida illustrates this relationship between faith and practice, through the concepts of obedience and oppression.* In order to have faith, there must be practice.

In another narration, Imam al-Baqir discusses features of faith and Islam as they relate to the human condition, as well as the relationship between man and God.

> Faith is what settles in the heart and what has been shown to God Almighty. It is what has been truthfully proven by action through obedience to God and submitting to His commands. Islam [on the other hand] is [simply] what is apparent through words and actions. It is what is upheld by the masses of the people from all sects. Through [Islam] blood was protected, the right of inheritance was granted, and marriage was allowed. [And because of Islam, people] were united in prayer, zakah, fasting and hajj, and thus were taken from nonbelief and into belief.[4]

---

* The reference of oppression is a common theme within Islam, and particularly Shi'ism, as one to warn believers from, in that adhering to the faith and practicing it should ward off one's own carnal inclinations which can lead to transgression of rights and the oppression of others. It is also used to distinguish the believers from those who are oppressors, be it private piety or in the public domain of rulership and governance.

Simply embracing Islam does not necessarily translate into having faith. However, if one has faith then they are within the fold of Islam. Essentially, Islam is a necessary condition of faith, but is not the only condition of faith. It is important to note that both religion and faith can be seen in what we say and do, and that faith itself requires much more than simple testimony. God illustrates this understanding through the example of some of the early Bedouins that embraced the message of Islam during the life of the Holy Prophet.

> The Bedouins say, 'We have faith.' Say, 'You do not have faith yet; rather, say, "We have embraced Islam," for faith has not yet entered into your hearts. Yet if you obey God and His Apostle, He will not stint anything of [the reward of] your works. Indeed, God is all-forgiving, all-merciful.'[5]

One of the companions of Imam al-Baqir struck a conversation with him on this very subject. He wondered about the rights and privileges of a Mu'min when compared to a Muslim. So, he asked the Imam candidly, "Does the Mu'min have more privileges in terms of virtues, rulings and punishment than a Muslim?"

The Imam replied, "No, they are both the same when it comes to these affairs. But the Mu'min is favored over a Muslim in terms of their actions and what makes them closer to God Almighty."

The companion followed up by reciting the following verse, "Whoever brings virtue shall receive [a reward] ten times its like."[6] He then asked, "You said that a Muslim is the same as a Mu'min in terms of prayers, zakah, fasting and pilgrimage. [Thus, per the verse, they should be rewarded in the same manner.]"

The Imam replied, "Did He, the Almighty, not say, 'That He may multiply it for him several fold'? The believers are the ones for whom God Almighty will multiply their rewards seventy-fold. That is the status of a believer, and God will increase his reward manifold in accordance with the truthfulness of his belief. Indeed, God will do as much good as He pleases for the believers.

The companion followed up by asking, "Is it not that whoever embraces Islam embraces belief as well?" To this the Imam gave a beautiful analogy.

> No, it is not. Indeed, he has [become closer] to faith and has moved away from *kufr* [nonbelief]. I will give you an example by which you can understand the difference between Islam and Iman. If someone were in the [Grand] Mosque, could you bear witness that they are inside the Kaaba? But if you see a person inside the Kaaba, can you not testify that he entered the [Grand] Mosque?

The companion replied, "Yes, I can testify to [the latter and not to the former] because he could not enter the Kaaba unless he entered the [Grand] Mosque."

Imam al-Baqir replied, "That is accurate and well-said. It is the same when it comes to Iman and Islam."[7]

Jamil ibn Darraj, a companion of Imam al-Baqir's son – Imam Jaʿfar al-Sadiq – narrates a conversation that he had with Imam al-Sadiq about faith. Imam al-Sadiq said, "[Faith] is to witness that there is no god but God and Muhammad is His Messenger."

Ibn Darraj then asked the Imam, "Isn't this an action as well?" The Imam said, "Yes it is… Faith is not truly attained [by a believer] except through action…"[8]

This particular narration goes to emphasize how faith does not come simply through the basic acceptance of Islam, but by actually acting on the belief that one is accepting and testifying to. By truly embracing that there is no god but God, and Muhammad is His messenger, one would align his conduct and lifestyle in a way that reflected that belief. Such an alignment would translate into having faith, or *Iman*.

Hammad ibn ʿAmr al-Nasibi narrates another conversation between Imam al-Baqir and an individual who beseeched him for some answers. The inquirer asked him, "O' knowledgeable one, what are the best acts before God?" The Imam replied, "It is the act that no other will be accepted except through it. "And what act is that?" the man asked. Imam al-Baqir replied, "It is faith in God, which is the greatest of deeds… Faith is entirely in practice and what is said is only part of that practice…"

"Describe this for me so I can understand it," the inquirer requested. The Imam said, "Faith comes in different situations, levels, degrees and categories. Thus, there is complete faith that is perfect in its realization. There is also faith that is not complete…" The man interjected, "Is it possible that faith can be added to and subtracted from?" The Imam answered,

> Yes… God obliged faith on the faculties of the children of Adam, dividing and distributing it amongst them. Thus, there is no faculty of the faculties [of mankind] except that it is given a responsibility towards the faith that is not given to its sister [faculties]. Amongst them is the heart* through which [the individual] reasons, learns, and understands. It is the commander of his body, and none of the other faculties may [act], except by its opinion and command. And amongst them are his hands which he strikes with and his feet which he walks with… As for what the heart has been obliged with of the faith, it is acquiescence, knowledge, belief, submission, resolve, and contentment in that there is no god but God – solely and without partner – the One and All-sufficing who has not taken to Himself neither a partner nor a son. And that Muhammad, may the blessings of God be upon him and his family, is His servant and messenger.[9]

If the reader looks closely at the words of the fifth Shiʿa Imam, there is a practical understanding of the Shiʿa view on how every part of the individual plays into the lifestyle of a believer. To believe in God is not simply the

---

* The "heart" here is a literal translation from the word *qalb*. Within context this is a reference to the intellect.

responsibility of the heart or intellect. The heart leads that first step, because without the heart nothing else could follow. To be a believer, however, one must use every other organ and limb in their own responsibility to practice the faith. Each part of an individual's being plays a role in the practice of faith. It is a total engagement of one's self.

Shi'a Islam teaches that the Prophet and his Household delivered a complete system for the believers to embrace and utilize throughout their lives. Much of this is observed through conscientious worship and reflection. The Shi'a community maintains these practices on a daily (such as the five obligatory ritual prayers*), weekly (such as Friday congregational prayers,† weekly supplications like Du'a' Kumayl‡ on Thursdays and Du'a' al-Tawassul§ on Tuesdays), monthly (certain days of the month being recommended to fast**), and yearly (certain days being held as 'Id, or holidays, for the community to come together in gift-giving and prayers). The traditions of the Shi'a Imams provide their followers guidance on how to fully

---

* Muslims pray five daily prayers. Each prayer has a prescribed number of units, within each of which there are verses from the Quran and short supplications recited. The first prayer Fajr (2 units) is prayed at the time of dawn; the second prayer Zuhr (4 units) and third prayer 'Asr, are performed in the afternoon; the fourth prayer Maghrib (3 units) and the fifth prayer 'Isha' (4 units) are prayed after sunset. Each unit of prayer is comprised of reciting the first chapter of the Holy Quran (al-Fatihah) and a second chapter while in a standing position. One then proceeds to go into state of ruku', followed by two prostrations with one's forehead, palms, knees, and toes touching the ground. Muslims must maintain a state of purity and perform ablution before they begin their prayers. For details on religious rulings regarding prayers see: al-Sistani, *A Code of Practice for Muslims in the West.*

† Muslims generally hold Friday prayer congregations in observance of the Quranic instruction: "O you who have faith! When the call is made for prayer on Friday, hurry toward the remembrance of God, and leave all business. That is better for you, should you know. And when the prayer is finished, disperse through the land and seek God's grace, and remember God greatly so that you may be successful." The Holy Quran, 62:9–10. Muslims will hold congregational prayers during other days of the week as well in mosques, community centers, safe public spaces, and homes.

‡ Du'a' Kumayl was a supplication taught by Imam Ali to his close companion, Kumayl ibn Ziyad. The supplication would become attributed to Kumayl and today is known as Du'a' Kumayl. The supplication is usually recited every Thursday night in mosques and homes across Shi'a Muslim communities.

§ Du'a' al-Tawassul is a supplication of intercession invoking the 14 Immaculates, starting from the Holy Prophet Muhammad and his daughter Lady Fatimah, and continuing with the Twelve Immaculate Imams. It is recommended and observed on Tuesday nights according to Shi'a tradition.

** Fasting is recommended in the beginning, middle, and end of every month generally in Shi'a Muslim tradition.

engage themselves in faith, through the complete engagement of all their faculties.*

THE UNDENIABLE TRUTH

The guidance of the Holy Prophet that continued with the vicegerents of his Household is central to the Shi'i discourse on faith. Following them is often considered to be the turning point for an individual that truly embraces faith within Islam. The concept of following them again is not lip service but rather practice and action that manifests the instructions and guidance of the Prophet himself.

Zurarah, a companion of the Imams, narrates a discussion with Imam al-Baqir. The Imam was speaking about Islam and its foundations. He said, "Islam was built on five things: prayer, alms, pilgrimage, fasting, and *wila-yah* [allegiance]."† Zurarah followed by asking, "What is the best out of these things?" Imam al-Baqir replied that, "Wilayah is the best, as it is the key to all of them. The *wali* [immaculate Imam] is the guide for them." The Imam continued by explaining that prayer, alms, pilgrimage, and fasting all followed after wilayah.[10]

Shi'a tradition cites to the verses of the Quran to draw on and point to the significance of the Ahl al-Bayt, in addition to what is explicitly shown in the hadith evidenced in both Sunni and Shi'a sources. Shi'a scholars maintain that the significance of Ahl al-Bayt is illustrative in the verses of the Holy Quran, especially when examined within context. In the following

---

* Shi'a piety observes three primary books: The Holy Quran, *Nahj al-Balaghah* (The Peak of Eloquence): Sermons, Letters, and Sayings of Imam Ali ibn Abu Talib, and *al-Sahifat al-Sajjadiyyah* (The Psalms of Imam Ali al-Sajjad). In addition to these books, many Shi'a Muslims in the past several decades have utilized an early 20th century book of rituals called *Mafatih al-Jinan* (The Keys to the Heavens) by Shaykh 'Abbas al-Qummi (1877 – 1941). This book was unique in that it provided a compilation of recommended prayers, *ad'iyah* (singular: *du'a'*) or supplications, and *ziyarat* (singular: 98iyārah) or visitations of the Immaculates and the saints of Islam, for the entirety of the year. Shi'a Muslims could look up any day of any month of the year and see the recommended rituals and spiritual acts to perform, as well as the significance of each act and the corresponding day or time it is attached to.

† Wilayah refers to allegiance to the Household of the Holy Prophet, beginning with Imam Ali and continuing with the rest of the eleven Imams, as one of the primary tenets of Shi'ism. Al-Hakeem, *al-Jama'at al-Salihah*, 1:64.

verse God provides the Prophet with a response to those who wish to confer reward and gifts upon him for his virtuous deeds.

> Such is the good news that God gives to His servants who have
> faith and do virtuous deeds! Say, 'I do not ask you any reward for it
> except the love of [my] relatives.' Whoever performs a good deed,
> We shall enhance its goodness for him. Indeed God is all-forgiving,
> all-appreciative.[11]

Thus, the Prophet would reply to his own people, "I do not ask you any reward for it except the love of [my] relatives." This verse has also been referred to in Shi'a piety as the *ayat al-mawaddah*, the verse of love or adoration for the Prophet's family. On numerous occasions the Holy Prophet would be heard speaking about his love for his family and how that love was a part of faith. "Everything has a foundation, and the foundation of Islam is to love us, the Ahl al-Bayt."[12] Applying ideas to practice the Prophet emphasized to his followers, "Whoever loves us will act like us."[13]

It was not because they were merely his blood, but rather it was embedded in the prophetic tradition that God had ordained. They were the household of truth and excellence – the highest example offered to the followers of the faith and humanity at large. The Prophet did not want anything from his people, except that they love and honor his family – because through that love they would realize their own excellence and salvation.

Imam Muhammad ibn Idris al-Shafi'i (767–820 AD), the leader of the Shafi'i* sect of Sunni Islam, praised the Household of the Prophet as the undeniable pinnacle of faith. A few lines of his poetry in their honor is widely known across the Muslim world and has been recited generation after generation.

> O Household of the Messenger your love
> is mandated by God, revealed in the Quran

---

* The Shafi'i school of thought is one of the four primary jurisprudential schools of thought within Sunni Islam. The others are Maliki, Hanbali, and Hanafi.

It is enough of grand purpose that you are who you are

Who does not mention you in prayer has no prayer at all[14]

The Holy Prophet was quite detailed and direct when it came to describing faith and the relationship his household played in its regard. The more complete version of the narration above on the "foundation of Islam", is relayed from the Prophet as follows,

> Islam is bare. Its clothing is bashfulness. Its adornment is dignity. Its ethic is practicing virtuous deeds. Its pillar is the fear of God. Everything has a foundation, and the foundation of Islam is the love of us, Ahl al-Bayt.[15]

Imam Ali masterfully ties this principle and the verse of *mawaddah*, love or adoration, as an expression of God's right upon the Muslims.

> Love the progeny of your prophet, for it is the right of God on you and what [God has obliged himself to reward you for]. Do you not see the verse of God, 'Say, I do not ask you any reward for it except the love of [my] relatives'? [16]

True belief follows through application and action. God poses a central "self-check" question in the Holy Quran. "O you who have faith! Why do you say what you do not do? It is greatly outrageous to God that you should say what you do not do."[17] Aligning one's words and actions is key to successful piety, a universal principle that Shi'a faithful share. Muslims believe that the Prophet Muhammad set the immaculate example in this. But what did he, and his family, do to bring this all into practice? What kind of framework did they provide their followers?

PRACTICES AND RITUALS

In examining the books of *fiqh*, or Islamic jurisprudence, one of the first topics a researcher will come across is the principle of ʿadalah – a standard of justice and virtue applicable in essential roles such as that of a judge (*qadi*), jurist (*faqih*), and prayer leader (*imam jamaʿah*). ʿAdalah can be

translated simply to mean justice; however, it is more practically understood as a standard of virtue, justice, and integrity required for sensitive
positions in Islam. Most if not all positions of leadership in the faith require
that the individual live by this standard of virtue. That standard of virtue
translates to having the integrity to behave in accordance with the faith at
all times. It is, as related to the discussion above; "to do what you say and
believe".

This standard is seen across the board in Islam. First and foremost, the requirement is seen in the institution of *Marji'iyyah* – religious authority and
emulation in the Shi'a school of thought. In order to be a *Marji'*, a jurist
that is followed by others in matters of Islamic law, the scholar has two primary requirements: First, the scholar must be a *mujtahid* – a jurist who has
reached a level of skill and ability to deduce the religious rulings from the
primary sources without need of following the verdicts of another jurist.
Second, the scholar must be *'adil* or just. In a more technical sense, he must
be an individual who abstains from committing any forbidden acts and fulfills all his obligations.[18]

'Adalah is also relevant when it comes to a number of elements affecting
the community such as the process of *ru'yat al-hilal*, or moonsighting,[*] or
the testimony needed for any matter. On a monthly basis, individuals from
the community go out to sight the crescent to identify the start of the next
lunar month. This is especially relevant for the holy month of Ramadan
when the Muslim community commences its annual month-long fast.[19][†]
The primary condition for eye-witness testimony of the individual

---

[*] The sighting of the crescent or the new moon is a practice that dates back to before the days of Islam. It is a ritual
that announces the beginning and ending of the lunar months for the Islamic lunar calendar. "The month of Ramadan
is one in which the Quran was sent down as guidance to mankind, with manifest proofs of guidance and the Criterion.
So let those of you who witness it fast [in] it, and as for someone who is sick or on a journey, let it be a [similar] number
of other days. God desires ease for you, and He does not desire hardship for you, and so that you may complete the
number and magnify God for guiding you, and that you may give thanks." The Holy Quran, 2:185.

[†] Muslim piety notes that it is important to say "the month of Ramadan," instead of merely saying Ramadan. The word
Ramadan is one of the names of God according to Islamic tradition. There are numerous of sources, both Sunni and
Shi'a, that substantiate this notion of prohibition to merely say "Ramadan" and practice saying *Shahr Ramadan*, or
the month of Ramadan.

moonsighting to be accepted is having two *'adil*, or just, individuals witness it. One *'adil* individual is not sufficient, nor is 100 individuals that do not qualify as *'adil*.

On another level, Shi'a piety maintains that the Ahl al-Bayt established space for religious projects to flourish within the practices of the faith. Practices are usually described as either *sha'a'ir* or *'ibadat*. *Sha'a'ir*, or rituals, refers to the ritual activities celebrating and commemorating significant tenets, events, and personalities of the faith. *'Ibadat*, or worship, refers to acts of worship, whether they are obligatory or recommended. Both rituals and worships are abundant in the domain of Shi'a doctrine and practice.[20]

Many of the prominent rituals practiced are seen in connection to the reverence of the Holy Prophet and his family. The greatest example of this is the annual commemoration of the massacre of Imam Husayn ibn Ali, his family, and companions. The massacre took place on the 10th of Muharram, the first month of the Islamic calendar in the year 680 AD, when thousands of Umayyad forces loyal to the caliphate of Mu'awiyah and his newly posted son Yazid besieged Imam Husayn's caravan in what is modern-day Karbala on their way to the city of Kufa. This day is known as the *Day of 'Ashura'*.[21]

The caravan consisted of Imam Husayn's companions, women, and children. They were cut off from water for three days. Finally, the battle commenced whereby Imam Husayn and his men were slain. After the massacre, the Umayyad army took the women and children as captives, dragged in chains across the deserts from Karbala to Kufa and then Kufa to Damascus. One man did survive, Imam Ali al-Sajjad, a son of Imam Husayn who fell ill along the way to Karbala. The Umayyad soldiers attempted to kill him as soon as they discovered his bedridden state in one of the tents; however, Lady Zaynab, Imam Husayn's sister, saved his life by telling them they would have to kill her first to take him under their sword.

The personalities in this story continue to be influential in the Shi'a consciousness today. Imam Husayn was the valiant and immaculate leader who sacrificed himself to awake a nation that had gone astray. Lady Zaynab was that strong and fearless advocate for truth and justice. Imam Ali ibn Husayn became a force of spiritual awakening and the preservation of truth for a nation that witnessed the slaughter of his whole family. Still, he would live amongst the people and be a spiritual doctor to their ailing souls.[22]

For 1400 years, Muslims have commemorated this tragedy year after year. It drives the identity of a worldwide community of Muslims and has inspired Muslim and non-Muslim alike. Mourners around the world come together in *majalis*, functions or places of gathering to recite the saga of 'Ashura'. From those *majalis*, communities have been built. The commemoration of 'Ashura' has become a feature of the Shi'a Muslim identity, serving as a central part of its culture and dogma.[23]

Muslims' commitment to celebrating or commemorating these symbols of the faith is believed to be inspired by God's words. "And whoever venerates the sacraments of God—indeed that arises from the piety of hearts."[24] It is this piety and God-consciousness that mourners seek in commemorating Imam Husayn, and the rest of Ahl al-Bayt, whom they consider as the sacraments of God. With every majlis, or commemoration, there is a consistent theme and reminder that everything belongs to God and all the faithful's deeds only have significance when they are attached to Him. "Indeed, we are from God and to Him we shall return."[25]

Other than the ritual commemoration of 'Ashura' and the anniversaries of the martyrdoms of the eleven Imams, as well as celebrating the lives of each of the Immaculates usually through their birthdates, there are numerous rituals observed.* *Laylat al-Qadr*, or the Night of Ordainment, during the holy month of Ramadan is a prominent example.† In these nights,

---

* Shi'a tradition records that each one of the eleven Imams, before the living and awaited Twelfth Imam al-Mahdi, was martyred by their adversaries. Imam Ali was assassinated, while Imam Husayn was killed and beheaded with his men in the Battle of Karbala. The rest of the nine Imams were all reportedly poisoned. See: Tabataba'i, *Shi'ite Islam*.

† In Shi'a tradition, there are three narrated nights for Laylat al-Qadr, reportedly the "small night" 19th, "middle night" 21st, and the "great night" 23rd of the month of Ramadan. Ysuf, "Laylat al-Qadr", *The Oxford Encyclopedia of the Islamic World*.

adherents stay awake until dawn busying themselves in supplication, recitation of the Holy Quran, and active reflection. It is a time dedicated to spiritual development and enrichment giving Muslims self-renewal and rejuvenation.

God speaks of the value of these nights in the Quran with a chapter dedicated to its significance – *Surat al-Qadr.**

> Indeed, We sent it down on the Night of Ordainment. And what
> will show you what is the Night of Ordainment? The Night of
> Ordainment is better than a thousand months. In it the angels and
> the Spirit descend, by the leave of their Lord, with every command.
> It is peaceful until the rising of the dawn.[26]

Days later, Muslims celebrate *'Id al-Fitr* – marking the end of the holy month of worship and fasting. Families come together, celebrating their faith, health, and community. After the annual pilgrimage of *hajj*, in which Muslims are obligated to perform a pilgrimage to the Holy City of Mecca at least one time in their lifetime, *'Id al-Adha* is celebrated as well.† Just about a week later, Shi'a Muslims go on to celebrate 'Id al-Ghadir – the day marking the Prophet's designation of Imam Ali as his heir and successor in the last year of his life, 632 AD – also considered to be al-'Id al-Akbar, or the Greatest 'Id, by some Shi'a traditions.[27] ‡

In Islam, there are also certain places that serve as reminders for the practice of the faith – the most central of which are mosques. The mosque is the house of God and the main place of public worship for a Muslim.[28] In addition to being sanctuaries of worship, they also serve as monuments of the religion of Islam.§ People yearn to build mosques for the great reward that

---

* Surah is the equivalent of "chapter" in the Holy Quran.

† 'Id al-Adha is celebrated on the 10th of Thu'l-Hijjah. This holiday also honors the willingness of Abraham to sacrifice his own son for God. In Jewish and Christian tradition, this story is shown in Genesis 22:2.

‡ 'Id al-Ghadir is celebrated on the 18th of Thu'l-Hijjah on the Islamic lunar calendar and is observed by Shi'a Muslims for the date marking Prophet Muhammad's appointment of Imam Ali as his successor.

§ "Monument" here is not to imply an inactive or stoic role; to the contrary, mosques are monuments in their symbol of pride and identity for Muslims. Going to mosques around the world, be it in the Middle East, North America,

comes from erecting a place of worship in the name of God. Both Sunni and Shi'a hadith corpus venerate building houses of worship. The Prophet is reported to have told his followers, "Whoever builds a mosque for the sake of God, then God will build for him a house like it in Paradise."[29] *

The practice of Friday prayers, general congregational prayers, *i'tikaf*, group supplications, and many other rituals are all traditionally held in mosques.† From the onset of the faith, the mosque was a focal point of Muslim society and central to the sense of community in Islam. There are mosques in specific geographic locations that are highlighted by the religion for their significance as well. Some of these mosques include: *Masjid al-Haram* in the holy city of Mecca (Saudi Arabia), *Masjid al-Rasul* in the holy city of Medina (Saudi Arabia), *Masjid al-Kufa* and *Masjid al-Sahlah* in Kufa (Iraq). The actual shrines or mausoleums of the Imams are also very significant in this regard in the Shi'a spiritual conscience.

The holy cities of Najaf, Kadhimiya, Karbala, Mashhad, and the Baqi' Cemetery are some of the major ones. The relatives of the Ahl al-Bayt are also of significance, venerated as champions of the faith and some of the greatest supporters of the Prophet's holy household. Prominent examples of such relatives include Abu al-Fadl al-'Abbas ibn Ali, whose shrine is steps away from his brother Imam Husayn's shrine in Karbala; and Lady Fatimah al-Ma'sumah, Imam Ali al-Rida's sister, who is buried in the holy city of Qum, Iran.

Visiting these places, along with the rituals associated with them, are believed to add blessings in a believer's life. These sacred places are beacons

---

Europe, South Asia, etc. show an observer that they are far from stoic in the passive sense, and rather stoic in the enduring and formidable meaning of the word, with Muslims holding prayers and spiritual rituals on a regular basis.

* A discussion in the next chapter will follow on the history and development of mosques within the Shi'a community, and how an alternative space (i.e. the *husayniyyah*) developed as well.

† *I'tikaf* is a type of spiritual retreat where Muslims devote a period of three days or more to worship in the mosque. They live, eat, and sleep in the mosque for that period of time. They are to refrain from all worldly affairs and discussions and fast from food and drink during the hours of the day. The purpose is to dedicate oneself in that short period of time to acts of worship, spiritual rituals, and contemplation.

of hope and inspiration for the people today, connecting to and learning from the servants of God par excellence.

With regards to acts of worship, the Prophet and his family provided detailed instructions guiding their followers on the best practices to maintain their connection with God and their faith. Daily, weekly, monthly, and annual acts of worship are part and parcel to the practice of Islam. First and foremost, Muslims observe the five daily prayers – *Fajr* at dawn, *Zuhr* and *'Asr* prayed in the afternoon or midday, *Maghrib* and *'Isha'* prayed after sunset. The five daily prayers are coupled with additional recommended units of prayer, which add up to a total of 51 units of prayer each day.

Beyond the daily prayers, prophetic tradition encourages reading or reciting the Holy Quran daily. Infusing one's day with the reminder of the Word of God is central to the preservation of its thought to maintain a God-centric lifestyle. In addition to prayers and Quran, there are designated days out of the month and throughout the year that are highly recommended to fast in. The months of *Rajab* and *Sha'ban* for example are such times. They come right before the month of Ramadan.*

The tradition and practice provided by the Prophet, preserved and protected by the Imams, was a complete and comprehensive system. The Shi'a maintain that though the Prophet and the Imams did not necessarily provide an encyclopedia of information filled with exact answers to people's everyday challenges and frustrations; they did, however, provide the divine inspiration and complete framework of guidance to help humanity achieve its moral excellence and lead lives of virtue and purpose. The individual is empowered to carry these principles into his or her life and meet the challenges of their day.

---

* The reader can find more details on this discussion in books such as *Mafatih al-Jinan* (The Keys of the Heavens) or in some renditions titled, *Call on Me and I Shall Answer*, where they lay out all the recommended acts of worship throughout the year instructed by prophetic tradition.

CHAPTER 6

THE HERITAGE OF RELIGIOUS EDUCATION

Seek knowledge from the cradle to the grave.

The Holy Prophet

EDUCATION AND NARRATION

Thought can be encapsulated in an individual. But naturally an individual will only live for so many years. The creation of institutions and organizations, as perpetual entities, safeguard those thoughts and values to survive generations. The Prophet and his Household established their own institutions to do just that. Thus, the methods they used in disseminating and preserving their thoughts and values, and ultimately their strategies for growth and development of a virtuous community, have been enshrined by way of these institutions.

In this chapter, the reader will develop a broader understanding of the principles and values that the Prophet Muhammad and his Household embedded in their institutions. They will further see the quintessential focus of the Ahl al-Bayt on education, as the overarching objective of the institutions they built. The following chapter will examine the actual institutions built, as well as the types of individuals the Ahl al-Bayt empowered by agency to help carry on these institutions of education and guidance.

The movement of Ahl al-Bayt fundamentally revolved around learning and education – specifically the teachings of the Quran, the Holy Prophet, and the Immaculates. From the very start of the faith, education and the pursuit of knowledge was emphasized like no other endeavor. The revelation that Prophet Muhammad himself received was, "Read." He was commanded through Angel Gabriel to,

> Read in the Name of your Lord who created; created man from a clinging mass. Read, and your Lord is the most generous, who taught by the pen, taught man what he did not know.[1]

That was the very first divine message to the Prophet Muhammad. This was the message that conveyed the importance of knowledge and its proximity to the Creator. God "taught by the pen, taught man what he did not know." In this same light, the Prophet and his Household would lead and inspire their followers through education.

After the Holy Prophet, Imam Ali would stress to the Muslims the importance of seeking knowledge and acting according to it.

> O' people, know that the fulfillment of religion is seeking knowledge and acting according to it. Surely, seeking knowledge is more incumbent upon you than seeking wealth. Wealth is divided and guaranteed for you. A just being [God] is the one who divided it amongst you, guaranteed it for you and will fulfill it. Knowledge [however] is stored with its people. You were commanded to seek it from its people, so seek it.[2]

Imam Ali was the first disciple of Islam's Prophet. In fact, Ali was the first male to accept the religion of Islam. The first individual to accept the message of the Prophet was Khadijah bint Khuwaylid, the Prophet's first wife and first supporter. The Prophet was monogamously married to her for 25 years, before her death in 619 AD. When she passed away, the Prophet entered a deep state of sorrow. Also being the same year that his uncle and protector Abu Talib passed away, the Prophet later called that year the "Year of Sorrow."[3] She had owned one of the largest trading enterprises in Arabia. With the rise of Islam, she dedicated her entire fortune to support her husband's divine message. A Muslim axiom states, "Islam did not soar except by the wealth of Khadijah and the sword of Ali."[*]

As taught by his Master Muhammad, Imam Ali emphasized that, "Seeking knowledge is an obligation."[4] It is not simply something admirable or virtuous but rather it is part and parcel to upholding one's duties and responsibilities as a Muslim. There is a dynamic with seeking knowledge that is more than mechanical. Seeking knowledge brings the seeker closer to the Almighty, and closeness to God can be summarized in one word – love. Imam Ali said, "Indeed, God loves the seeker of knowledge."[5]

Seeking of knowledge and the love for God, are deeply connected. For the one who seeks knowledge is ultimately seeking his Lord. When God spoke to Prophet Moses about love, He said to him,

> O' son of ʿImran, the one who claims to love me but when night
> falls sleeps without remembering me, has lied. Does not every lover
> long for the company of his beloved? I am here, O' son of ʿImran,
> looking over my loved ones. If the night falls upon them, their
> hearts are not distracted from Me by what their eyes see; my
> punishment would manifest before their sight, they address me out
> of vision, and they speak to me out of presence. O' son of ʿImran,
> give me the piety of your heart, the obedience of your body, and
> the tears of your eyes in the darkness of the night. Call on to me,
> you will find me near… answering your call.[6]

Having shown his valor on the battlefield, Imam Ali would compare seeking knowledge in a context that the admirers of bravery and valor would appreciate. "A person who sets out seeking knowledge is like the one who struggles [in battle] on the path of God."[7]

Knowledge was synonymous to struggling in the way of God, to give oneself for His cause. The Prophet Muhammad instructed his companions and

---

[*] Khadijah's wealth was instrumental in providing much of the basic infrastructure to support the early Muslim community. Ali's "sword" referred to his defense of the faith in all the battles the Muslims faced (most of which were waged on the Muslims by the pagans of Mecca).

followers to seek knowledge. "Discuss, meet, and narrate [our traditions], as narration [of our traditions] is a cleanser of the heart. Surely, hearts rust just as swords rust. Their cleanser is narration…"[8]

Islam emphasizes freedom of thought and expression in scholarship and education. It also advises that knowledge is to be sought from the people of knowledge. Otherwise, without referring to the proper and legitimate sources the seeker may be misled by arbitrary leanings. Objectivity is essential in the pursuit of knowledge. Lacking direction when it comes to this would be counterintuitive to the basic premise of preserving the faith and its authentic sources of guidance.[9]

Imam al-Sadiq stressed the gravity of the consequences of opinionated or arbitrary verdicts. "Whoever interprets a [single] verse of the Book of God by his [opinion alone] has disbelieved."[10]

Though this principle may seem obvious to some, to others it could be revelation. Shiʿa consciousness warns against the arbitrary interjection of one's own opinion, ra'y, in interpreting the words of the Holy Quran and religious law. Skewing religion to what "makes sense" on subjective preconceived notions is a dangerous slippery slope. Even for those who are generally educated or informed, it does not necessarily simplify the interpretation of the Holy Quran nor does it warrant personal opinion in the space of religious laws or decrees. Of course, everyone has the freedom to say or feel whatever they want, but there are natural implications to the decisions individual's make and how arbitrarily they interact with their religion.[11]

To provide more context and exhibit the importance of knowing the sources of knowledge and religion the Holy Prophet said, "The religion of God cannot be achieved [solely] by the intellect…"[12]

Islamic teachings maintain that human beings cannot arrive at true and complete faith by the mere intellect alone without utilizing any other outside sources. Of course, there are many truths that can be realized by mere reflection and contemplation – like the manifest order of the universe, purpose and accountability, and the necessary existence of God. However, there are intricate details of guidance that require the aid of guides such as prophets and messengers to deliver God's message and exemplify those heavenly principles. That is why, Islamic theology explains, the sources of religion are so important, as they are integral to the guidance of man on his journey towards success in this life and the next.[13]

In this vein, the Prophet described his household as that ship of salvation that is the key to people's success. "My household amongst you is like the Ark of Noah; whoever boards [the Ark] is saved and whoever falls behind will drown…"[14]

It is for this reason that the Prophet himself emphasized their significance – for his people's salvation. And anything the Prophet says is an extension of revelation, a decree from God and a command of the Divine. "He does not speak out of whim, it is nothing but revelation."[15]

As much as the Prophet stressed the importance of going back to his household, the reader will find that in the corpus of hadith, the Ahl al-Bayt stressed that everything goes back to him and the word of God. Imam Ja'far al-Sadiq said, "Everything is returned to the Book of God and the Tradition of the Prophet. Any tradition that does not concur with the Book of God is a [false] embellishment."[16]

Shi'a doctrine establishes that the Household was not some additional or extrajudicial source of religion, but rather it was an extension of the Holy Prophet. Their role was protecting what the Prophet brought forth and guarding it with their lives. They respected, honored, lived, and died according to the authority of God, the guidance of His Prophet and His Holy Book. That connection to the Book of God is a key principle in Shi'a creed, because nothing that contradicts it is accepted in the school of thought. Imam al-Sadiq said, "Whatever of our narrations that reach you and that do not conform to the Book of God is void."[17]

The sixth Imam had an enlightening exchange with one of his companions, Abu Basir. In this conversation the Imam spoke of the "*al-Jami'ah*". He said, "We have al-Jamiʿah! And how would they know what al-Jamiʿah is?" So, Abu Basir asked him, "What is *al-Jamiʿah*?" The Imam explained in some detail,

> It is a scroll which is seventy arm-spans long, measured by the arms of the Messenger of God, may peace and blessings be upon him. It was dictated by the Prophet directly and written by Ali's right hand. It contains all which is permissible or impermissible and everything which people need even [things as small as] the monetary damages of a scratch.[18]

The scroll illustrates the source and extent of the Imams' knowledge. Imam al-Sadiq shared with his companions the words of his father, Imam al-Baqir, on knowledge and value. He stated that the value of a person lies in his knowledge and that knowledge is connected to understanding the narrations of the Holy Prophet.[19]

> My son, know the status of the Shiʿa by the level of their narration and knowledge. Surely, knowledge is in the understanding of the narrations, and with [deeper] understanding of the narrations the believer will ascend the highest levels of faith. I have read in a scroll from Ali that 'the value and status of each individual is in his knowledge.'[20]

"The value of each person is in his knowledge" is a theme that the reader will see carried through within the institutions of the Ahl al-Bayt. The Imam expounds on this principle with some detail when discussing the status or level of his followers based on their knowledge of prophetic traditions or narrations. He explained, "Know the status of our followers based on their proficiency in narrating from us. Surely, we do not consider a scholar amongst them to be a [true] scholar unless he is a [true] narrator."

Someone in the gathering then asked if every individual that is a believer is also considered to be a narrator. To that, Imam al-Sadiq replied, "A believer is one who understands, and the one who understands becomes a narrator."[21]

Beyond simply learning or memorizing the narrations of the Holy Prophet, the Imams frequently underscored the importance of writing down the text of those narrations. It is noteworthy to keep context in mind, as the previous caliphs had many of the prophetic narrations compiled and burned, so the challenge was greater and the responsibility even more significant. Generation after generation, the Prophet's household highlighted the necessity that their companions narrate and keep record of the narrations through writing.

A great compilation of narrations written by the companions of Imam Jaʿfar al-Sadiq and Imam Musa al-Kazim would form a collection that became known as *al-Usul al-Arbaʿmiʾah*.* These primary resources in the 8th century would inspire the works that would become central references for the Shiʿa school of thought in narration and jurisprudence in the 10th and 11th century. Those books are:

1. *Kitab al-Kafi*† by Shaykh Al-Kulayni,
2. *Man La Yahdaruh al-Faqih*‡ by Shaykh al-Saduq,
3. *Tahthib al-Ahkam*§ by Shaykh al-Tusi, and

---

* *Al-Usul al-Arbaʿmiʾah* literally translates to "The Four Hundred Principles". The compilations were books of narrations that served as the early sources for Shiʿa Muslims.

† Compiled by Shaykh Muhammad ibn Yaʾqub al-Kulayni (864 AD – 941 AD), *al-Kafi* is a collection of Twelver Shiʿa narrations. The work has a total of 16,199 narrations and is divided into three parts: *Usul al-Kafi* (topics on history, supplications, theology, epistemology, and the Quran), *Furuʿ Al-Kafi* (topics on practices and legal issues), and *Rawdat al-Kafi* (includes speeches and letters of the Imams). It is considered to be the most comprehensive collection of Shiʿa traditions from the formative period of Islamic scholarship.

‡ Abu Jaʿfar Muhammad ibn Ali ibn Babawayh al-Qummi (923 AD – 991 AD), also known as Ibn Babawayh and more commonly as Shaykh al-Saduq, is the author of this famous work. The title of this book literally means "For him who is not in the presence of a jurist." This book is mainly comprised of matters dealing with the practices of religion, as summary of the study of the narrations. It does not include the chain of narrations which is usually present in books that have compiled narrations. The work is meant to be a more practical reference for Shiʿa Muslims to understand their duties, as well as what is permissible and not permissible in the practices of their faith. Regarding this Shaykh Al-Saduq says, "I compiled the book without chains of narration so that the chains [of authority] should not be too many [and make the book too long] and so that the book's advantages may be abundant. I did not have the usual intention of compilers [books of traditions] to put forward everything which they [could] narrate but my intention was to put forward those things by which I gave legal opinions and which I judged to be correct." *Man La Yahdaruh al-Faqih* is comprised of 9,044 narrations.

§ *Tahthib al-Ahkam* was compiled by Shaykh Abu Jaʿfar Muhammad ibn Hasan Al-Tusi (996 AD – 1067 AD), commonly known as Shaykh Al-Tusi and Shaykh Al-Taʾifah (The Leader of the School of Thought). The title of the

4. *al-Istibsar** by Shaykh al-Tusi.

In taking a closer look at many of the narrations from these books, as well as those cited in more contemporary works, there are recurring names relayed. Some of the famous narrators, or *muhaddithun*, of these traditions were the closest companions of the Imams, specifically the contemporaries of the fifth and sixth Imams, Imam al-Baqir and Imam al-Sadiq, respectively. These narrators include: Burayd ibn Muʿawiyah al-ʿIjli, Abu Basir Laith al-Rawi, Muhammad ibn Muslim, Zurarah ibn Aʿyun, Aban ibn Taghlib, and ʿUbaydullah ibn Ali al-Halabi. Much of Shiʿa heritage and the corpus of Shiʿa hadith is owed to these men for ensuring the narrations of the Imams continued to be recorded and learned across Muslim society, particularly amongst the Shiʿa.

The Imams also focused on different specialties of education and sciences with their companions and students. They did not merely teach jurisprudence and Islamic law to their followers. The education they provided spanned from philosophy and theology to chemistry and physics and much in between.

Hisham ibn al-Hakam, a companion of Imam al-Sadiq and Imam al-Kazim, specialized in theology. Zurarah ibn Aʿyun, a companion of Imam al-Baqir and Imam al-Sadiq, and Muhammad ibn Aslam, a companion of Imam al-Sadiq, specialized in studying jurisprudence. They were regarded as experts in Islamic law and were authorized to issues *fatawa* (singular: *fatwa*), or verdicts, by the Imams. Aban ibn Taghlib, also a companion of

---

book means "The Refinement of the Laws." It is one of the four major collections of narrations in Shiʿa tradition, with 13,590 total narrations.

* *Al-Istibsar* is also authored by Shaykh Al-Tusi. This work followed *Tahthib al-Ahkam* to summarize the previous work and determine discrepancies between some of the narrations. Explaining the purpose of the book Shaykh Al-Tusi says, "It would be useful that there should be a reference book which a beginner could use in his study of jurisprudence, or one who has finished, to remind himself, or the intermediate [student] to study more deeply. Thus, so that all of them could obtain what they need and reach their souls' desire, what is connected with different traditions would be set in an abridged way. Therefore, they asked me to summarize [*Tahthib al-Ahkam*] and devote care to its compilation and abridgement, and to begin each section with an introduction about what I relied on for the legal decisions and traditions in it; then I should follow with those traditions which disagree and explain the reconciliation between the two without leaving out anything which was influential." *Al-Istibsar* has a total of 5,511 narrations.

Imam al-Sadiq, was known for his knowledge in the sciences of the Holy Quran. He was notable for Quranic exegeses in addition to being a narrator of the traditions of the Prophet. A companion of Imam Ali ibn Abu Talib, Salim ibn Qays specialized in studying history. The same was said about Lut ibn Yahya, a companion of Imam al-Sadiq, who was regarded as one of the greatest historians of his time. Lut ibn Yahya was also the grandson of Mukhnif ibn Salim, a companion of Imam Ali who died fighting by his side in the Battle of the Camel during Imam Ali's caliphate. Aban al-Ahmar al-Bajli, a companion of Imam al-Sadiq and Imam al-Kazim, was also a notable scholar of history.

In the domain of natural sciences, Imam al-Sadiq focused on teaching and empowering his students to become leading authorities of their time. One of the most notable of Imam al-Sadiq's students in natural sciences was Jabir ibn Hayyan. Jabir was a regarded as a prominent polymath, one whose expertise spanned a vast array of sciences. He was a physician, physicist, geographer, astronomer, engineer, and chemist. He is widely regarded as the father of early chemistry.[22] Another companion of Imam al-Sadiq, Mufaddal ibn 'Umar was also widely regarded as a leading authority in natural sciences, particularly in chemistry. Most of these companions mentioned here were contemporaries to Imam al-Sadiq. The remainder of the disciples of the Prophet were also quite comprehensive in the breadth of sciences they taught their companions and followers.

SUPPLICATIONS AND PSALMS

Shi'a scholars maintain that the education involved with learning and recording the prophetic traditions was instrumental to the preservation of the pristine message of the Prophet. Still, there were other methods utilized by the Imams to educate, protect and preserve the faith. One of the most striking methods employed was the use of supplications and psalms.[23]

Imam Ali ibn al-Husayn, also known as al-Sajjad* and Zayn Al-'Abidin,[†] became widely regarded for his immaculate and prolific publication of supplications. His psalms, compiled in the book *al-Sahifat al-Sajjadiyyah*,[‡] form one of the oldest prayer manuals in Islam. Moreover, his work is considered the most formative book on spirituality from early Islamic history. It is revered so much that it follows only after the Holy Quran and *Nahj al-Balaghah* according to Shi'a doctrine and tradition.

The tradition of supplications, as well as its deep impact on the life of Muslims, is found throughout the history of the Prophet's disciples especially amongst the earliest Imams. One of the most profound supplications was taught by Imam Ali to his close companion; Kumayl ibn Ziyad. The supplication would become attributed to Kumayl and today is known as *Du'a' Kumayl*; usually recited every Thursday night in mosques and homes across Shi'a Muslim communities. Imam Husayn's supplication, *Du'a' 'Arafah*, holds a special place in the collection of supplications in the tradition of the Ahl al-Bayt as well. This supplication was recited by Imam Husayn on the 9th of Thu'l-Hijjah, the month of the hajj pilgrimage in Mecca. Ascended on Mount 'Arafah, Imam Husayn directed himself to the Holy Kaaba. He raised his hands in supplication, palms open before his reverent face, and recited to his Lord. His companions and family members would learn the verses of the supplication directly from him and continue the tradition of reciting it every year on the 9th of Thu'l-Hijjah, also known as the Day of 'Arafah.

---

* A title of Imam Ali ibn Husayn, al-Sajjad means "the one who prostrates extensively."

[†] Another title of Imam Ali ibn Husayn, Zayn al-'Abidin means "the best of the worshippers," or "the adornment of the worshippers."

[‡] *Al-Sahifat al-Sajjadiyyah* is the compilation of supplications and psalms by Imam Ali ibn Husayn. The title means "The Book of al-Sajjad." Imam al-Sajjad taught his supplications to his children, particularly Imam Muhammad al-Baqir as well as Zayd ibn Ali. The text would disseminate and continue to be spread amongst Shi'a communities. Experts in narration would refer to the text as *mutawatir*, which means that the text has been narrated so frequently and relayed from numerous chains.

Observed in Shi'a piety today, books of supplication are characteristically seen in mosques and libraries, as well as in people's homes along with the Holy Quran and *Nahj al-Balaghah*. In addition to *al-Sahifat al-Sajjadiyah*, there is a more contemporary book known as *Mafatih al-Jinan* that is widely used for supplications. *Mafatih Al-Jinan* was compiled by Shaykh 'Abbas Al-Qummi (1877 – 1940), putting together a comprehensive manual of the prayers, supplications, and worship rituals recommended by the Prophet and Ahl al-Bayt for practically every day of the year. Legend has it that Shaykh al-Qummi delayed the publication of his work for an entire year, in order to practice every one of the rituals in his book before sharing it with the world. Such works contribute to the central importance of education within the Shi'a school of thought.

SPIRITUAL DIRECTIVES, WILLS AND LETTERS

Another significant method used by the Prophet and his disciples was the use of spiritual directives, wills and letters.[24] Throughout their lives, the Prophet and his disciples were characteristic of advising one another with the use of spiritual directives in their conversations. One such example can be seen in a particular incident when the Prophet visited his daughter, Lady Fatimah, and son-in-law, Imam Ali, at their home. He found Imam Ali helping his wife in cleaning and preparing lentils. The Prophet turned to his son-in-law and said,

> Listen, and I do not say anything but what my Lord has
> commanded! Any man that helps his wife in [the chores of] her
> home, will be rewarded for every hair on his body a year's worth of
> worship, fasting its day and staying up [in worship] throughout its
> night. [In addition,] God will give him of rewards like He gave the
> Patient Ones, David the Prophet, Jacob, and Jesus (peace be upon
> them all). O' Ali, whoever was in service of his family without
> resentment, God will write his name in the book of martyrs. God
> will write for him for every day and night the recompense of a

thousand martyrs. For every step he takes, God will write for him
the reward of hajj and 'umrah.' And God will give him for every
vein in his body a city in Paradise.[25]

Through his own family, the Prophet established what kind of dynamic
should exist within the home. Every member of Ahl al-Bayt also left the
next Imam after him a will, with directives and advice on how to lead his
fellow man, advance society, and maintain one's excellence through their
divinely guided principles. After Imam Ali was fatally wounded by the blow
of 'Abdulrahman Ibn Muljam, a Kharajite,[†] in the Grand Mosque of Kufa,
he gave specific instructions on how Ibn Muljam should be dealt with.
Imam Ali advised his sons, Imam Hasan and Imam Husayn, in his dying
will.

> I advise you [both] and all my children and members of my family
> and everyone whom my writing reaches, to fear God, to keep your
> affairs in order, and to maintain good relations among yourselves
> for I have heard your grandfather [the Holy Prophet] saying,
> 'Improvement of mutual differences is better than general prayers
> and fasts....' O' sons of 'Abdulmuttalib,[‡] certainly I do not wish to
> see you plunging harshly into the blood of Muslims, shouting 'The
> Commander of the Faithful has been killed.' Beware! Do not kill on
> account of me except my killer. Wait and see if I die by this strike
> of his [Ibn Muljam], then strike him one strike for his strike and do

---

' 'Umrah is a set of rituals performed by Muslims out of devotion to God. Like Hajj, 'umrah may be obligatory in
certain cases and may be recommended in others. Also like Hajj, it is of two types, *ifrad* and *tamattu'*. For details, see
Manasik al-Hajj (Rulings on Pilgrimage) by Grand Ayatollah Sayyid Ali al-Sistani.

[†] Kharajites were a dissenting group after the Battle of Siffin (657 AD) between the forces of Imam Ali and Mu'awiyah.
The Kharajites wanted Imam Ali to unconditionally continue the pursuit against Mu'awiyah's forces without regard.
When Imam Ali chose not to, they deserted his army and went on to wage war against him in the Battle of Nahrawan
(659 AD). 'Abdulrahman Ibn Muljam was the Kharajite who assassinated Imam Ali. He waited until Imam Ali was
head down in the state of prayer at dawn as he led prayers in the Grand Mosque of Kufa, then struck him on the head
with a poisoned dagger.

[‡] 'Abdulmuttalib Shaybah (497–578 AD) ibn Hashim was the grandfather of the Prophet Muhammad. 'Abdulmuttalib
raised the Prophet in his early years. He was the leader of the Hashimite clan, as well as the custodian of the Kaaba
protecting it from the attack of Abrahah of Himyar and his army of elephants. See: Ibn Ishaq, *Sirat Rasul Allah*.

not mutilate the man, for I have heard the Messenger of God
saying, 'Avoid mutilation even it is to rabid dog.' [26]

Before he was assassinated, Imam Ali had ruled as the fourth caliph of the
Muslim nation from 656 – 661 AD. Though his reign was plagued with civil
wars waged by his adversaries, most notably Mu'awiyah ibn Abu Sufyan,
Imam Ali focused on establishing a universal standard of just governance.
He carefully selected his governors and representatives to be the most ethical, just, and fair leaders for the community. One of the most prominent
examples of this was shown through his letter to Ali's newly appointed governor in Egypt, Malik al-Ashtar.* This letter is seen as one of the greatest
instructions on just governance in human history.

> Then, know, O' Malik, that I have sent you to an area where there
> have been governments before you, both just as well as oppressive.
> People will now watch your dealings as you used to watch the
> dealings of the rulers before you. People will criticize you as you
> criticized the rulers [before you]. Surely, the virtuous are known by
> the reputation that God circulates for them through the tongues of
> His creatures. Therefore, the best collection with you should be the
> collection of good deeds… Habituate your heart to mercy for the
> subjects and to affection and kindness for them. Do not stand over
> them like greedy beasts who feel it is enough to devour them, since
> they are of two kinds, either your brother in faith or your equal in
> creation… you are over them and your responsible Commander
> (Imam) is over you while God is over him who has appointed you.
> He (God) has sought you to manage their affairs and has tried you
> through them. [27]

Imam Ali showed his governor an important principle: maintaining perspective. He reminded Malik of how he used to think and act before he was

---

* Malik al-Ashtar was one of the most prominent and loyal companions of Imam Ali ibn Abu talib. He came into Islam
during the lifetime of the Prophet and remained a committed companion of his Household. He was one of the
commanders of the Caliphate's army in the Battle the Camel and the Battle of Siffin. See: Sayyid and 'Alyawy, *Malik
al-Ashtar*.

assigned governorship; how he used to criticize governors for their greed and oppression. Thus, he should keep in mind that his citizens will look at him the same way as he looked at previous governors. He should aim to provide for his citizens in the same way he wanted the governors before him to provide for him and his family.

Moreover, Imam Ali reminded Malik of the virtuous characters that he must abide by – not only as a governor, but as the representative of a divinely appointed Imam. More importantly, the Imam emphasized the need to exercise mercy, kindness, and affection towards all – regardless of their creed or philosophy.

It was a tradition of the Imams to write letters to their companions. Imam al-Baqir wrote a letter to a group of his followers and companions, providing them everlasting guidance and inspiration. Imam al-Sadiq penned a letter for the readership of the entire public. Imam Ali al-Hadi addressed a letter to people in the community who believed in a widely discussed topic in theology at the time, *al-Jabr* or predestination.* All in all, these letters and directives were utilized by the Imams to protect the universal principles of Islam and ensure the preservation of the Prophet's message.

---

* A prominent Shi'a scholar, al-Fayd al-Kashani, compiled all of the known letters of the Imams in a multivolume book. See: al-Kashani, *Ma'adin al-Hikmah.*

CHAPTER 7

RELIGIOUS INSTITUTIONS

To this day we still feel the deep effects of sincerity and pragmatism in creating har-
mony between the maraji'. They emphasized working with one another in coopera-
tion and avoided negativity and division.

Grand Ayatollah al-Hakeem

HAWZAH: THE ISLAMIC SEMINARY

The institutions that Ahl al-Bayt developed to promote education were fundamental to the dissemination of their message and the preservation of the principles of the faith. The central establishment to this all was the Islamic seminary – *al-Hawzat al-'Ilmiyyah.*

Across Islamic history, there have been seminaries in numerous cities including Kufa, Medina, Basra, Mecca, Cairo, and Andalusia.[1] The concept of the seminary began in the Grand Mosque of Kufa, the heart of Imam Ali's capital in Kufa, Iraq. Kufa was known as the hub of Shi'a Islam, both for the sheer number of loyalists to Imam Ali and his family as well as the living presence of the Prophet's disciples in the metropolitan area. The governors assigned to administer the affairs of Kufa, and other surrounding cities were mostly close companions of the Prophet and Imam Ali. Some of the most prominent amongst them were Salman al-Farisi,* who was

---

* Salman al-Farisi (The Persian), also referred to as Salman al-Muhammadi, was one of the close companions of the Holy Prophet. He was so close to the Prophet that the Prophet considered him to be a member of his household, Ahl al-Bayt. He would continue to be a loyal companion, supporter, and representative of Imam Ali. He died in 656 AD.

assigned as the governor of al-Mada'in, and Ammar ibn Yasir[*] who governed over Kufa. The Grand Mosque of Kufa would prove to be a central place for learning and education. In fact, it was the headquarters of Imam al-Sadiq's seminary. Imam al-Sadiq taught over 4000 students in the Grand Mosque of Kufa alone.[2] His students even included the founders of the Hanafi and Maliki schools of Sunni jurisprudence, Abu Hanifah and Malik ibn Anas.[3]

With pressure from the Abbasids over several years, the seminary would end up moving from Kufa to Baghdad particularly during the lifetimes of Imam Hasan al-'Askari and the four ambassadors of Imam al-Mahdi. It then moved to the Holy City of Najaf during the tenure of Shaykh al-Mufid and his student Shaykh al-Tusi during the beginning of the 11th century. For centuries, the concentration of the Islamic seminary would move to and from a number of key cities in Iraq including Najaf, Hilla, and Karbala.[4] The past two centuries, however, have seen the Islamic seminary's primary locations consolidated to two cities; Najaf and Qum.[5] [†] Each city rising almost in turn as dictated by the political circumstances faced in each nation.[‡]

The precise structure of the Islamic seminary is quite unique. It does not necessarily have what most universities and academic institutions have in

---

[*] Ammar ibn Yasir was a close companion of the Holy Prophet, and a loyal companion of Imam Ali. He is considered in Shi'a tradition as one of the Four Companions of Imam Ali, those who stayed loyal to the Imam after the death of the Prophet. In addition to Ammar they include: Abu Thar al-Ghafari, Miqdad ibn Aswad al-Kindi, and Salman al-Farisi. Ammar ibn Yasir was born in the same year as the Holy Prophet, 570 AD. He died about 25 years after him however in 657 AD, martyred in the Battle of Siffin fighting in the army of Ali ibn Abu Talib against Mu'awiyah ibn Abu Sufyan.

[†] The seminaries of the Shi'a school of thought would also expand to other areas such as Jabal 'Amil (Lebanon), Damascus (Syria), Isfahan (Iran), Mazar-e-Sharif (Afghanistan), Hyderabad (India), Karachi (Pakistan), amongst many others in the modern day.

[‡] During the reign of Shah Reza Pahlavi (1919-1980) in Iran in the 20th century, the seminary in Qum faced definite political pressure that caused it great difficulty and struggle in its growth. At the same time, the rise of the Baathists in Iraq with Saddam Hussein put tremendous pressure on the Najaf seminary and the religious institutions of Iraq. With circumstances like these you found the scholars between the two regions, creatively working with what was before them to continue building the seminaries and promote religious learning to the greatest extent possible. When greater political pressure was exerted in one seminary, the other would often be a safe haven for the scholars and students wishing to continue pursuing their religious studies and education.

formal admissions, evaluation, and processes whereby individuals apply on a yearly basis and a percentage are accepted based on the merit of their applications. The Islamic seminary is, in a sense, an open university. This, of course, does not mean that anyone can become a student and remain in the seminary. The system is more fluid, functional, and self-correcting instead of formalistic or sanctioned by written procedures.

One of the reasons for this is the circumstances in which the Islamic seminary has developed throughout history. The Prophet's disciples were at many times considered to be enemies to the state and a threat to any sitting caliph. Though they minimized any impression of threat they could have posed, the fear of their ability to mobilize the masses with anti-state sentiment was always prevalent in the minds of the ruling elite. Thus, the Prophet's disciples were not able to freely establish their own institutions under the governments of their time due to the great hostility directed towards them from state authority. Affiliation with the Imams was grounds for persecution and state-sanctioned punishment. Tightening and loosening of the authoritative grip by the state varied from one administration to another. Thus, there were some brief moments to increase enrollment into their educational institutions and engage more publicly with the masses.

Still, official recognition by the state was not viable. Therefore, the institutions of the Imams, particularly the seminary, were forced to be a nonformal association of sorts that organized and conducted its programs without formal recognition. Keep in mind, the Ahl al-Bayt were banned from open expression or protest. There was no freedom of speech or expression sanctioned by the government, so individuals and groups discontent with the political establishment could not officially organize – even if their practices were peaceful, nonviolent, and educational.

As mentioned previously, there were times where their activities expanded more freely depending on the political climate. The strongest movement took place during the lifetimes of Imam al-Baqir and Imam al-Sadiq, due to the decline of the Umayyad dynasty and the rise of the challenging

Abbasids. The Abbasids had come to power with rallying cry of taking vengeance against the Umayyads for their crimes against the Ahl al-Bayt and their Shiʿa. The Abbasids, claiming lineage from the Prophet's uncle ʿAbbas, claimed this narrative as the cousins of the Prophet. After the Abbasid revolution overthrew the Umayyad dynasty, however, they quickly turned against the Shiʿa groups that helped them against the Umayyads. They were suspicious of Imam al-Sadiq whose following had grown substantially both amongst the scholars and public.[6]

Like the experiences of the Imams, the Islamic seminary was required to adapt to the various regimes that would come to rule. Under the Abbasids, the Ottomans, colonial powers, monarchies, and contemporary dictatorships, the Islamic seminary faced similar pressures which perpetuated the nonformal style of its institution. However, starting in the later part of the 20th century and early 21st century, institutions were more freely able to formalize in a way that is more like what we see in universities with standardized admissions and evaluation. Nonetheless, the traditional nonformal association of the Islamic seminary continues to exist in the seminaries of Najaf, Qum, and elsewhere in the Shiʿa world.

The academic structure of the Islamic seminary has been heavily focused on a mentor-mentee system. Anyone can come into the seminary; however, the student must find a teacher and mentor that will take them under their wing to pursue a study program that will yield true substance. The student has the freedom to choose his teachers and mentors. The mentor-mentee structure practiced in the seminary has promoted a system that focuses more on comprehensive individual growth given the commitment involved by both the mentor and the mentee. Though efficiency and allowing for a greater number of students at a given time may be sacrificed, it is argued that this system provides for greater quality in learning and development for the seminary students.[7]

Students attend the courses taught by their teachers and colleagues daily. Traditionally, classes were not typically held in a "classroom," instead instruction is often conducted in the courtyards of mosques or in homes. Today, classroom settings are more common. Outside of class instruction and engagement with their teachers, instructors, and lecturers, students meet regularly in what are called *mubahathah* (sessions where they essentially gather as study groups).* The students challenge each other's understanding of the books they are studying, as well as their comprehension of their professors' instruction during class. After these sessions, students often write their findings and compile their notes into what are known as *muqarrarat* (written reports to be presented to their professor). The student goes forward to present his work to the professor for evaluation. Throughout instruction, as well as in and out of class, teachers usually ask their students questions to constantly gauge their understanding and evaluate their participation.

In addition, the Islamic seminary is characteristic of scholarly gatherings called *al-barrani*, (open forums and discussions between scholars, professors, and students of the seminary). These forums are an opportunity for students to engage with the scholars of the seminary. In their engagement they can ask questions, participate in unique discussions, and showcase their grasp on the concepts they have been studying and put those concepts to practice. Traditionally, there is no official standardized method of evaluation and testing of the seminary students, though it is changing in some seminaries. Therefore, these non-formal methods are utilized to evaluate the students and their level of subject mastery. Engagement here is key. To show mastery of subject-matter, students must participate and engage. Such engagement is not effective unless the student properly prepares and exhibits that he understands what he is discussing. The scholars are very attentive, and the level of scrutiny is high, so students do their best to make

---

* The word *mubahathah* means deliberation in Arabic. In the seminary context, it refers to students meeting together and discussing their notes after lecture as well as reviewing the content of the books they are studying. The style of the discussion usually consists of the students taking turns teaching each other the material. By taking the role of the instructor amongst peers, they are forced to learn the material to a level of proficiency that will allow them to adequately teach it to the next person.

use of their study groups and spend the necessary time to prepare themselves.

MOSQUES AND HUSAYNIYYAHS

Beyond the Islamic seminary, the next primary institution established and utilized by Ahl al-Bayt were the mosques. Mosques hold a very high level of sanctity in Islam. They are integral to religious practice and central to the religious community. The mosque is not merely a house of worship. It has traditionally been a place of gathering, celebrating, educating, and providing various social services to the community. People got married in the mosque. People solved their problems in the mosque. People found help at the mosque. It was the center of Muslim society. In the absence of a "mosque" in a Muslim community, there is often a "community center". These community centers were derived from the functional use of the mosque going all the way back to the early days of Islam. The mosque was a part of every Muslim's life.

The first mosque in Islam was built by the Prophet Muhammad in Medina – *Masjid Quba*. Many other mosques were built in Medina during the Prophet's lifetime as well, including *Masjid al-Nabi* (the Prophet's mosque), *Masjid al-Qiblatayn* (where the Qibla was changed), *Masjid Imam Ali, Masjid Fatimah*, and *Masjid Salman al-Farisi* among others. Outside of Medina there were numerous other mosques built as well in the early days of Islam. Some of these included *Masjid al-Kufa* and *Masjid al-Sahlah* in Iraq. Each of these mosques, while varying in sanctity and domain, were central to their communities and used as place of solidifying and growing the community.

Throughout history, however, Shi'a Muslims have been barred from building their own mosques under various repressive governments. The policy of banning Shi'a communities from building mosques in those situations came with the intent to denigrate Shi'a image in general Muslim society. Mosques play central role in Muslim piety, and with Shi'a having no mosques they would seem irreligious and distant from the faith in the eyes of the general Muslim public. Nevertheless, Shiʿa Muslims would historically come to establish alternative spaces in the face of these odds to continue practicing their faith. These spaces were called the *Husayniyyah.*˙

Shiʿa Muslims would continue to gather and perform their rituals, regardless of being ostracized by the regimes they lived under or the policies that marginalized them. The concept of the *Husayniyyah* has predominantly morphed into what many Shiʿa communities have in the "Islamic center", or *al-Jamiʿ*, across North America and Europe. The centers are not necessarily mosques, with the unique religious rulings pertaining to the sanctity of the mosque, but many of the same functions take place in the center as a practical way for Muslims to gather and practice their faith throughout the year.

SCHOLARS AND MARJIʿIYYAH

Organizations and institutions are made up of individuals. Individuals come together to honor and serve the purpose of their institution or they can neglect it and fall short of its purpose. Thus, there is a great deal of responsibility in serving an organization. The Prophet's disciples were aware of that. Therefore, they established certain qualifications to ensure the future leaders of their institutions were capable and to be expected to protect and serve its faith and values.

Since its inception, Islam has emphasized the importance of scholars and the role they serve the in Muslim consciousness. The Prophet Muhammad augmented their position in the minds of the faithful through his sayings. "The scholars are the lanterns of the Earth and the successors of the prophets. They are my inheritors and the inheritors of the prophets," the Prophet is reported to have said.[8] In that same light, Imam al-Sadiq stated, "The

---

˙ The Husayniyyah was a place dedicated for holding gatherings to mourn the tragedy of ʿAshuraʾ, as well as other occasions significant to Shiʿa Muslim doctrine and tradition.

scholars are the inheritors of the prophets. Indeed, the prophets did not bequeath [gold or silver], but they bequeathed narrations from amongst their narrations. Whoever took any of it has taken a great fortune. So be careful of where you take your knowledge…"[9]

In examining the role of the Twelve Imams as the first and foremost scholars of Islam, it is essential to do so in the context of their circumstances and the sociopolitical climates they lived in. Still, the reader will find a common theme throughout, that of a continuous effort to preserve the faith through education and ultimately better the human condition.

The Commander of the Faithful, Imam Ali, brought back to life Islam's standard of just governance during his tenure as Caliph in the last years of his life (656-661 AD).[*] Before that, and for 24 years after the death of the Prophet Muhammad in 632 AD, Imam Ali educated his followers, and foes, on the principle of the greater good and what it meant to sacrifice for the preservation of true Islam.[10] Imam Hasan followed in his father's footsteps in teaching people about strategy and long-term planning through the peace accord he struck with Mu'awiyah, which saved the faith from destruction at the hands of the Umayyads.[11] Imam Husayn would go on to offer the greatest sacrifice, manifesting a university of lessons and principles on the Day of 'Ashura', after following the policies of his brother and father and continuing to implement the strategy of preservation and protecting the faith.[12] Imam al-Sajjad would witness the tragedy of his father and the massacre of his family in Karbala, but would nonetheless persevere. He would go on to spread knowledge and enrich people's souls through the supplications and psalms he developed. He led a spiritual revolution,

---

[*] Commander of the Faithful was a title given to Ali ibn Abu Talib by the Holy Prophet Muhammad. Al-Majlisi, *Bihar al-Anwar*, 37:339, hadith 81. The original Arabic, *Amir al-Mu'minin*, is also sometimes translated to the Prince of the Believers. This title in Shi'a tradition is reserved for Imam Ali ibn Abu Talib. See: Al-'Amili, *Wasa'il al-Shi'a*, 14:600, stating, "This is a title only suitable for Imam Ali."

reviving people from the dead slumber they had entered.[*] Imam al-Baqir and Imam al-Sadiq had the opportunity to educate thousands of seminary students through direct instruction, given the squabbling of the Umayyads and their imminent decline against the Abbasid revolts. They enriched the intellectual domain of society and became the teachers of anyone who claimed to be a scholar of religion or science.[13] Imam al-Kazim and Imam al-Rida tackled issues on governance and how to deal with government through their engagement with the Abbasids, which was often witnessed by the public.[14] Imam al-Jawad, Imam al-Hadi, and Imam al-'Askari would go on to set the stage and prepare their followers for the occultation of the Twelfth Imam, as it became more imminent with the passing of each Imam. All in all, the Imams laid the groundwork and prepared an institution for their followers to have during the era of the occultation. That institution would become the *Marji'iyyah* – one that has existed for over a thousand years now.[15]

Marji'iyyah is the institution of religious scholars that form the spiritual and religious leadership for Shi'a Muslims, particularly in the era of occultation since 941 AD. Shi'a Muslims adhere to the system of *taqlid*, emulating a religious scholar in matters of Islamic law. Before entering his major occultation with the death of his last ambassador al-Samari, Imam al-Mahdi advised his followers, "As for current affairs, go back to the narrators of our traditions. They are my proof on you and I am the proof of God."[16] [†]

Shi'a tradition maintains that the "narrators", or jurists, must have certain qualifications for people to do *taqlid*, or emulate them, in matters of religious rulings. For safeguarding the faith and the community of the faithful

---

[*] The fourth Imam, who is also referred to as Zayn al-'Abidin, continued to teach in Medina and produced Islam's earliest works on spiritual psalms through *al-Sahifat al-Sajjadiyyah*, and on human rights called *Risalat al-Huquq*, or the Treatise on Rights. For the full treatise, see: al-Harrani, *Tuhaf al-'Uqul*, 255-72.

[†] With the death of his last ambassador, Abu al-Hasan Ali ibn Muhammad al-Samari, in 941 AD the door to direct deputyship with the Imam closed and the major occultation began.

during the occultation era, the Ahl al-Bayt established two major conditions for jurists. The first condition is called *ijtihad*, or the ability of a scholar to derive the religious rulings from the original sources of Quran and hadith. A scholar who has reached the level of *ijtihad* does not need to follow another jurist, or *Marji'*, because they are able to independently arrive at the religious rulings to relieve their burden before God.[17] A scholar who has reached this level is also referred to as a *Mujtahid*, in legal terms, and sometimes assumes the title of *Ayatollah*. Assuming this status is not an easy task and requires a lifetime of dedication to the pursuit of religious learning for most.[*]

The other condition required of jurists is called *'adalah*.[†] One who practices 'adalah is *'adil*. This term refers to the scholar being an individual of high moral character, known for virtue and justice. In practical terms, this is the condition that acts as a safety net for the religious institution, and a means to ensure corruption, fraud, or any form of moral decadence is prevented. Theoretically, one who is 'adil would refrain from even entertaining the possibility of misusing the traditions of the Prophet, offering misguided rulings to the faithful, or changing anything in the religion or its message. *'Adalah* is a standard of virtue, piety, and justice that the jurists commit themselves to, and in turn the faith is protected by way of that commitment to moral excellence.

These are the substantive conditions for *taqlid*, though there are additional technical requirements of the *Marji'* that can be found in the books of jurisprudence. Some examples of those include being alive, sanity, age, and depth of knowledge amongst one's peers when there is more than one jurist

---

[*] Some scholars have been exceptional in the time that they reached the level of ijtihad. Grand Ayatollah Sayyid Ali al-Sistani, for example, reportedly became a mujtahid at the age of 30.

[†] The literal translation of the word *'adala* in Arabic is justice. In jurisprudential terms, it refers to a standard of moral uprightness whereby the individual is one who fulfills all his religious obligations and abstains from committing any sins or forbidden acts by the religion.

in that era. However, the aforementioned are the most fundamental two requirements.[18]

Even during the lifetimes of the earlier Imams, it was tradition for the Imams to defer their followers to the scholars.[*] Imam al-Sadiq discusses this idea of deferring to scholars in matters of religious law by advising his followers to,

> They should look for someone amongst you who narrates our traditions, has studied what [we have taught to be] permissible and forbidden, and knows our rulings, and accept him as a judge [amongst themselves].[19]

With further emphasis on the narration of the Prophet's traditions, or *hadith*, Imam al-Baqir relays the following tradition on behalf of the Holy Prophet. The Holy Prophet said, "May God send blessings to my successors." The Prophet was asked, "And who are your successors?" He replied, "Those who come after me and narrate my words and traditions."[20]

In Shi'a belief, the chief narrators of the prophetic traditions were the Prophet's household, starting with Imam Ali and continuing with the rest of the Twelve Imams. However, this seems to tie in with the rest of the narrations mentioned that discuss and emphasize the authority and responsibility of scholars serving the school of Ahl al-Bayt. The Prophet Muhammad said,

> [Leadership] is not fit for a person except that he has three characteristics: fear that keeps him away from sinning against God, forbearance by which he can control his anger, and a good guardianship over those he leads so that he is like a merciful father among them...[21]

Muhammad ibn Muslim narrates that Imam al-Sadiq told him,

---

[*] The scholars the Imams referred their followers to were companions and students of theirs that they trained and taught.

> By God, O' Muhammad, whoever from this nation wakes up in the
> morning and does not have an Imam (leader) appointed from God
> Almighty who is present and just, wakes up misguided and lost. If
> he were to die in this state, he dies the death of a disbeliever and a
> hypocrite. Know, O' Muhammad, that the leaders of oppression
> and their followers are isolated from the religion of God, are
> misguided [themselves] and are misguiding [the people].[22]

The significance of religious leadership is paramount in Shi'a doctrine. The role of the scholars would be to continue to protect the tradition of the school of thought through their blessed positions as ambassadors, directly or indirectly, of the Imams and be guardians of the community. They would be ones to promote justice, equality, and the protection of all people's rights – as that was a central focus of the Prophet's message.

To ensure all of this, there are responsibilities assumed by the jurists in the role of the *Marji'iyyah*. Some of the most important responsibilities include the following. One, *Ifta'* – providing religious verdicts by deriving the rulings from the sources of the religion – is one of the most fundamental duties of the jurists. The primary relationship between the public and the *Marji'* is seeking the religious rulings to understand what their obligations and responsibilities are, according to the faith.[23]

Two, the jurists engage in spiritual and religious guidance. They have the responsibility to explain the religion and its principles, in the absence of the Imam, to the followers of the school of thought. This is done in their own direct capacity, through their students, educational initiatives, and outreach projects that they establish. This function has been essential for Shi'a society's educational, spiritual, and social development.

Three, the jurists are responsible for teaching and mentoring the next generation of scholars. This has historically been done through the context and domain of the Islamic seminary. The jurists are expected to remain long-term in their thinking, which is characteristic of the scholars of the seminary.[24] They measure their actions and activities by their effect beyond today and tomorrow, but rather by how it will set precedents and affect the generations after us. The jurists focus on preparing the next generation of scholars and passing the knowledge of Ahl al-Bayt to them. Passing on the proverbial torch of guidance is characteristic of the seminary, considered part and parcel to its continuity and permanence. Today, the Islamic seminary of the Holy City of Najaf celebrates over 1000 years of scholarship and leadership since its inception under the headship of Shaykh al-Tusi (996 – 1067 AD).

It is worthy to note that when Ahl al-Bayt referred the Shi'a public to the scholars, they made sure that they were acknowledged with the highest esteem and respect. Within the corpus of Shi'a hadiths, the status of their scholarly companions was often established by the Imams noting their own love and respect for them. For example, Abu 'Ubaydah al-Haththa' narrates that Imam al-Sadiq praised four of his closest companions as such.

> Zurarah, Abu Basir, Muhammad ibn Muslim, and Burayd are
> those whom God [described in the verse], 'The Foremost of the
> Foremost. They are the ones brought near [to God].'[25]

Jamil ibn Darraj, also a companion of Imam al-Sadiq, spoke of a personal conversation he had with the Imam. He expressed that Imam al-Sadiq was furious about a particular individual who had insulted his companions and done wrong by them.

> [I pray that] God does not bless his soul or the souls of those who
> are like him! He had spoken [ill] of a people whom my father
> [Imam al-Baqir] had entrusted with [the knowledge of] what is
> permissible and prohibited. They were the carriers of his
> knowledge. They are [still] today the keepers of my secrets, as they
> were the real companions of my father. If God wanted [to punish]
> the people of Earth, He would stop [the punishment] because of
> them. They are the stars of my Shi'a, whether they are alive or
> dead. They are the ones who revived the mentioning of my father.
> Through them, God uncovers every fabrication. They dispel away

from the faith the expropriation of falsifiers and the interpretations of fanatics.

The Imam began to cry. Ibn Darraj asked him, "Who are they?" Teary-eyed, the Imam replied, "They are those who the blessings of God is upon them... Burayd al-ʿUjali, Abu Basir, Zurarah, and Muhammad ibn Muslim."[26] Imam al-Baqir and Imam al-Sadiq trained their companions in a manner that prepared them to guide people by the religious rulings. They were directly educated by the Imams to provide *Ifta'* to the public.

Maʿath ibn Muslim Al-Nahwi, a *muhaddith* and a jurist of his time, narrates his conversation with Imam al-Sadiq in one of his visits to him. The Imam said to him, "I was told that you sit in the mosque and give rulings to the people." Maʿath replied, "Yes, and I wanted to ask you about this before I leave. I sit in the mosque and a man comes up to me asking about a certain matter. If I know that he is in opposition to you, I answer him based on his school of thought does. When a man comes with a matter, and I know that he is an admirer and a follower of yours, I answer him based on what has been relayed from you. And when a man comes with a matter and I don't know who he is or have a background of him, I answer him as such, 'It has been relayed from this person as this and from the other person as that...' and so I include your words amongst those."

The Imam said, "Do just that, for that is what I do."[27] *

Ali ibn al-Musayyib also had a conversation with Imam Ali al-Rida on a similar subject. He asked the Imam, "My home is far away, and I am not able to reach you at all times. So, who should I take my religious teachings from?" The Imam replied, "From Zakariyyah ibn Adam al-Qummi, the one who is trusted over religious and worldly affairs." Thus, when Ibn al-

---

* This particular conversation with Imam al-Sadiq is also very insightful into the practice of *taqiyyah*, pious dissimulation, that was diplomatically exercised by the Imams and their companions to maintain the peace, preserve and protect the persecuted Shiʿa. A more detailed discussion on taqiyyah is in Chapter 8: Assimilation and Isolationism in Shiʿism.

Musayyib left, he went to Zakariyyah ibn Adam and asked him all the things he needed.[28]

As mentioned previously, the jurists assume other responsibilities toward the faith and the people as well. Jurists reside as judges over people's affairs, especially in matters of conflict or disagreement. This role is referred to as *qada'*, or adjudication. For an individual to judge between parties and provide a verdict pertaining to rights or obligations, the presiding judge over the matter must be a jurist according to Islamic law.[29]

Jurists also assume a certain level of authority and guardianship over the general affairs of Muslims during the time of occultation. This is particularly relevant to orphans, those who do not have legal guardians, and the responsibility of spending religious dues.[30] The jurists are the indirect representatives of Imam al-Mahdi and thus, responsible for how the religious capital of the community is spent.[31] The institution of religious dues is hugely significant.

KHUMS AND FINANCIAL AUTONOMY

The Holy Quran established a financial system that would serve the advancement of the Islamic seminary, community projects, and caring for the needy and less fortunate. This was implemented by the Holy Prophet and his Household. Moreover, this financial system was formed to ensure that the religious establishment would be self-sustained and remain independent from external powers that may wish to influence it through monetary pressure. Although the Shi'a maintain that their religious leadership is fallible, this system of financial autonomy is a means to ensure that they remain sovereign and without infiltration or undue influence. The Shi'a argue that the system of religious dues was designed by the Imams in this manner to ensure the functionality, authenticity, and independence of the seminary throughout the era of the occultation.

*Khums** is one of the primary forms of alms paid by individuals in Islam. The obligation for this form of alms is directly derived from the following instruction in the Holy Quran.

> Know that whatever thing you may come by, a fifth of it is for God and the Apostle, for the relatives and the orphans, for the needy and the traveler, if you have faith in God and what We sent down to Our servant on the Day of Separation...[32]

There are different forms of charity in Islam. They include *sadaqah* (general alms), *zakah* (obligatory alms) and *khums* (obligatory fifth of net profits alms). In all these categories, much of the money goes to helping poor and needy families and public charities. Khums is split into two halves, *Sahm al-Sadah* (the portion for poor Sayyids)† and *Sahm al-Imam* (the portion for the Imam). Sahm al-Imam is spent on the poor and needy, as well as faith-based projects, like the Islamic seminaries, mosques, community centers, educational programming, and other functions that benefit the religion and its principles. This portion of *khums* is under the supervision of the *Marji'iyyah*, as it is responsible for how the money is spent.

These institutions have been essential for the preservation of the Shi'a school of thought. Over the past millennium, scholars have witnessed external forces, foreign or domestic, try to influence their seminaries and institutions. Because of both the principled and practical strength they had, sourced in what they inherited from prior scholars and ultimately the Imams, they were able to remain autonomous and ward off such pressures. Though financial hardship would weigh on them often, they remained resolute with their faith and chose their independence over all else.[33]

---

* Khums literally means one fifth in Arabic. In terms of the alms due, it means "one-fifth of certain items which a person acquires as wealth, and which must be paid as an Islamic tax." Rizvi, *Khums: an Islamic Tax*, 6-20.

† Sayyid is an honorary title given to the descendants of the Hashimite family - the family of the Holy Prophet Muhammad. It is impermissible for a Hashimite to take general charity; however, poor Sayyids may receive from the alms paid from khums.

PART 3:
Shiʿa Muslims

CHAPTER 8

IDENTITY

One who knows himself, knows his Lord.

Imam Ali

DEFINING IDENTITY IN CREED

The discussion of *al-hawiyyah*, or identity, can be relevant to every human being. The way individuals see themselves, within their communities and societies, is a great contributor to their behavior in both private and public contexts. Individuals that identify with one another are often more likely to work together for common goals. Even if their dominant identities do not necessarily coincide, so long as parts of their identity do, it increases their chances of mutuality and cooperation. The more encompassing one's identity and worldview, the greater likelihood for tolerance and peaceful coexistence.[1]

So how do Shi'a Muslims see themselves? How do they define their identity within the context of creed? And how does their creed contribute to the way they see the world around them? What does it mean to be a "Shi'a", a "Muslim", a "believer in God"? The discussion that follows will help the reader better understand the Shi'a Muslim identity and the way Shi'a Islam teaches its followers to see the world around them. The reader will see that Shi'a identity and worldview is based in the principles of tolerance and co-existence.[2]

Though many discussions on identity encompass ones of class, country, culture, ethnicity and race, this discussion is based in the socio-religious context; and thus, the focus is on creed. The distinguishing factor of creed from the other categories is that identity being empowered from the individual's choice. While a person is born into a certain race, ethnicity, class, or culture, a person ultimately chooses his or her creed. Even if an individual is born into a religion, whether they truly believe in it or not is their choice alone. The Shiʿa identity, and worldview, is based in that conception.

The underlying goal of the Shiʿa Muslim community is to protect and preserve the message of Islam's Prophet, and ultimately serve the advancement of humanity. Shiʿa consciousness observes the criteria, guidelines, and tools inspired by their Imams to protect its community. The stronger it is in its faith and identity, the stronger it will be in helping the development of mankind. The Shiʿa polity's desire to protect and preserve itself is a universal pursuit that extends to the rest of humanity. To maintain itself is to preserve the original message of the Prophet Muhammad, which the Imams vowed to protect, inspired by the Muhammadan purpose as the "mercy to all the nations."[3]

THE FOUR SPHERES OF IDENTITY

Shiʿa consciousness emphasizes the pursuit of self-awareness and understanding oneself. It is embedded in the *fitri*, or intrinsic, desire to come closer to the Creator. The Prophet Muhammad told his followers that the "one who knows himself, knows his Lord."[4] Thus, the quest to define one's identity is sourced in the desire to better understand oneself as an individual and collectively in the community he or she belongs to. More practically, to define and better understand the dimensions of oneself helps the individual in their journey of self-development which leads to societal advancement. Based on their understanding of the teachings of the Imams, Shiʿa scholars have developed a model for identity and how they see the world around them through Four Spheres of Identity.[5]

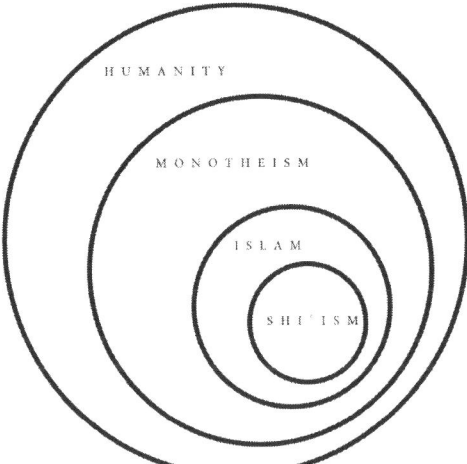

Figure 1. The Four Spheres of Identity. Note: the identity in Shiʿism, as the core sphere for a Shiʿa Muslim, is embedded in the rest of the spheres that are part and parcel to the Shiʿi worldview. The identity in, and connection to other that share in the same identity, Islam, monotheism, and humanity, are all dimensions to Shiʿa consciousness.

Identity is multi-dimensional, even within the context of creed which is our focus here. Humanity is one sphere encompassing multiple spheres within it. For this discussion, the authors will begin with the smallest sphere within the four spheres and expand outward. The smallest sphere of identity falls within belonging to Shiʿism – adhering to the teachings of Prophet and His Holy Household, the Ahl al-Bayt. This is the core of Shiʿa identity, where the individual derives their values and principles and sets the tone for their lifestyle and worldview. This core identity, in theological terms, also manifests itself in the self-awareness as servitude to God. Shiʿism delivers its adherents to arrive at that intrinsic awareness in the universe of, "We are for God and to Him we shall return."

The second sphere of identity, which encompasses the first sphere as followers of Ahl al-Bayt, is the dimension of Islam. The Shiʿa identify as Muslims just as any other adherent of other schools of thought within Islam. Shiʿism is not isolated, independent, or outside of the religion of Islam. Rather, it sees itself as the necessary vehicle and parcel, within the body of Islam, purposed with the task of preserving and protecting the faith. This is an essential point to emphasize and clarify. There is a mistaken notion that if an individual prides himself on belonging to something more specific, that individual is forgoing what is more general. Shi'a Muslim scholars teach that the Imams sacrificed and lived for the sake of Islam – nothing else. The affinity and allegiance Shi'a have to their Imams is derived from the desire to follow the perfect example of adherence to the Prophet and his message – Islam.[6] *

The third sphere of identity within the Shi'a worldview is belonging to the broader faith tradition of monotheism. Muslims are monotheists, believing in the core tenet that there is no other god but God. Muslims share this identity and belief with billions of other believers around the world. As Muslims belong to this broader sphere of identity, they understand that Islam came as a religion to complete the other faiths delivered to humanity. Islam is seen as a culmination of the other faiths and beliefs, as an enhanced and more complete version of the messages that came before it. Thus, its roots are derived from the other divine Abrahamic religions. Islam is seen as a continuation and completion of Judaism and Christianity. Muslims share the universal belief in the oneness of God and ultimate servitude to Him alone.

The fourth and final sphere is the Shi'a identity in humanity at large. Shi'a Muslims consciously see themselves in affinity and in connection to the broader human race. That consciousness values and cherishes that belonging as not a mere connection of being born in the same form as one's fellow man; rather, it acknowledges the connectivity that all human beings have to one another in the deepest of ways. That connectivity is an intrinsic brotherhood and equality. In his instructive letter to his governor in Egypt, Imam Ali said, "People are of two types, either your brother in faith or your equal in humanity."[7] Shi'a Muslims do not believe that they are better than

---

* In a meeting with Grand Ayatollah al-Hakeem in his home in December 2018, he emphasized to the authors the reality of Shi'ism as the heart of Islam and Imam Ali ibn Abu Talib as the safeguard whose mission was to honor and protect the message and legacy of Islam's Prophet Muhammad. Shi'ism is not a reformation movement to Islam, rather it is a safeguard to meant to protect and preserve the true message of the Prophet Muhammad.

anyone else, nor do they believe that they have a greater right than anyone else. Shiʿa belief is simple when it comes to its social dynamic and engagement with the world around them. Brothers or equals. Thus, the Shiʿa Muslim sees himself or herself as having a natural self-mandate to respect, regard, and look out for their fellow human being, regardless of their faith.

Looking at these spheres of identity, it can be seen both internally and externally that Shiʿa Muslims do not see themselves as an isolated community. The Shiʿa see themselves as being connected to every human being on this planet – whether it be a fellow follower of Ahl al-Bayt, a brother in the faith of Islam, a neighbor who shares belief in God, or another human being who merely shares similar desires, hopes and aspirations for a good life. Shiʿa Islam teaches that the connection people have as human beings is too sacred not to live and thrive together in harmony. The differences that human beings experience is a beautiful reflection of diversity that can be respected and honored, within the framework of commonality instilled in the Four Spheres of Identity.

THE SHIʿA IDENTITY

To identify similarly brings an associated label and a particular belonging to some set of values and perhaps a group of individuals. Additionally, each identity holds a certain significance as seen within the broader sociological context. With respect to the Shiʿa identity, there are a few names or labels ascribed to them as a group. Some of them include *Shiʿa* (Follower), *Muʾmin* (Believer), *Muwali* (Supporter), and *Rafidi* (Rejecter).˙

Abu Basir narrates that Imam al-Baqir stressed that his followers should be proud of their identity and the name associated with it. The Imam told him, "Be proud of your name." Abu Basir asked, "What is our name? May my soul be your ransom." He said, "It is the *Shiʿa*." Abu Basir exclaimed, "The

---

˙ The term Shiʿa literally means 'follower of' in the Arabic language. It is the most widely used term to refer to the followers of Ahl al-Bayt possibly for its simplicity and direct meaning.

people make scorn us for using that name." Imam al-Baqir then recited Quranic verses, "Indeed, Abraham was among his [Noah's] Shi'a [followers].[8] The one who was from his followers sought his help against him who was from his enemies."[9] Imam al-Baqir then repeated, "Be proud of your name."[10]

In another conversation with Imam al-Baqir's son, Imam al-Sadiq, Abu Basir narrates that the Imam said,

> We are the household of mercy, blessing, and [divine] grace. We are a foundation on this Earth, and our Shi'a are the anchors of Islam. Indeed, the prayer Ibrahim was not made except for us and our Shi'a. God [made us and our Shi'a] the exceptions to Iblis [and his ability to influence mankind] when He said, 'As for My servants you do not have any authority over them.'[11]

Ammar al-Kufi, also a companion of Imam al-Sadiq, was dismissed as an improper witness before Abu Layla, a state appointed judge in Kufa. Ammar was allegedly an improper witness because he was labeled a "*Rafidi*".* The judge singled him out and shouted, "Get up Ammar! We all know that your testimony is not accepted here. You are a *Rafidi*." Ammar got up and headed for the doors. As he walked away, he was visibly shaking and crying. The judge noticed this and called out to him. Bewildered he said, "Ammar, we also know you to be a brave and knowledgeable man. If it hurts you so much that you are called a *Rafidi,* then renounce it and become one of our brothers." Ammar looked up to Abu Layla as he wiped away his tears and responded with the following monologue.

> You misunderstand me. It is not because of spite that I cry. I cry because I am not worthy of being associated with the *Rafidah*. It is a lofty status that I do not deserve. It is such a great attribute. Woe to you, Judge! My Master told me, 'The first people that were called

---

* *Rafidi* – rejecter – was a title given to the group of individuals who rejected the legitimacy of the first three caliphs – Abu Bakr, 'Umar, and 'Uthman. Thus, followers of the Prophet's Household were seen as those who rejected the three caliphs' legitimacy and authority – *Rawafid* (plural).

Rafidah were the magicians who witnessed the miracle of Moses.
They believed in him and rejected the commands of Pharaoh.'
They accepted the punishment of Pharaoh so he called them the
Rafidah when they rejected his religion. The word Rafidah refers to
those who reject everything that God does not like. I cry over
myself out of fear that God will look at my heart and ask, 'O
Ammar are you really a rejecter, one who rejects everything that is
wrong and obeys everything that is right and ordered of you?' That,
I know, would lead to a grave chastisement.

Ammar then walked out of the court, leaving it in utter silence. When
Imam al-Sadiq was told about the exchange between Ammar and Abu
Layla the Imam testified,

If Ammar had sins greater than all the heavens and the earth they
would be wiped out because of these words. [These words] will
increase his good deeds before his Lord, the Almighty and
Majestic, so that He will make every [small deed the size of a]
mustard seed a thousand times greater than this world.[12]

The term *Rafidah* was not only used to describe the magicians that would
follow Prophet Moses and reject the Pharaoh. In fact, it was used to describe the followers of Moses, and his brother Aaron, who would not ac-
quiesce to the whims of those who abandoned the faith and began worshipping the calf in Moses's absence.

The relationship between Moses and Aaron is often referenced as an analogy for the relationship between Prophet Muhammad and Imam Ali. The
Holy Prophet would tell Imam Ali, "You are to me as Aaron was to Moses,
except that there is no prophet after me."[13]

When Moses left his people for forty days, he left his brother and vicegerent, Aaron, to lead the people. He bestowed upon him the same authority
he had over the people and let the people know as such. Aaron was a
prophet in his own right and Moses's right hand. Aaron was his supporter
and advocate; however, many of their followers quickly turned against

Aaron and the commandments of Moses within days of Moses' departure. There was, nonetheless, a small group of people that stayed loyal to Aaron. The majority began calling this small group *Rafidah* because they rejected worshiping the calf with them. Thus, the *Rafidah* at that time were the followers of Aaron, Moses's vicegerent.[14]

Relevant to this discussion is the origin of the term Shiʿa from a Quranic context. The term, Shiʿa, is used in the Holy Quran to describe followers of individuals and groups at different times. The Holy Prophet was the first to use the term in describing the followers of Imam Ali. The distinction or emphasis provided for the followers of Ali, was authored by the Prophet himself. One of the Prophet's closest companions, Abu Thar al-Ghafari,* narrated that the Prophet said,

> O' Ali, whoever loves us is the Arab, and whoever dislikes us is the [foreigner]. Our Shiʿa are the ones of [noble] families, mettle, honor, and pure birth. There are no followers of the creed of Ibrahim except us and our Shiʿa. The rest of the people have disowned it. Surely, God and His angels are demolishing the [built-up] sins of our Shiʿa just as people demolish any building...[15]

The reader should note that the use of the term "Arab" in this tradition is not a reference to ethnic Arabs or being of Arabian descent; rather, it is the connotation of authenticity and legitimacy. When people wanted to belittle someone, they would say that he was *Ajami* (a non-Arab or foreigner). Arabs were regarded and respected, or at least not belittled, even though tribalism was characteristic of the pre-Islamic era and continued to be reinforced to some degree by those who came to rule after the Prophet's death.[16] Through this quote, the Prophet clarified that having status is not established by lineage, but rather it is by one's actions and convictions.

---

* Abu Thar al-Ghafari was one of closest and loyal companions to the Prophet Muhammad and Imam Ali. He was known as a vocal opponent of the third caliph, ʿUthman ibn Affan, until he was exiled and died in the desserts of Rabathah in 652 AD.

Ibn al-Harith narrates from Imam Ali that he heard the Holy Prophet say,

> My likeness is as a tree; I am its root, Ali is its branch, Hasan and Husayn are its fruits, and the Shi'a are its leaves. Indeed, nothing will spring from what is good except what is [similarly] good![17]

Ibn 'Abbas also narrates that the Messenger of God spoke directly to Imam Ali, describing the fate of the Shi'a on the Day of Judgment and the status they assume. The Prophet said,

> O' Ali, your Shi'a are the victors on the Day of Judgment. Whoever insults one of them has insulted you. Whoever insults you has insulted me. And whoever insults me, God will settle him in hellfire where he will eternally stay – what a wretched fate! O' Ali, you are from me and I am from you. Your soul is from my soul, your clay [of creation] is from my clay, and your Shi'a were created from the remainder of our clay. Whoever loves tham has loved us, whoever hates them has hated us, whoever opposes them has opposed us, and whoever shows them affection has shown affection toward us.[18]

THE ATTRIBUTES OF THE SHI'A

In examining the corpus of hadith about the qualities or attributes of the "Shi'a", the Prophet and the Imams used specific terms. Some of those attributes included the following: *al-Salihun* (the Virtuous), *Uli al-Albab* (Those of Intellect), *Awliya' Allah* (the Friends of God), *al-Musallin* (the Prayerful), *Ashab al-Yamin* (the People of the Right), and *Khayr al-Bariyyah* (the Best of People).

Shi'a teachings elucidate that numerous verses from the Holy Quran described the Prophet's Household, as well as their followers. The Imams directly explained some of those verses to their companions, indicating the deeper meanings involved in those pieces of revelation. Abu Basir narrates from Imam al-Sadiq in explaining the following verse,

Whoever obeys God and the Apostle—they are with those whom God has blessed, including the prophets and the truthful, the martyrs and the righteous, and excellent companions are they![19]

Imam al-Sadiq explained the parts of the verse saying,

The Messenger of God is, in this verse, referred to as 'the prophets.' We are the 'truthful' and the 'martyrs.' You are the 'virtuous' and by God you are our Shiʿa. God mentioned you in His Book when he said, 'Are those who know equal to those who do not know? Only those who possess intellect take admonition.' It is us who are 'those who know.' Our enemies are 'those who do not know.' Our Shiʿa are 'those who possess intellect.'[20]

The intellect observed in this verse is a reference to practical intellect, as opposed to conceptual intellect. There are generally two types of intellect recognized in this discussion – the conceptual intellect, which all people possess, and the practical intellect, which is connected to manifested through excellent decision-making aligned with divine commandments.*

God speaks of those who will not fear or grieve in the Quran. Individuals who are safe from any sort of psychological distress, protected from what many will experience in dread and anguish. It is narrated that Imam Ali explained the following verse from the Quran, "Look! The friends of God will indeed have no fear nor will they grieve."[21]

Imam Ali asked the companions sitting with him, "Do you know who the friends of God are? They are us, our followers, and those who follow us after them. Glad tidings to us. And glad tidings to them [that the reward they receive will be] better than ours.

The companion asked, "Why is the reward for them better? Are we not on the same?" The Imam replied, "No, as they will be made to carry that which

---

* Conceptual intellect refers to the faculties of learning, abstract thinking, rationalization, and all cognitive functioning. This type of intellect is naturally possessed by all people. The practical intellect – what is referred to above in the verse, is the faculty of decision-making utilized to adhere to God's expectations of us. Those who utilize this intellect will meet those expectations and fall within the grace of God.

you were not asked to carry, and they will bear that which you have not borne."[22]

Muhammad ibn Fudayl, a companion of the 8th Imam of the Ahl al-Bayt, Imam Ali al-Rida, had a conversation with the Imam regarding some verses from the Holy Quran. Those verses focused on individuals' that were characteristic of prayer.

Ibn Fudayl recited, "[All are such] except the prayerful, those who persevere in their prayers."[23] The Imam said, "By God, they are the ones of Fifty from amongst our Shiʿa."* When Ibn Fudayl mentioned the verse, "And [those who] are watchful of their prayers,"[24] the Imam replied, "By God, they are the ones of the five [daily] prayers of our Shiʿa." Finally, Ibn Fudayl asked, "And the People of the Right Hand — what are the People of the Right Hand?"[25] Imam al-Rida said, "By God, they are from our Shiʿa."[26]

Imam al-Sadiq described what it meant to be Shiʿa in some more detail.

> Our Shiʿa are the people of piety. They are the people of loyalty and
> trustworthiness. They are the people of austerity and worship.
> They are the people of fifty-one rakʿah in every day and night.
> They [spend their nights in prayer] and fast during the day. They
> purify their money [through charity]. They perform the hajj
> toward the House [of God] and they avoid every forbidden act.[27]

The Holy Quran expresses that a people's identity is contingent on what they believe in and who they follow. God says this within the context of Prophet Abraham: "Indeed the nearest of all people to Abraham are those who follow him and this prophet and those who have faith, and God is the guardian of the faithful."[28]

In Shiʿa teachings, there is a great deal of emphasis on the relationship of an individual to others, for example, what group they belong to and what

---

* Fifty refers to the fifty-one total rakʿah, or units of prayer, that is characteristic of the devout followers of the Prophet and his Household. They include the 17 mandatory units of prayer encompassed by the 5 daily prayers, with an additional 34 units of prayer that are highly recommended to perform between those mandatory prayers.

affinity exists with them. There are two relevant ancillaries of faith for Shi'a Muslims here: *tawalli* and *tabarri*.* Tawalli refers to the obligation to love the Ahl al-Bayt, while tabarri refers to the practice to disassociate oneself from the enemies of the Prophet and his family. Ultimately, these two practices are based in the principle of loving what God loves and detesting what God detests.[29]

The Prophet honored some of his own companions by considering them to be a part of their own family. The Holy Prophet set that precedent with one of his closest companions, Salman al-Farisi. Salman had proven time and time again his loyalty and dedication to the Prophet and the message of Islam. For that, the Prophet considered him to be a member of his own family saying, "Salman is from us Ahl al-Bayt."[30]

The Imams would mention their own select companions in a similar light, based on their merit and character. 'Umar ibn Yazid, a companion of Imam al-Sadiq, was one of such individuals of merit. Imam told him one day, "By God, You are of the family of Muhammad." 'Umar replied with astonishment, "May my soul be sacrificed for you, from the [family of Muhammad] themselves?!" Imam al-Sadiq assured him, "Yes, by God, you are from their souls. O' 'Umar, God, the Blessed and High, says in His Book, 'Indeed the nearest of all people to Abraham are those who follow him and this prophet and those who have faith, and God is the guardian of the faithful.'"[31] †

---

* The ten ancillaries of faith, or *Furu' al-Din*, are 1. Salah/Prayer (the five daily prayers), 2. Sawm/Fasting (in the holy month of Ramada), 3. Hajj/Pilgrimage (pilgrimage to Mecca once in a lifetime, 4. Zakah/Alms (obligatory alms), 5. Khums/Fifth Alms (one fifth of net profits alms), 6. Jihad (struggling in the way of God), 7. Enjoining the Good (enforcing or speaking for good works), 8. Forbidding the Evil (acting against, speaking against, or at the very least disassociating from evil deeds), 9. Tawalli (loving the Ahl al-Bayt), and 10) Tabarri (disassociating from the enemies of the Ahl al-Bayt).

† On another similar occasion, Sudayr narrated that Imam al-Sadiq was amongst his close companions and followers. The Imam pointed to his Shi'a and said to them, "You are the family of Muhammad, you are the family of Muhammad." Al-Barqi, *al-Mahasin*, 1:238.

INTRINSIC VALUE IN THE CORE-IDENTITY

There is a great deal of value associated with fulfilling the qualities and attributes as a follower of the Prophet and his Household. The reward, blessing, and grace bestowed upon genuine devotees are unmatched. On a theological level, this is promised by the Holy Prophet as evidenced in the narrations relayed by his family and companions. Salman al-Farisi narrates a particular occasion when he was sitting with the Holy Prophet. When Imam Ali arrived, the Holy Prophet greeted him and asked him, "O' Ali, should I give you some good news?" Imam Ali said, "Yes, O' Messenger of God."

The Prophet shared the news,

> My beloved Gabriel is informing me on behalf of God, Exalted by
> His Majesty, that He has given your devotees and followers seven
> traits; ease during death, companionship during loneliness, light
> during darkness, safety during fear, equity during judgment, a pass
> along the path [of Paradise], and entry into Paradise before the
> people of all nations by 80 years.[32]

Shi'a doctrine accepts that each one of those elements reflects the favor and grace received by this group in this life and the next. The Prophet and his family's emphasis of pride, honor, and reward with the genuine identity of being Shi'a was clear and distinct. Zayd ibn Ali[*] narrates from his fathers that the Commander of the Faithful Imam Ali said,

> I lamented to the Messenger of God about the envy of those who
> envied me. He said to me, 'O' Ali, are you not content with that fact
> that the first four to enter heaven are: you and I, our progeny
> [following closely] behind us, and our Shi'a will be at our rights
> and our lefts.'[33]

---

[*] Zayd ibn Ali was one of the sons of Imam Ali al-Sajjad and brother of Imam Muhammad al-Baqir.

During the Prophet's lifetime, Ibn ʿAbbas had the opportunity to ask the Prophet many questions of theology and creed. He asked the Holy Prophet about the following verse from the Holy Quran, "And the Foremost of the Foremost; they are the ones brought near [to God], [who will reside] in the gardens of bliss."[34] He wanted to know who was referenced by "the Foremost." The Holy Prophet responded, "Gabriel told me, 'Those are Ali and his followers. They are the ones who [enter] foremost to heaven. They are the ones who are brought near to God because of the status of Ali.'"[35]

Imam Ali describes the state of his true followers during Resurrection and the Day of Judgment. While many may imagine this day of reckoning to be a daunting one, it is illustrated as a time of ease and comfort for the followers of Ali.

> Those who follow us will come out of their grave on the Day of Judgment with their faces bright, their private areas covered, their fears alleviated, their struggles relieved, and their affairs eased. All the people will be afraid while they will not be afraid. All the people will be sad but they will not be sad. They have been given safety and faith, and all sorrows have departed them… They will sit on Pulpits of Light in the shadow of the Throne of the All-Merciful. Before them will be a spread which they will eat from until all people are dismissed from their judgment.[36]

Shiʿa doctrine attributes great value, weight, and responsibility to those who assume the Shiʿa identity. But it also requires much sacrifice as seen in the context of narrations. To claim the title is much different than owning it and living it. Sacrifice is not the only character trait required to fulfill this identity. Mercy, compassion, and empathy are top priorities for any person who wishes to live on the path of Muhammad and Ali.[37]

The directive of Imam Ali to his companion Malik al-Ashtar reigns true as a testament to the essence of what it means to be a follower of Ali. It is to live by the principles and values that Ali lived and died for, and that ultimately came down to the service of one's fellow man. Shiʿa identity enjoins the faithful to only further value and appreciate their common identity with their fellow Muslims, fellow believers in God, and fellow human beings. The belonging to each one of these spheres is significant and essential to the Shi'a worldview, and their ultimate pursuit to better the human condition. The community of the Shi'a faithful was founded on the understanding of "your brother in faith or equal in humanity."[38]

CHAPTER 9

COMMUNITY RELATIONS

Indeed, you cannot escape [your need for] people. No one can be independent of people during his life, as people need one another.

Imam al-Sadiq

THE SIGNIFICANCE OF COMMUNITY

A community has a responsibility to protect itself from negative forces within. If the community does not ensure its own protection, then no one else will. The strength of a community is often derived from the commitment of its members to one another. Individuals come together and create a collective and the nature of that collective will often dictate the type of community they form. Strong ties between individuals and groups will more likely result in a community that protects itself and its members from harm. It will endure the challenges it faces and advance its members forward on the levels it deems to be important, be it material, intellectual or spiritual. Islamic doctrine has placed a great deal of emphasis on strengthening the ties between community members on several levels. This is evident in the corpus of hadith and the verses of the Holy Quran.

This chapter will focus on the significance of the notion of community, the principles that make up a community in Shiʿa doctrine, as well as some of the highlighted relationships evidenced in the corpus of Shiʿa hadith.

Marriage is the institution communities are built on in their most basic and literal forms. The union of two individuals creates a family. That union of families creates more families, and the collective of families can form a community. One of the first verses that stands out in this regard is found in chapter 30 of the Quran, *al-Rum* (the Romans), which describes the blessing of God's union of individuals in marriage.

> And of His signs is that He created for you mates from your own selves that you may take comfort in them, and He ordained affection and mercy between you. There are indeed signs in that for a people who reflect.[1]

In Chapter 49, *al-Hujurat* (the Rooms), God speaks of the diversity of mankind. From males and females to different tribes and nations, God affirms that diversity as one to be acknowledged and celebrated within humanity. In that diversity, what reigns supreme is one's piety and virtue – not a belonging to a particular classification within humanity's diverse makeup.

> O mankind! Indeed, We created you from a male and a female, and made you nations and tribes that you may identify yourselves with one another. Indeed the noblest of you in the sight of God is the most Godwary among you. Indeed God is all-knowing, all-aware.[2]

In the light of celebrating diversity and embracing one's community, the Prophet's disciples spoke extensively about the virtue that lies in caring for others. They emphasized a spirit of active engagement and involvement in community life. Imam al-Sadiq said,

> Make sure you perform the prayers in the mosques, be good neighbors to people, testify as witnesses, and attend funerals. Indeed, you cannot escape [your need for] people. No one can be independent of people during his life, as people need one another.[3]

Human beings are social beings. They are wired to belong and be part of communities. It is human nature to gather and congregate, and the need for connection is part of what it means to be human. It goes against human nature to live isolated from one another. Human connection is essential.[4] Shi'a doctrine advises against people distancing themselves from one another, and instead emphasizes the notion of community and engagement with fellow human beings.

Imam Ali advised his followers, "Beware of controversy and enmity, as they sicken the hearts of brothers and are fodder for hypocrisy."[5] This wisdom can be coupled with the verses in the Holy Quran that state,

> Then We followed them up with Our apostles and We followed [them] with Jesus son of Mary, and We gave him the Evangel, and We put kindness and mercy into the hearts of those who followed him. But as for monasticism, they innovated it—We had not prescribed it for them—only seeking God's pleasure. Yet they did not observe it with due observance. So, We gave to the faithful among them their [due] reward, but many of them are transgressors.[6]

Islamic teachings express that closeness to God, piety, does not come by way of one's isolation from society. The faith does not encourage its adherents to be isolationists, as that essentially allows for avoidance as a mode of operation considering the tests and trials in life. Islam teaches that tests and trials exist for the faithful to endure and triumph over. The character of a believer is built because of the tribulations they overcome and their commitment to godly principles and values when they are tested.

THE RIGHTS OF A COMMUNITY

There are certain principles and rights by which the notion of community is built on. The Prophet and his disciples stressed that their followers ought to be helping hands to one another. Supporting and helping each other as believers, is a fundamental part of the Muslim identity and conscience. Further, Shi'a belief is not complete without fulfilling the rights and obligations of their counterparts and fellow man.[7] Imam al-Sadiq said,

> It is incumbent on the Muslims to strive in communicating with each other, to commit to sympathy and consolation to those who are in need, and to be sympathetic amongst one another. Thus, you would be as God Almighty has commanded you – merciful amongst yourself and to one another, sorrowful for what you do

not know of [the struggles that each faces]. In that, you would be like the Ansar at the time of the Messenger of God.[8]

The Muslim narrative maintains that this idea of community was near and dear to the Prophet Muhammad, especially as he raised a community from the deserts of Arabia to become one of the greatest civilizations in the world. He wanted every Muslim to empathize with his fellow Muslim. He let all the believers know how much he despised the possibility of ignoring each other's needs or requests. The Prophet said, "Whoever hears a Muslim calling, 'O Muslims!' [i.e. calling for help] but does not answer, is surely not a Muslim."[9] Imam al-Sadiq would also go on to say that, "Whoever does not care about the affairs of the Muslims is surely not a Muslim."[10]

This sense of care, empathy, and greater consciousness to what is going on with others – their struggles, worries, and challenges – is an essential part of the worldview that the Prophet taught his followers. If the concern of an individual does not rise above himself, his family or his group, then what use is he to the community he belongs to? In fact, what use is the community at all? Other than being a collective in quantity, what value does the community of individuals provide the collective itself?

Everyone has a role to play as he or she belongs to the greater group that potentially provides for him materially, psychologically, intellectually, and spiritually. As social beings, people engage with their communities on all these levels and have an intrinsic expectation in this regard. However, if everyone chooses not to engage and not to care, then that fabric would be dismantled, and those needs would not be provided for.

This duty of care also stems from two of the Ten Ancillaries of Faith in Shiʿa doctrine, known as *al-Amr biʾl-Maʿruf* and *al-Nahi ʿan al-Munkar*, or enjoining the good and forbidding the evil. These tenets are derived from the tradition of the prophets and the lifestyle of the virtuous servants of God. One of the unique features about this practice is that through it, other obligations are observed and promoted as well.

It is a great obligation. Through it all other obligations are
established, the faith is secured, earnings are legitimated, what is
usurped is returned [to its rightful owner], and [cities] are built.
[Through it], justice is [established among] enemies and [all
matters are] made upright.[11]

One of the essential components to enjoining what is good and forbidding
what is evil is one's own implementation of the duties he calls others on to.
Before one can promote certain good deeds or deride certain injustices, one
must act by the words they preach. This standard forces practicing Muslims
to not only care for one their spiritual and moral wellbeing, but to
check their own selves and ensure they are practicing what they preach.

There are times and situations where people's interactions with one another
allows for reading into intentions and possibly doubting the intentions
of others. It could be within the context of the pious adherent attempting
to enjoin the good and forbid the evil. Take the example of seeing
a friend in a seemingly suspicious place or situation. Perhaps the reader is
driving and happens to see a friend walking out of an unbecoming place,
somewhere that is not appropriate for families or children, for example.
What reaction does the reader have? What kind of judgment crosses their
mind? More importantly, how does the idea of community influence how
the reader reacts to such observations?

In such situations, Shi'a Islam teaches the doctrine of *husn al-zan*, which
essentially means to think the best of someone and to give them the benefit
of the doubt. The Prophet taught his followers to give each other the benefit
of the doubt. It may be such a simple concept, but in practice, it can prevent
the drama and distress to families and individuals' reputations. Benefit of
the doubt is given as a social mechanism of protection to the individual.
That mechanism fosters harmony and a culture of positivity in a community.
Instead of being ready to thrust into negativity and suspicion, this doctrine
provides for an encompassing positive attitude that reinforces trust
and confidence as opposed to qualms and suspicion.

The notion of giving each other the benefit of the doubt extends beyond suspicious situations. It can be applied even in the subtlest and simplest conversations. Sometimes people misunderstand each other and are not able to communicate articulately or effectively. A lack of communication or misunderstanding of some sort can lead to frustration and resentment. Giving the benefit of the doubt transcends the frustration and allows people to be forgiving and more open to understand one another. Be it between a husband and wife, a father and son, or two colleagues. Muslims are raised in the tradition of consciousness of thinking the best of people. So when they hear something that can be understood negatively, but consciously choose to give the person the benefit of the doubt and seek to understand what they truly mean, they are allowing positivity to remain the focal point of the relationship.

Imam Ali said, "Keep [your consideration on] the matters of a brother in the best [light] until you see of him what prevails over [all justifications]. Do not think ill of any word that comes out of him so long as you find a possible good meaning for it."[12]

People owe it to one another to look at each with goodness instead of spite. If someone hears something that can be interpreted negatively, the listener is advised to strive to find the positive interpretation and build the outcome on that basis instead. This principle alone is quintessential to the Ahl al-Bayt's worldview on community. This mechanism of *husn al-zan*, a mere shift in attitude and perspective, is central for an individual's spiritual and social wellbeing. Abu Basir was advised by Imam al-Sadiq to "not examine people [for their faults], as you will remain without friends."[13]

The Shi'a perspective on community relations and development has a returning principle of the individual's accountability and introspection. Islamic ethics reinforces the idea that believers should be wary of their own deeds and nonjudgmental of others. If they wish to do good, that is great, and of course required of them. If they wish to prevent injustice and wrongdoings, that is also expected and a noble cause. However, these noble pursuits should not be confused with being suspicious of one's friends, family, and community members. Nor should it be used as an excuse to pry into people's business and the problems they face. It is a balancing test for the individual's own intentions and a contemplation that one ought to constantly undertake, to ensure compliance with divine guidance.

Islam teaches its followers to acknowledge and be appreciative of the individuals that have preceded them in experience, wisdom, and knowledge. It encourages them to tap into their wealth of knowledge and wisdom, to learn from their experience and benefit as they carry on in their own life journeys. Seeking advice from wise and intellectual individuals was promoted by the Prophet and the Imams. Sulayman ibn Khalid narrates an instruction provided by Imam al-Sadiq in this regard.

> Seek advice from the intellectuals of men who have fear of God, as [such an individual] not command except with what is good.
> Beware of going against [that advice], for going against the advice of a God-fearing intellectual will lead to ruin in this life and the hereafter.[14]

It is narrated that Prophet Muhammad would describe what value is found in seeking advice from the wise and intellectual. He told his companions, "A consultation with a sincere intellectual is [a sign of] rectitude, blessing, and success. If a sincere intellectual advises you, beware of contradicting [his advice] as that will surely lead to ill."[15]

To neglect the experience and wisdom of the wise is juvenile and immature. It is no wonder why the Prophet stressed that such neglect would lead to a person's failure. Islamic scholars caution their followers who may find themselves at odds with the advice above, when they decide to neglect divine wisdom and tread their own paths. This is sometimes observed under the pretenses of "individuality" or "wanting to experience things on their own." The teachings of Islam are not at odds with recognizing uniqueness and the power of the individual. Imam Ali is reported to have said,

> Your cure is within you, but you do not know,

> Your illness is from you, but you do not see,
> You are the 'Clarifying Book'
> Through whose letter becomes manifest the hidden.
> You suppose that you are a small body
> But the greatest world unfolds within you.
> You would not need what is outside yourself
> If you would reflect upon the self, but you do not reflect.[16]

People are encouraged to live their life knowing the power that lies within; however, that individuality should not be misguided by whim. If one's attitude or experience would be to one's detriment, what is its use? Divine guidance, by way of the Prophet and the Imams, are prescriptions for the individual's success and happiness. A person has the free will to follow that path or not, but also bears the responsibility of their choices and their implications.

The Shiʿa take on community not only enforces ideals of moral support between its members, but also provides an infrastructure of financial and material support. The doctrines of *khums* and *zakah*, as discussed in the previous chapter on Shiʿa institutions, make it an obligation for the faithful to look after the needy and destitute. Through these practices, each person is obligated to give a percentage of their income to help support the less fortunate members of society. One who does not care for his brother or sister, cannot claim to be of the faith. As Imam al-Sadiq said, "Whoever does not care about the affairs of the Muslims is surely not a Muslim."[17]

OBSERVING THE RIGHTS OF OTHERS

The Prophet told his companions of a group of people that will be known as *Jiran Allah*, or the Neighbors of God, when they are resurrected on the Day of Judgment. Imam al-Baqir narrates the Prophet's illustration as follows.

> On the Day of Resurrection, a caller will call by the command of
> God Almighty, so that the furthest will hear him just as [clearly as]

the closest. [He will call out,] 'Where are the neighbors of God, Exalted by His Majesty, in His Abode?' A group of people will stand up. A group of angels will receive them and ask, 'What was your deed in the first life so that you became the neighbors of God Almighty in His Abode?'

They will respond, 'We used to love each other for the sake of God and support each other for the sake of God Almighty.' Then a caller will call on the command of God Almighty, 'My servants are truthful. Leave them. Let them proceed towards proximity to God in Heaven without any accounting [or judgment].'

Imam al-Baqir followed his narration by saying that "Those are the neighbors of God in His Abode. People will be afraid, but they will not be afraid. People will be judged, but they will not be judged."[18]

The love of God is directly connected to one's parents, and thus parents hold a great deal of importance in the Muslim conscience. In the Holy Quran, God brings the discussion of parents alongside the worship of God.

Worship God and do not ascribe any partners to Him, and be good to parents, the relatives, the orphans, the needy, the near neighbor and the distant neighbor, the companion at your side, the traveler, and your slaves. Indeed, God does not like those who are arrogant and boastful.[19]

God lays the order of relations here. God, parents, relatives, orphans, the needy, neighbors, and so on and so forth. Parents come second only to God himself. Respecting and adhering to parents, as well as doing good by them, is an essential component to a healthy and successful lifestyle. Implementing this on an individual level leads to community application and ultimately to a trait that a community can be characteristic of. To align oneself and community with the pleasure and favor of God, is to ensure that our relationships with our parents are taken care of and kept at the highest priority.

In his book *Risalat al-Huquq*, the Treatise on Rights, Imam al-Sajjad describes the rights of numerous individuals and even entities. His work, which dates to the later part of the 7th century, is considered to be one of the earliest publications on individuals' rights in human history. Regarding the rights of mothers, the Imam eloquently wrote the following.

> As for the right of your mother, it is that you know that she carried you where no one carries anyone, she fed you of the fruit of her heart that which no one gives to anyone, and she protected you with her hearing, her sight... and all her organs... She was content to remain hungry as long as you were fed, to remain naked as long as you were clothed, to remain thirsty as long as you drank, and to remain in the sun as long as you were in the shade. She ensured your happiness though she remained woeful and ensured that you enjoy your sleep though she remained wakeful.... You wish to thank her for all this, but you will not be able to [give her justice] unless through God's help and support.[20]

The Prophet Muhammad told his followers that, "Heaven lies at the feet of your mother."[21] One day, a man came to the Prophet seeking advice on where he should spend his time and what he should give his focus to. The Prophet simply answered, "Your Mother." When the inquirer asked who he should devote his time to next, the Prophet gave the same answer. The inquirer repeated his question a third time, but again the Prophet advised him to care for his mother. When the inquirer asked the fourth time, the Prophet said, "Then to your father."[22]

Imam al-Sajjad also described the rights of fathers when he wrote,

> As for the right of your father, it is that you know that he is your root, that you are his branch, and that without him you would not be. Whenever you see anything in yourself which pleases you, know that your father is the root of its blessing upon you. So praise God and thank Him in that measure.[23]

In acknowledging the rights of parents, the Imams also recognized that children have rights that must be observed. The Imam said,

> As for the right of your child, it is that you should know that he is from you and will be ascribed to you, through both his good and his evil, in the immediate affairs of this world. You are responsible for what you teach him of good conduct, pointing him in the direction of his Lord, and helping him to obey Him in [all of God's divine commands]. You will be rewarded for that [if you teach him well] or punished [if you teach him ill].[24]

Islam places a great deal of importance on family unit, but no doubt that significance also extends to the rest of the community as well. Families make up communities, and if the rights of families are neglected it would contribute to the decline of that community. Islamic doctrine attributes a connection between neglecting familial rights and relations with the hastening of death. Abu Hamza al-Thumali,[*] one of the close companions of Imam al-Sajjad, narrates that the Commander of the Faithful Imam Ali said in one of his sermons, "I seek refuge from the sins that hasten death…"

One of the Kharijites stood up and questioned Imam Ali, "Are there sins that hasten death?" The Imam responded decisively,

> Woe to you! Yes, [of course]! It is neglecting family relations [which hastens death]. A household that gathers and comforts one another, even while they sin publicly, God will still bless [despite their transgressions]. And a household that is divided, where each neglects the familial rights of the other, God will deprive them from His mercy even if they were pious.[25]

In identifying the deep importance of familial rights, Shiʿa doctrine pays special attention to brotherhood and the rights of siblings. Imam al-Sajjad

---

[*] Famously known as Abu Hamza al-Thumali, his birth name was Thabit ibn Safiyyah. He was a very close companion of Imam al-Sajjad, Imam al-Baqir, and Imam al-Sadiq thereafter. Narrations say that he was like the Salman of his time in knowledge and closeness to the Prophet's progeny. One of the most notable supplications of Imam al-Sajjad was taught to him and named after him – Duʿaʾ Abu Hamza al-Thumali. He passed away in 150 AH.

discussed the rights of brothers upon one another. On the rights of one's brother the Imam said,

> As for the right of your brother, it is that you know that he is your hand with which you give, your support on which you lean, your honor on which you rely, and your might with which you strike. So do not take him as a weapon with which to disobey God, or as means with which to wrong God [and His creatures]. Do not neglect to support him against himself, aid him against his enemy, separate between him and his demon [i.e. his ill thoughts], or give him good counsel and grow close to him for the sake of God. If he returns to God and succeeds in obeying Him, [that is well and good.] Otherwise, let God be of a higher priority and greater honor over you than him.[26]

As previously mentioned, Imam Ali once wrote that people are of two types – either a "brother in faith or [an] equal in creation." But what does it mean to be a brother? On another occasion, Imam Ali described exactly what it meant. He explained that brothers are of two kinds: brothers of trust and brothers of company. A man visiting from Basra made a request of Imam Ali. In the company of the Imam he said, "Tell us about brothers." Imam Ali replied,

> Brothers are of two types: brothers of trust and brothers of company. Brothers of trust are like your hand, your limbs, your family, and your wealth. If you trust your brother, make sure you give him from your wealth and your support. Be a friend to all of his friends and an enemy to all his enemies. Keep his secrets. Help him and show whatever is good of him. And know, O' inquirer, that they are rarer than red sulfur. As for the brothers of company, they are the ones through which you attain your enjoyment [of socialization]. Do not disconnect from them. Do not seek to understand their intention behind this. Show them the same as what they show you of cordial demeanor and pleasant conversation.[27]

Family and kin are the cornerstone of a community in Shiʿa Islam. Still, there are several other relationships that are essential and hold a great deal of importance. Neighbors, friends, colleagues, partners in work, scholars, and teachers all play significant roles in day-to-day life. Thus, Shiʿa faithful are instructed to be mindful of their rights and duties towards them.

One night, Imam Hasan stayed awake to observe his mother Lady Fatimah in prayer. She prayed from nightfall until dawn, while the curious young Imam took note of her supplicative whispers. When she finally finished her prayers at dawn, he stood up and approached his dear mother to ask a question. The hours that he spent watching and listening to her prayers, he only heard her ask God to help others. She prayed for the poor to gain wealth and sustenance. She prayed for the sick to be cured. She prayed for the orphans to be cared for with kindness. She prayed for the needy, asking that their wishes to be fulfilled. She prayed for God to protect her neighbors and strengthen her community. She prayed for peace and justice. She prayed for humanity. She prayed for all but herself.

So, the young Imam said to his mother, "O' mother! You have not prayed for yourself as you prayed for others!" Lady Fatimah smiled at her son and simply said, "My Son, [put] your neighbor before your household."[28]

In that spirit, Imam al-Sajjad would outline the rights of neighbors.

> As for the right of your neighbor, it is to safeguard [his interest] in
> his absence, honor him in his presence, and support him if here
> oppressed. Do not look for his concealed defects and if you come
> to know something ill about him, conceal it for him. If you know
> that he will accept your advice, counsel him [in private]. Do not
> abandon him in times of hardship, excuse his missteps, forgive his
> wrongdoings, and accompany him with honorable
> companionship.[29]

Neighbors can be friendly, but not always. Still, their rights must be observed. The friends that a person does have will prove to be a great contributor to a person's identity. "Tell me who your friends are, I will tell you who you are," is a saying often attributed to Imam Ali. Indeed, friends reflect one another. Those friends have rights upon one another. These rights are illustrative of what kind of friendship adherents of the faith look for, and what they expect of themselves as they look for those traits in others.

> As for the right of [your] friend, it is to deal with him with grace as much as possible, and, if it is not possible, then at least with justice. You should honor him as he honors you and protect him as he protects you. You should strive hard that he does not go ahead of you in any good deed between you and him, and if he surpasses you, you should repay it [with grace] and do not fall short in the love which he deserves.[30]

Social relationships and responsibilities extend into the professional and commercial settings as well. Shi'a doctrine regards business colleagues and partners as ones that are owed respect and consideration. Imam al-Sajjad describes the rights of business partners in the following words.

> As for the right of your partner, it is that you should take his burden upon yourself if he is absent, and be amiable to him when he is present. Do not decide anything contrary to his decisions and do not act according to your opinion without consulting him. Safeguard his wealth for him and do not be unfaithful to him in whatever matter, be it great of paltry. Verily, the hand of God [i.e. His blessing] remains upon the hands of the partners as long as they do not act unfaithfully to one another. And there is no power but with God.[31]

Educators, teachers, and scholars play a tremendous role in the Shi'a community as it would in any society. They hold a position that is deeply regarded in the faith and must be appreciated by all. Historically, much of the Shi'a community's engagement with their scholars came during the season of the hajj pilgrimage. This was often due to the political climate of the time that did not allow for the followers of the Imams to meet with them openly and regularly. Thus, hajj was a highly valued time not only in the traditional sense of pilgrimage but for the rare opportunity to connect and communicate directly with the scholars and even the Imams. On the role of scholars and the respect owed to them in the community Imam Ali stated,

> It is of the right of the scholar that you do not ask him too many questions, hasten to answer [a question that is asked of him without giving him the opportunity to answer], or insist on an answer if he rejects to answer. Do not [bother him] if he is tired. Do not point at him with your hand or wink at him. Do not become very comfortable at gatherings in his presence. Do not seek to find his faults… If he is in need, rush to fulfill his need before anyone else. Do not feel bored sitting long with him. For he is like a palm tree, wait and see what good will drop from him to you… When the scholar dies, Islam loses a fragment which will not be recompensed until the Day of Judgment. The seeker of knowledge will be carried by 70 thousand angels [when he dies]…[32]

Imam al-Sajjad also discussed the rights of scholars, or more specifically the rights of the one who trains others in knowledge, in the Treatise on Rights. He said,

> The right of the one who trains you in knowledge is to honor him, respect his sessions, listen well to him, and attend to him with devotion. You should not raise your voice at him. You should not answer anyone who asks him [a question], in order that he may be the one who answers. You should not speak to anyone in his session nor speak ill of anyone with him. If anyone speaks ill of him in your presence, you should defend him. You should conceal his faults and make manifest his virtues.[33]

All in all, Shi'a doctrine stresses the aforementioned obligations as a means to protect individual's rights and liberties. Such protections contribute to community development as the Prophet envisioned. Such a movement towards change, development and betterment cannot take place without individual action. "Indeed God does not change a people's lot, unless they change what is in their souls."[34]

CHAPTER 10

INTEGRATION & COEXISTENCE

Indeed, We created you from a male and a female, and made you nations and tribes that you may identify yourselves with one another.

The Holy Quran, 49:13.

THE FAMILY OF HUMANITY

Shi'a Muslims see themselves as belonging to the general body of Islam. They are taught to engage with their brothers and sisters from other schools of thought wherever they may be. The Shi'a also see themselves as belonging to the greater faith tradition of monotheism, a belief in one creator that blesses this world. Shi'ism teaches its followers, that to their very core, they belong to the family of humanity, as their identity is embedded in their origin as the sons of Adam. With that context in identity, how do Shi'a Muslims see themselves practically interacting with other groups in society?

It is important to realize the position of Shi'a Muslims from a historical backdrop. The Shi'a have long coexisted with other communities within the societies they lived in, be it during the normative period of the Muslim community in Arabia, Syria, and Iraq or elsewhere in their migration throughout the eastern and western worlds. Historically, the Shi'a have found themselves under the ruling authorities of the Umayyads, the Abbasids, the Ottomans, colonialist mandates, authoritarian regimes, modern-day democracies, and other forms of government and rule. All in all, the collective Shi'a community's experience with government and civic society has been diverse. The common theme in its history, however, has been a tradition of tolerance and coexistence. Both in doctrine and in practice, the Shiʿa have notably been advocates for a homeland as opposed to being advocates for power or authority, as one contemporary scholar of the seminary calls it.[1] Being advocates for a homeland, has positioned the Shiʿa community to be one that expects all people to be treated as citizens of nations under the equal protection of the law. Coexistence in society is intrinsic to Shiʿa Muslim identity and its worldview.

Nonetheless, groups may question as to what mode of operation is best for them regarding societal engagement. This discussion is not reserved for "minorities" alone in a traditional sense, as every individual in society is "part of a minority in some respects and of a majority in others."[2] It can be observed that groups generally navigate social engagement on the spectrum of assimilation and isolation with primarily two interests in mind. One, the interest of preserving values, customs, and origins. Two, the interest of being accepted by greater society and belonging to the broader milieu. Isolation may be reasonable means to protect the integrity of one's customs, beliefs, and group identity. Assimilation, on the other hand, may be chosen to get ahead and be more easily accepted into the greater fabric of that society. There are costs, however, to both approaches.

In this discussion, the authors propose a third option that has essentially been the doctrinal mode of operation for societal engagement in Shiʿism. That alternative approach is called integration, as opposed to straight assimilation or absolute isolation. The reader will also come to learn that integration can be passive or active in practice. Passive integration would be the choice not to assimilate and not to completely isolate oneself or group from society. But the individual who chooses passive integration does not make any active steps to engage outside of their immediate community. Thus, the impact of the individual or group outside of their direct circles is minimal. They do not seek to engage with others, nor do they seek to isolate themselves from others. Active integration, on the other hand, is a mode of societal engagement that requires the group to keenly connect, communicate, and collaborate with other groups in society. Awareness of the group's context and the need for partners, allies, and friends outside of their immediate circles is real. They acknowledge this and engage proactively, while preserving and affirming the group's identity within their society.

In the American context, the ideas of identity, citizenship, and societal engagement has long been negotiated in various communities. Catholics, Jews, and Mormons are some faith groups that lived and continue to experience the significance of this discourse.[3] Other ethnic and racial groups such as Latin Americans and African Americans have their own experiences that others can benefit from in this context. W. E. B. Du Bois, an African American thinker and activist, would express the idea of integration in what he called "assimilation through self-assertion," a method he attributed to the brave outlook and program of Frederick Douglass.[4] * Practically, assimilation through self-assertion is very relevant and relatable in the context of this discussion. For the purposes of this framework, the authors prefer to distinguish the positive product of assimilation, but avoid the downsides of its connotation, using the term *integration* instead. Thus, the idea of integration is to actively participate within society while asserting one's values, principles, practices, and beliefs; all the elements that make them distinct.

As a faith community, Shi'a Muslims asks themselves how their Prophet and Imams wanted them to live and engage. Are they to isolate themselves from society, pushing for self-containment, to ensure their values are absolutely protected, and consequently avoid societal engagement altogether? Are they to push forward their shared interests as a group by blending in

---

* Du Bois's (1868 – 1963) work, *The Souls of Black Folk*, was a collection of 14 essays he wrote on the African American experience and visions for that community. His work is considered as a seminal work in African American literature. Frederick Douglass (1818 – 1895) was an African American abolitionist, social reformer, statesman, writer, and orator. He escaped slavery and became a leading figure in the abolitionist movement. He was the excellent counterexample to Southerner's argument that African Americans were inferior and justified their enslavement. Northerners even were bewildered and amazed by his oration given the fact that he had been a slave for so many years. His writing and oratory skills were admired and much of what he expressed set the tone for African American thought during his era.

with the rest of society so that they are not perceived as different, foreign, or a threat to those around them? Or do they proactively engage and integrate within their societies in such a manner that their identity, values and principles are not compromised? Shiʿa consciousness sees itself as having a responsibility to protect and preserve its community, greater society, and humanity.

OPPOSED TO ISOLATIONISM

Shiʿa doctrine is sternly opposed the idea of isolation. The Imams stressed that their followers must not fall into being an isolated community. It does not serve them, nor does it advance their cause. Marazim and Huthayfah ibn Mansur, close companions of Imam al-Sadiq, relay two separate narrations from the Imam on the ideas of isolation and self-containment, as well as the way he advised his followers to see society.

> Indeed, you cannot escape [your need for] people. No one can be
> independent of people during his life, as people need one
> another...[5] Whoever holds his hand from [cooperating with] people
> has surely only held a single hand [i.e. his own] from them. Yet
> they shall hold many hands from [cooperating with] him.[6]

Choosing to isolate oneself from the community brings the most harm to the individual. If a group's choice is to isolate itself from society, it will be getting the short end of the stick. It is true that the group may save itself from the harms or side-effects that may come from society; and though society would be deprived of engaging with the group, in the end the world will go on. The choice to isolate one's group from the greater community deprives the group from the opportunity and potential to protect, preserve, and advance its cause. It denies the group the ability to help its community grow. In fact, though the decision of isolation may be intended to protect the community of the faithful, it is innately a selfish and shortsighted choice. Avoidance is not a solution for the potential challenges a community face. Instead, it may be a veiled excuse and an easy escape from facing the trials that come with living in a world of differences and diversity.[7]

> O mankind! Indeed, We created you from a male and a female, and made you nations and tribes that you may identify yourselves with one another. Indeed, the noblest of you in the sight of God is the most Godwary among you. Indeed God is all-knowing, all-aware.[8]

As previously mentioned, an essential point within this verse is to encourage appreciation, acknowledgement, and engagement of diversity. God created the world this way so that humanity can appreciate its differences and celebrate its diversity. People should not yearn to become carbon copies of one another, nor should they wish to avoid one another out of fear of losing that diversity. God wants people to interact and engage with individuals and groups that are different from their own. He wants mankind to learn from those differences and enjoy that diversity. He wants people to see that everyone is different, and there is nothing wrong with that. There is no superiority over any person or group by the mere virtue of belonging to a certain tribe, race, or culture. The only virtue that reigns supreme is piety, and the pious do not deem themselves supreme – supremacy and glory is to God alone.

To isolate oneself from society is a likely contributor to animosity. One will find that most individuals that possesses racist, prejudice, or discriminatory views often have little to no engagement with the group they are biased against. This can affect both sides of the conversation. For example, if the average White American chooses to isolate himself from greater society, he will likely be ignorant of the culture and way of life of those outside of his group. He will probably not meet or interact with other groups like Jews, Muslims, or Latinos, so long as he is isolated to his group. Due to lack of exposure, he may develop unfavorable or at least stereotypical views of said groups. Further, if Jews, Muslims, or Latinos chose to isolate themselves from society, it may further contribute to the stereotypes held of them because they did not afford themselves the opportunity to proactively engage and dispel preconceived notions.

Shi'a doctrine acknowledges that ignorance is not bliss. Imam Ali said, "People are enemies of what they do not know."[9] Ignorance is a wretched thing that turns man against his fellow man for merely not knowing enough about him. Ignorance makes people scared and reactive. Most hate crimes that take place in the United States are often attributed to xenophobia – an intense and irrational dislike or fear of people from other nations or countries.[10] An example of this includes the profound number of Sikhs that have been victims of anti-Muslim hate crimes even 15 years after the terrorist attacks of September 11, 2001. The first revenge killing after September 11 took the life of Balbir Sing Sodhi who was an Indian Sikh immigrant. "The assailant said he wanted to 'go out and shoot some towel heads' for the actions of Osama bin Laden."[11] It just goes to show the ignorance behind these actions. The man was not even a Muslim, yet he was killed by someone who harbored resentment towards Islam. To the assailant, a Muslim looked a certain way and a Sikh immigrant fit that description – dark skin, long beard, and wearing a turban. Fear and ignorance go together, usually leading to devastating outcomes for people across the world. Isolation, be it by those perpetuating hate or those receiving it, only fuels the sensational fire of fear and ignorance.

THE PERIL OF ASSIMILATION

Assimilation is an experience discussed in virtually every group entering or existing in a society. It is part of the social experience involved in migration and there are many sides to the subject. As the authors understand it, assimilation refers to the course of a group adopting the culture, values, and customs of others to become more like them. To be a part of a society, it seems that one would need to share the predominant features, values, and characteristics of that society. The challenge of assimilation is it also tends to eradicate or replace the values the individual or group brings with them.

The negative result of that, especially in immigrant communities, is that the person loses their heritage and traditions to assimilate leading do a departure from one's identity. From a religious perspective, the loss of one's faith-based identity is tantamount to a loss of salvation.

Given the context of the discussion, it brings forth the discourse of compatibility of other societies with Islam and other faith traditions for that matter. How can a secular or non-religious society engage with faith? Can one lead a religious lifestyle while being assimilated in one's society? These questions will be addressed in greater detail in the discussion that follows on integration and model citizenship.

Nonetheless, as the idea of assimilation is entertained, it is important to realize what the possible effects it entails. One of the adverse examples of assimilation discussed is pertaining to members of the faith group attending establishments such as bars, pubs, and clubs. Though such an activity may be widely considered a norm in nonreligious American or British life, it is deeply abhorred and prohibited in religious tradition. A person looking to assimilate may likely accept an invitation from colleagues or classmates to go to a bar or pub, because the mode of operation is to immerse fully into the broader culture. This is the very crux of the concern from the religious perspective. When assimilation is prioritized over religious values, it slowly etches away at the individual's religious identity.

Though assimilating may guarantee or help ensure one's presence and social acceptance in society, it risks far greater things such as faith, beliefs, and identity. Assimilation, in this discussion, does not mean a temporary means to integrate into society. The reference is more in its pure sense of adopting a host culture and replacing one's former values, customs, and traditions with new ones. Assimilation sacrifices the individual's identity for a desire to be a part of something new.

The concern of losing one's identity by moving to another community or society was seen from the very birth of Islam during the lifetime of the Prophet. In the Prophet Muhammad's will and directives to Imam Ali before he died, the Prophet spoke of faith after enlightenment. He said, "There shall be no *ta'arrub* [faithlessness] after *hijrah* [migration]."[12] *

The Prophet wanted to make it clear that one's faith was a priority to be maintained. Those who migrated to escape religious persecution should remember that. A person's aim should be to live a wholesome and faithful life. Migration is welcome and those who choose it are empowered, so long as they remember the purpose for which they migrated. That purpose, according to Islamic belief, should be to protect and preserve one's faith. Identity must be reinforced after migration, not compromised. That is what the Prophet advised.

Imam Ali al-Rida wrote,

> God forbade [the return to nomadism] after migration, as it would mean abandoning the faith and neglecting to support the prophets and [vicegerents of God]... That is why a man who may have a comprehensive understanding of the religion is not permitted to associate with the people of ignorance. One should be uncertain of his matter, as he is not safe from the possibility of abandoning knowledge and [fully assimilating] with the people of ignorance.[13]

After reading some of these narrations, the reader may get the impression that migration to a "non-Muslim" land is prohibited or loathed. That is simply not the case. Rather, if an individual knows that they will lose their faith by moving to a certain area, regardless of where it may be, then it is religiously prohibited. However, moving or migration is not forbidden or prohibited. In fact, there are several examples in the Quran where individuals sought to protect their faith and wellbeing by means of migration to other regions. One primary case is Prophet Moses.

---

* *Ta'arrub* is an Arabic word meaning nomadism but is used in this context to refer to the lack of faith or guidance that is associated with primitive and nomadic pre-Muslim Arabia. *Hijrah*, or migration, in that context refers to the different migrations that the Muslims undertook in order to escape persecution to Medina. The Prophet is thus declaring that a person who left to Medina in order to escape persecution should not compromise his faith by returning to the old habits and culture of origin – or by adopting the habits and culture of his new found home if they are similarly contrary to the teachings of Islam.

> So he left the city, fearful and vigilant. He said, 'My Lord! Deliver
> me from the wrongdoing lot.' And when he turned his face toward
> Midian, he said, 'Maybe my Lord will show me the right way.'[14]

His move to Midian was to flee persecution and protect his faith and well-being. God supported him in this and cleared the path for him. Similarly, when the Prophet Muhammad and his followers went through intolerable measures of religious persecution during their days in Mecca, the Prophet instructed a group of his followers to seek haven in the land of Abyssinia – modern-day Ethiopia.[15] When Ja'far ibn Abu Talib, Imam Ali's brother, led a band of Muslims to Abyssinia in 615-616 AD, the Prophet instructed Ja'far regarding their stay in Abyssinia. The Prophet's directives emphasized respect and regard for their host's faith and explicitly ordered that the Muslims not push their beliefs on anyone. "The king of Abyssinia welcomed the Muslim refugees from Makkah into his kingdom. He gave them sanctuary, and they enjoyed peace, security and freedom of worship under his aegis."[16]

INTEGRATION AND MODEL CITIZENS

The polar approaches of pure isolation and complete assimilation are both counterintuitive and do not truly serve the interest of preservation of faith. Isolating one's group as to avoid any possible challenge or trial to one's faith is not prescribed in the prophetic tradition. Nor is sacrificing one's principles and identity to fit in with the rest of society. Instead, the Prophet and his disciples advised their followers to integrate in society, rather than isolate or assimilate. From one generation to the next, the Ahl al-Bayt stressed the principles of coexistence and harmonious living. They did not settle for passive integration in their instructions to their followers. They themselves actively integrated within their societies and encouraged their followers to do just the same.

The Imams themselves lived in the center of society and did not isolate themselves from people. They encouraged active engagement in their societies. Isolation was never an option, neither was assimilation and a loss of identity. Even amidst all their challenges and tribulations, active integration was the way forward. Through integration they showed how to engage in society and thrive as the model citizens and leaders that they were.

In another instance of instruction to those in "foreign lands", Imam al-Sadiq had an enlightening conversation with a companion of his named Hammad al-Samandari. Hammad told the Imam of a disconcerting situation he faces whenever he travels abroad. In the conversation, he complained to the Imam that he was being chided by fellow Muslims for traveling to lands where Islam was not prevalent. They told him that he would be resurrected with the nonbelievers that he lived with.

Imam al-Sadiq asked him, "When you [are there], do you remember our cause and call for it? Hammad replied, "Yes, I do." Then the Imam asked, "If you are in these cities – the cities of Islam – do you remember our cause and call for it?"

"No, I do not," Hammad replied simply. Imam al-Sadiq then reassured him, "If you die there, you will be resurrected as a nation of your own with your light beaming before you."[17]

It is not merely about where a person lives. The country or nation of residence is relevant to the extent of its effect on one's faith and relationship to God. It is better for one to live in "foreign country" that has no outwardly Muslim presence but allows one to fulfill their duties as a believer (like the companion Hammad al-Samandari); rather than living in a Muslim country where one is complacent, apathetic, and has become heedless of their relationship to God and their faith.

Muhammad ibn Abu Hamza narrates the story of a blind man seeking help from people in the market of Kufa during the tenure of Imam Ali's caliphate. That day, as he did from time to time, Imam Ali was humbly walking amongst the people in the market when he saw this man begging. The poor man went from one person to the next asking for assistance. Not a single person stopped to help the old man. Outraged, Imam Ali looked at the people around him and exclaimed, "Who is this?"

They responded simply, "He is a Christian." Imam Ali then retorted, "You used him until he grew old and unable [to work], then you cut him off?! [Give him] from the treasury!"[18]

Regardless of one's religion or creed, people are to be treated with dignity, respect, and honor. If one human being suffers, all are suffering. If one human being succeeds, all succeed. Simply because another individual has a different belief or worldview does not justify apathy towards him or her. Imam Ali showed that in his moral outrage towards the way people neglected that elderly Christian man. The story tells that Imam Ali would not leave the market until that man was cared for in every way. He would not rest until anyone that crossed his path with a need or request was indeed fulfilled. The life of Imam Ali tells of how he spent his days and nights during his rule. In the day, he fought for justice in government, in the marketplace, and on the battlefield.

Justice was blind and all men were to be treated equally. In distributing state funding from the treasury, Imam Ali instructed his deputies, "Begin with the *Muhajirun* and call them to receive their portion. Give each of them three dinars. Then call the *Ansar* and give them all the same amount. Do the same with everyone that comes to you – whether he is red or black."[19] In the marketplace, he would ensure that not even a beggar was neglected. And on the battlefield, he reminded his men of bravery and true faith in the Almighty.

> Mountains may move from their position, but you should not
> move from yours. Grit your teeth. Lend to God your head in
> fighting for Him. Give yourself to God. Plant your feet firmly on
> the ground. Have your eye on the remotest foe and close your eyes
> to their great numbers. Remember, your aid comes from God
> alone, the Glorified.[20]

Imam Ali ensured that his governors were instructed to treat people with the same dignity and respect that he gave to all people. Followers of Ali are taught that they should ache when another human being suffers, be it a "brother in faith or an equal in humanity." If a person is not to have compassion and show care to those around them, then what purpose does that person serve? The Holy Prophet Muhammad was sent as a mercy to all of mankind. Islam teaches that if a person wishes to be a follower of Prophet Muhammad, then such a person must strive to reflect him. "And We did not send you but as a mercy to all the nations."[21]

"He is a Christian," they apathetically said to Ali when he was enraged by the neglect heaped on to an old man. In that marketplace, Imam Ali showed humanity that the care and kindness of a true Muslim must extend to every human being – Christian, Jew, and Muslim alike. Through one's actions, the individual defines who they are. Through one's conduct, a person preaches their faith.

Shi'a doctrine maintains that the community of the faithful cannot be preserved, protected, and developed unless humanity is protected and advanced. To move forward as a community, Shi'a Muslims believe that they are not to make others insecure at their expense. The Shi'a are empowered when the communities around them are empowered. They are secure if the communities around them are secure. All people are to be respected in a society and preserved under the equal protection of the law.

About being model citizens and how Shi'a Muslims are encouraged to live within their communities, Safwan ibn Yahya narrates detailed instructions from Imam al-Sadiq.

> Deliver my regards to whoever you see that obeys me and accepts my word. I advise you all to practice piety before God Almighty. Fear God in your religion and strive in the way of God. Be truthful in your words, deliver the trusts [that you have been entrusted with], prolong your prostration, and be good neighbors. For this is what [Prophet] Muhammad came with. Deliver the trusts to

whoever entrusts you, whether virtuous or a sinner. The Messenger
of God would command to deliver back the remainder of the
sowing thread and the needle [along with the sown garment]. Be in
touch with your tribes, attend their funerals, visit their ill, and
fulfill their rights. Surely, if a person amongst you was pious in his
religion, truthful with his words, delivers the trusts [with which he
was entrusted], and was well-mannered with the people, he would
be called a *Ja'fari.*' That would please me and he would bring me
great happiness. The people would say, 'These are the manners of
Ja'far.' If a person was not like that, I would be saddened and
ashamed by him, as they will then say, 'these are the manners of
Ja'far.' By God my father told me, if a person was part of a tribe
and he was a follower of Ali, he would be the best amongst them.
He would be the most trustworthy, the most upright in fulfilling
the rights of others, and the most truthful. People would entrust
him with their wills and [wealth]. When the tribe is asked about
him they respond, 'Who is like him? He is the most trustworthy
and the most truthful amongst us!'[22]

Imam al-Sadiq also said,

O' Shi'a! Be an adornment [i.e. a good reflection] for us and do not
be a disgrace upon us. Speak kindly to people and preserve your
tongues, holding them from prying and abhorrent language.[23]

By practicing the ethics of Ahl al-Bayt, Shi'a Muslims become an integral
and positive part of their communities. They are to bring no harm and present no threat to their neighbors and friends. The role of a Muslim is to
bring peace and mercy wherever they live.

The prophets and messengers of God were always leading the way as the
role models for their people. "There is certainly a good exemplar for you in
the Apostle of God—for those who look forward to God and the Last Day,

---

' Ja'fari was the term used to describe the followers of Imam Ja'far al-Sadiq. It is still used today as a reference to the
Twelver Shi'a jurisprudential school of thought.

and remember God much."[24] Even when people doubted the prophets and accused them of being magicians, insane, or disillusioned, the prophets remained steadfast. God would reinforce them for their high morals and character. In the Holy Quran, God told Prophet Muhammad,

> By the Pen and what they write. By your Lord's blessing, you are
> not insane. And yours indeed will be an everlasting reward. And
> indeed you possess a great character. You will see and they will see,
> which one of you is insane. Indeed, your Lord knows best those
> who stray from His way, and He knows best those who are
> guided.[25]

In their active integration in their communities, the Imams and their followers protected themselves, their beliefs, and contributed to their societies. They emphasized certain key principles: model-leadership and citizenship, coexistence, and tolerance, and promoting change within systems as opposed to disrupting or destroying what exists.

THE DOCTRINE OF COEXISTENCE

The principle of coexistence with others is part and parcel to understanding active integration. Coexistence is not merely tolerating the presence of others; rather, it means to engage with others and seek to understand them. Seeking to understand others is the most effective way to be understood.[26] The more people engage and learn about others, as well as open themselves up to have others learn about them, the closer humanity gets to peace, harmony, and understanding.

Nonetheless, coexistence is not always advocated for or tolerated by others in a society. Like other marginalized groups, Shi'a Muslims have faced a great deal of discrimination, prejudice, and persecution throughout their history as a people. The Shi'a have been victims of terrorism, exile, imprisonment. Horrendous violations of human rights have been endured in Shi'a history, often for the mere fact that their communities identified as followers of a particular school of thought. There were different political motivations depending on the regime and the region in which some of these atrocities took place. The persecution the Shi'a faced came as early as the years immediately after the death of the Prophet and would rise monumentally with the rise of the Umayyads. It would continue under the Abbasids as well. For the preservation of life and the continuity of their message, the Imams and their followers often practiced what is known as *taqiyyah*, or pious dissimulation, in the face of such tyranny and extremism.[27]

Too often were the lives of the Imams and their followers under threat by the grossly reckless authority of tyrants. Thus, to preserve their lives, as guardians and ambassadors of the Prophet's message, they would conceal their faith at times until the whims of tyrants would pass. In fact, the practice of *taqiyyah* was first approved by the Prophet himself through the example of his close companion Ammar ibn Yasir.

During the early days of Islam, the Muslims were taunted and persecuted by the pagans of Mecca. After accepting Islam, Ammar ibn Yasir became the new target of the Meccans. They forced Ammar to recant his faith under duress after capturing and torturing him. When the matter came to the Prophet, he asked Ammar of the state of his heart. He told the Prophet that he did not disbelieve, and that faith still filled his heart and soul. The Prophet said that Ammar had done the right and that all would be well.[28] God then revealed the verse,

> Excepting someone who is compelled [to recant his faith] while his heart is at rest in it, those who disbelieve in God after [affirming] their faith and open up their breasts to unfaith, God's wrath shall be upon them and there is a great punishment for them.[29]

The Prophet and the Imams instructed their followers with the practice of *taqiyyah* as a practical means to save their lives from persecution. If an individual's life is in danger for a display of his faith, it is obligatory for that person to omit that display of faith to ensure his safety. Putting one's life in danger to proclaim their faith is not the tradition of the Prophet or his disciples. The practice of *taqiyyah* serves as a sensible practice authorized by

God's Messenger to protect the life and wellbeing of believers. People cannot control the actions of others, but individuals have the free will to dictate their own actions. This is a means to help gain control in an otherwise helpless situation. Note that once the danger on one's life ceases, the omission of one's display of faith or practice also stops.

On various occasions, Imam al-Sadiq stressed the significance of *taqiyyah* in as central part of faith. He stated, "Taqiyyah is my religion and the religion of my fathers;"[30] Imam al-Sadiq advised his followers to "safeguard your religion and protect it with taqiyyah. Surely, there is no faith for a person with no taqiyyah."[31] Moreover, he testified that, "God has not been worshipped with anything better than taqiyyah."[32]

What has been expressed here thus far is the practice of *taqiyyah* in its purest form. In Shi'a doctrine, there is also something that is called *al-taqiyyat al-mudaratiyyah.** This form of taqiyyah is applied in less serious situations like the ones described above. It is used to be courteous and kind to others, to be considerate of their sensitivities and things that they hold dear. Take the example of a mosque in a predominantly non-Muslim neighborhood in Georgia. The *adhan* plays from the speakerphones atop the minarets of the mosque for each of the five daily prayers.† Fajr prayer, prayed at dawn, comes as early as 4:00 AM sometimes of the year, if not earlier. As a practice of *al-taqiyyat al-mudaratiyya*, the mosque decides not to amplify the adhan during the early morning hours out of consideration for their sleeping non-Muslim neighbors. In that, they avoid risking their neighbors' agitation and added negativity to their impression of Muslims. The whole idea is to be aware of one's surroundings and working within the context that one lives in.[33]

Another topic of relevance within the discussion on coexistence is proselytism. What is the Shi'a view on actively trying to convert people to their

---

* *Al-Mudaratiyyah* comes from the word *mudarah*, which essentially means to be courteous, polite, or civil.

† *Adhan* is the Muslim call to prayer.

faith or school of thought? Are they instructed to proselytize or not? In a conversation with Imam al-Baqir, Abu Basir asked the Imam about this very subject. Abu Basir asked, "Should I preach to the people what I know?" The Imam replied simply, "No." Abu Basir followed up, "If someone sought my guidance, should I then?"

"Whoever seeks guidance from you, guide him. If he seeks more, give him more. If he turns away from you, turn away from him,"[34] Imam al-Baqir instructed.

Thabit ibn Sa'id narrates that Imam al-Sadiq was even more direct on the Ahl al-Bayt's position on proselytizing. He said,

> O' Thabit! What do you have with the people? Leave the people alone. Do not call anyone to your faith. By God, if the denizens of the heavens and the denizens of the earth all rallied to misguide a servant who God wishes to guide, they would not be able to misguide him.[35]

Instead, the Imam would instruct his followers to "Be callers [towards faith] without using your tongues. Let people see in you the fear of God, commitment, prayer, and virtue, as that is a method of calling [towards faith]."[36] Ahl al-Bayt wished for their followers to teach others their principles without needing to preach to them about them. Actions speak louder than words.[37]

Even when the Muslims migrated to Abyssinia from Mecca, the Prophet gave Ja'far ibn Abu Talib specific instructions on their stay in Abyssinia. He told Ja'far that he should not seek to convert anyone to Islam. His role in Abyssinia was to seek refuge for the Muslim community, appreciate the kindness of their hosts, and coexist with their new neighbors.

CITIZENSHIP AND WORKING IN THE SYSTEM

In both Biblical and Quranic tradition, Prophet Joseph's story of tribulation and triumph has inspired generations. Thrown to a well and forsaken by his brothers, he would not be forgotten by his Lord. He would become an honorable citizen of Egypt, even though his youth was plagued with turmoil and hardship. From a bought slave to high chancellor, Joseph would ascend to the highest ranks of Egypt's government. He changed the system that governed over his people from within. Joseph did not dismantle that government, nor did he overthrow the pharaoh. Instead, he ruled alongside him and ultimately under his reign. History would tell that the pharaoh would eventually become a believer in God and accept Joseph as the prophet of God.[38]

In the story of Moses, is yet another example of *taqiyyah* as well as working within the system to protect the wellbeing of the community of the faithful. There was a member of Pharaoh's family who worked under him as a minister. Unbeknownst to the Pharaoh, this relative was a believer in the religion of Moses. Throughout his tenure as minister, he continued to hide his faith to serve and save his community.

It is important to note here a very crucial point. Practicing taqiyyah and working within a system that is not friendly or open to one's faith essentially go together. If Shi'a Muslims are to conceal their faith, it is not for the purpose of harming the establishment or the opposition. Rather, it is only to protect their own lives and wellbeing. This practice cannot be used to harm others. It is only used to protect oneself and community.

Ali ibn Yaqtin (742–798 AD) was the son of a close companion of Imam al-Sadiq. His father was placed under house arrest by the Umayyad Caliph Marwan II. When the Umayyads fell and the Abbasids came to power in 750 AD, Ali ibn Yaqtin returned to Kufa as a young boy with his family. He grew up in Kufa and when he completed his education, he went on to gain employment in the Abbasid government. Ibn Yaqtin was ordered by Imam al-Kazim to stay in the Abbasid government to protect the interests of the Shi'a community. He was a close companion of Imam al-Kazim and his father Imam al-Sadiq. Imam al-Kazim told him of the great responsibility he had and the significance he served the Shi'a. To ensure that he would not be a potential threat to the Abbasids, and continue quietly protecting the interests of his community, he remained under the radar as much as possible. During that time, he was even instructed by the Imam to change the way he prayed to evade his counterparts' suspicions that he was Shi'a.[39] If Ali ibn Yaqtin had openly displayed his creed, he would be removed from his position, imprisoned, and possibly executed.

Delving into the corpus of Shi'a hadith will show that there are indeed some narrations that speak of people's hand in helping oppressors and supporting their tyranny. Is a person who works in an oppressive government a culprit himself to the crimes of that system? Imam al-Sadiq said,

> On the Day of Resurrection, a caller will call out, 'Where are the oppressors, the supporters of the oppressors, and the likes of the oppressors? Even an individual who [prepared] for them a pen or inkwell [will be called]. They will all be gathered in an iron coffin and thrown in hellfire.[40]

Abu Hamza Al-Thumali narrates that Imam al-Sajjad said,

> Be aware of befriending disobeyers, supporting oppressors, or taking transgressors as neighbors. Be careful of their sedition and stay away from their domains.[41]

Shi'a scholars explain that the Imams were not assigning guilt to an individual who works within an oppressive system by mere association. Rather, they were drawing the lines and reminding their followers to be prudent and cognizant of their responsibilities. An argument can be put forth that Muslims must fully oppose an oppressive or unjust system to change or fix it. But the Imams simply did not do that. Each one of them, to the fullest extent possible, worked within the system and circumstances of their time.

They worked within the system and sought reform through it, not outside of it.

The Prophet chose Imam Ali as his successor and the next caliph of the Muslims. The narration of the event of Ghadir is one of the most narrated traditions in Islam.[42] Even though nearly a hundred thousand individuals would be witness to the Prophet's proclamation of Ali as his heir, the community chose a different path after the Prophet's death. Imam Ali would not fill the position of political authority until 25 years later and under entirely different circumstances. As the legal and spiritual heir of the Prophet, Imam Ali tended to his burial and ensuring the Quran was properly arranged and preserved after it was completed and compiled in the Prophet's lifetime.[43] Though others were fixated on the transition of power and forming a new government, Imam Ali was pragmatic and mindful of the consequences of people's actions. He stepped back and heeded to the Prophet's directions not to rise against those who would turn against him.

> The Messenger of God told me, 'if they gather against you, do what I have commanded you. Stay your chest to the ground.' When they deviated away from me, I [persevered] despite the adversity. I closed my eyelids and endured the pricking in my eyes. I stayed my chest to the ground...[44]

Imam Ali was found as an advisor, with an active role, within the system even though it was a system created to replace him. Thus, Imam Ali would make his position clear, "By God, I will accede so long as the matters of the Muslims are secure, and so long as this transgression remains against me alone [as an individual]."[45] That was his goal – securing the affairs of the Muslims and Islam, even if it was at his personal expense. The second caliph would famously express Imam Ali's profound effect on his own caliphate. "If it were not for Ali, ʿUmar would have perished,"[46] he said of himself. Imam Ali took it upon himself to have an active role within that system, so that he could protect the principles of the faith and reform what others brought forth in misguided novelties and whimsical ventures in the name of Islam. Imam Husayn ibn Ali was just the same.

Though the narrative may be confused at times, Imam Husayn's mission was clear. He did not wage war, nor did he lead a rebellion against the Umayyads at the death of Muʿawiyah in 680 AD. He simply refused to give allegiance to the illegitimate caliphate of Yazid ibn Muʿawiyah. The caliphate of Yazid would be publicly recognized as a farce, given that it violated the final term of the peace accord between Imam Hasan and Muʿawiyah that allowed the latter to assume power and for Imam Hasan to abdicate.[47] The distinguishing factor here, given the context, was that Imam Husayn's acceptance of Yazid's caliphate would mean complete obliteration of the faith. The Umayyads had expanded in a way that was going to replace everything deemed sacred in Islam with a new brand of tribalism and kingship coined with conquest, military expansion, and economic growth. Like his father and brother, Imam Husayn's role was to protect the faith and the faithful.

In fact, even as he anticipated that he would need to sacrifice his life to stand for his principles and protect the faith from disintegrating, he would do so with the least casualties possible. Ahl al-Bayt valued the sanctity of life. They did not deal with the souls of people lightly. This is an essential part of belief and found throughout prophetic tradition and Quranic teachings.

> That is why We decreed for the Children of Israel that whoever
> kills a soul, without [its being guilty of] manslaughter or
> corruption on the earth, is as though he had killed all mankind,
> and whoever saves a life is as though he had saved all mankind.[48]

In the events leading up to the Battle of Karbala, Imam Husayn would not call onto the people of his community to topple the Umayyad regime and revolt against the establishment. The Imam did not mobilize forces as he embarked on his journey toward Iraq. Instead, when the news came of the execution of his ambassador to Kufa, Muslim ibn Aqil, he made sure to inform all those who accompanied him. He did not conceal the news to keep the morale of his company high. He wanted to make sure that all those who were with him knew of the possible fate that followed. This was not a venture to overthrow a government and establish a new rule. This was a movement to reinforce the principles he was tasked to protect and bring reform within a society to which he belonged.[49]

In today's context, the Marji'iyyah emphasizes a key jurisprudential concept – *hifz al-nizam* or maintaining public order. Inciting chaos, havoc and any form of anarchy is something that is forbidden by our faith. Keeping public order is not only preferred but obligatory.

As citizens of nations with participative systems, the Shi'a Religious Authority advises its followers to seize the opportunity to establish their presence and protect their rights and interests as a community. Civic engagement and actively participating in elections and voting is favorable to its community's preservation. If a community chooses to isolate itself from the systems that dictate laws and regulations that govern its day-to-day life, such a community is inadvertently choosing to exclude itself from the conversation.

It is imperative that people see things holistically and realize that they have tremendous potential as individuals and collectively as a community. Youth, especially, are advised to strive to best they possible can be at whatever they are doing. They should strive to attend the best universities and seminaries and attain high-ranking degrees. They should aspire to seek competitive jobs and secure employment in crucial positions of society. They should be top entrepreneurs and be examples of success and moral excellence in trading and business. All of these are advised with the goal to help and advance one's community and society. Regardless of one's craft, profession, or trade, they are encouraged to excel in whatever they do.[50]

The teachings and precedent of the Prophet and his disciples make the Shi'a a dynamic community. Given its dynamism, it can hold on to its principles and heritage while engaging with the rest of world. That translates to active integration. As an integrated community, its members naturally have an appreciation and a sense of obligation to the societies it lives in. That then translates to the principle of *citizenship*.

Citizenship, *al-muwatanah*, is part and parcel to Shi'a tradition and doctrine, though it remains a very nuanced study. Some scholars say that there is broad citizenship where one resides in a place with a social contract between the citizenry and their governors. Then there is legal citizenship, where this social contract is given more permanency. Yet, the implication of current state borders in the modern world on the concept of citizenship remains a matter of debate amongst Shi'a scholars. Is an individual a citizen of their city, province, or country?

Nonetheless, citizenship is not merely the observance of a social contract, and the deep respect the Prophet gave to the rights of others, but is seen as a relationship of adoration. Looking at the earliest days of Islam, scholars observe the affinity of Islam's Prophet to the places he called home. The Holy Prophet described early on the significance of *al-watan*, the homeland, and the deep feelings he had towards it.

The Prophet looked to his companions and said, "To love one's *homeland* is a part of faith."[51]

Mecca was the Prophet's home, but he was forced to leave it by those that persecuted him and his followers. He made a new home to the north, in Yathrib, which would later become known as Medina. This would be the new homeland, or *watan*, of the Prophet and his people. He loved Medina, many people also calling it Medinat al-Rasul, or the Messenger's City. It would also become the home of his immediate family and many that would come from his lineage. Still, the Prophet and his family never forgot about Mecca, it remained a place in their hearts – a *watan* that could not be removed from their psyche.

A community that integrates within its society is a community that understands and appreciates citizenship. The Shi'a see citizenship, wherever it may be, as a crucial component of community engagement. Islam teaches its followers to respect, honor, and protect the land they live on and the country they belong to. The body of laws and institutions that protect a society have a sanctity that to the community must uphold. Such observance is not optional, and it cannot be neglected by the community, as ethical members of society. Believing that integration is the mode of operation for societal engagement, Shi'a Muslims aspire to be the best citizens they can be in whatever nation or country they live in. It becomes part of their social identity and way of life, reinforced by the principle of integration and proactive engagement.

CHAPTER 11

THE DOCTRINE OF OCCULTATION

Imam al-Sadiq was asked, "How will people benefit from an Imam who is absent and concealed?" He replied, "They shall benefit from him like they benefit from the sun concealed behind the clouds."

THE PROMISE OF GOD

God's *promise* is reiterated in numerous places across the pages of the Holy Book. It is a promise to allow His virtuous servants to inherit the Earth. It is to empower them with what He has ordained and issued. God says in the Holy Quran,

> Certainly We wrote in the Psalms, after the Torah: 'Indeed My righteous servants shall inherit the earth.'[1]

In Chapter 24 of the Quran, al-Nur (the Light), He also describes his promise.

> God has promised those of you who have faith and do righteous deeds that He will surely make them successors in the earth, just as He made those who were before them successors, and He will surely establish for them their religion which He has approved for them, and that He will surely change their state to security after their fear, while they worship Me, not ascribing any partners to Me. Whoever is ungrateful after that—it is they who are the transgressors.[2]

The end goal of humanity is to reach the status of vicegerent – to represent God on earth. Someone who is empowered to use the resources created for him to manifest the attributes of God on Earth.

Inheriting the earth refers to using what God has created to manifest His principles and lead life in the way He approves and desires for His creation. It is to empower them to live in the way that God wishes for them – the best and most prosperous way to live. It is that path that leads to one's success and happiness, in this life and the next.

Islam teaches that when God gives His light, it may disturb those who live in darkness. It may irritate those who do not wish to see, and they may choose to shut their eyelids even harder than before. When people did not like what He approved for his servants in faith and provided for in guidance, He promised that the faithless would surely despair, disapprove, disagree, and disdain. But the prerogative of the faithful should remain with resilience and fortitude.

> Today the faithless have despaired of your religion. So do not fear
> them, but fear Me. Today I have perfected your religion for you,
> and I have completed My blessing upon you, and I have approved
> Islam as your religion. [3]

It is essential to note that religion and divine guidance cannot be established by force or coercion according to Islamic doctrine. "There is no compulsion in religion: rectitude has become distinct from error." [4] Instead, it is established through planning and strategy.

Upon the death of the Prophet, the Imams prepared for and implemented this grand project of religion. One after the other, each Imam had a different role depending on the context of the time. Imam Ali exemplified the principle of the greater good and what it meant to sacrifice for the preservation of true Islam. He said, "By God, I will accede so long as the matters of the Muslims are secure, and so long as this transgression remains against me alone [as an individual]." [5]

He went on to establish the standard of just governance during his momentous yet short-lived caliphate. Each of the succeeding Imams worked tirelessly to make the best of the circumstances of the time and preserve the message of Islam. As discussed in previous chapters, this meant that each Imam played his role and fulfilled his duty in a unique way dictated by his circumstances.

The adversaries of the Imams fought them with various methods and tactics; and they usually had the resources of an empire at their disposal. The regimes or authorities of the time tried to alter the interpretations of the religion to their favor via fabricated narrations and pseudo-scholars. This was especially utilized during the Umayyad dynasty, which reigned in the years 661 to 750 AD. The reader may recall that recording narrations was prohibited during the second caliphate, as discussed previously in the book. However, when the Umayyads reinstated the recording of narrations, they infused their own fabrications with the rest of texts of Islamic tradition.

Many of the ruling authorities pushed their policies and interests through the brutal means of persecution, unwarranted arrests, blackmail, exile, and execution. The targets of these unwarranted means of persecution were often the followers of the Imams. Both the Umayyad and Abbasid regimes targeted and attacked them consistently. Their primary target, of course, was the Imam himself and usually his close circle of companions and representatives. They would receive the death blow of shortsighted, power hungry tyrants, be it by sword as with Imam Ali and Imam Husayn or poison; the method used for the rest of the Imams before the Twelfth.

Shiʿa Islam maintains Twelve Imams, starting with Imam Ali and ending with the last and awaited Imam al-Mahdi. Each Imam prepared for the next. In that, they prepared their community of followers and taught them how to protect themselves. When the Twelfth Imam went into occultation, it was to protect his own life and wellbeing – a necessity for the preservation of the faith and carrying on the will of God that would persist against all the odds of tyranny, oppression, and injustice. According to Shiʿa belief, the occultation of the Imam certainly does not have a particular time limit. However, it will not last forever.

In the previously referenced verse, God says, "He will surely change their state to security after fear, while they worship [Him]…" According to Shiʿa scholars, this is a reference to the return of the Mahdi and the end of the occultation.*

There are several questions about the doctrine of occultation and what it really means within Shiʿa belief. Is this concept of "occultation" a new idea? And did occultations take place before Imam al-Mahdi? Understanding the doctrine of occultation is an essential part of Shiʿa creed and the focus of this chapter.

OCCULTATION AND THE CAVE

To understand the Shiʿa doctrine on occultation within a theological framework, the authors will reference several verses and stories from the Holy Quran that are often pointed to by scholars of the faith on this subject.[6] In the Holy Quran, there are different types of verses. Some of the verses are regarding worship, while others are instructions on beliefs and creed. Many other verses are narratives or stories of events that have taken place in history.

The verses of stories in the Quran are referred to as *Qasas*. A lesson may be derived from the story and the content of it could be fictional or nonfictional. *Qasas* comes from the root word of *Qassah*, which refers not merely to any story, but rather to an event that occurred in real time. It is not a parable of lessons but an account of a factual experience that can be relied on and can inspire.

---

* The promise God made in this verse has not yet been truly realized. It is a promise that God will fulfill through the awaited Twelfth Imam. For a more detailed discussion on this verse, see: Tabatabaʾi, *Tafsir Al-Mizan*, exegesis of verse 24:55.

God tells the Holy Prophet Muhammad in the Holy Quran, "We relay to you [O Muhammad] the best of narratives."[7] Later on in the same chapter God gives background to the Quran and its role as an "elaboration of all things."

> There is certainly a moral in their accounts for those who possess intellect. This [Quran] is not a fabricated discourse; rather, it is a confirmation of what was [revealed] before it, and an elaboration of all things, and a guidance and mercy for a people who have faith.[8]

The Quran does not have stories of fiction. What is relayed in it are historical experiences and a narrative of different dimensions of the human condition. Two primary purposes can be derived from the narratives in the Holy Quran. Firstly, the Quranic account of these stories provide a confirmation for these events that have already been mentioned in previous scripture but were changed. The purposes of relaying the same stories in the Quran was to clarify between fabrication and truth. Secondly, the stories chosen in the Quran all provide morals and lessons of guidance as a grace from God to teach the people through the examples of those that came before them.

The concept of occultation is not a new one. It is something that has happened on several occasions throughout history. The Quran shows that throughout the human experience, God directed some of His servants to go into a state of occultation for the sake of protecting them from evil and harm. The occultation was utilized to shield them from being abused or killed. Moreover, it is utilized as an essential requirement for the implementation of their mission at that time.

There are multiple Quranic stories relevant to the concept of occultation. Prophets, Imams, and ordinary individuals all experienced occultations – to protect and preserve them from harm's way and allow them to continue to work on God's path.[9]

One such occultation conveys the story of a group of young believers who sought refuge in God and wanted to protect their religion. They did not necessarily fear for their lives, but feared the possibility of becoming misguided. God answered their prayers and guided them to a cave.* Their entering and eventual sleep in that cave was a state of occultation. They did not die. They were not raised to the heavens. They were isolated from the world, protected, and kept in that cave for many years.

> Do you suppose that the Companions of the Cave and the inscription were among Our wonderful signs? When the youths took refuge in the Cave, they said, 'Our Lord! Grant us a mercy from Yourself, and help us on to rectitude in our affair.' So We put them to sleep in the Cave for several years.[10]

This was merely a group of youth, not vicegerents or prophets of God, and they entered a state of occultation to be protected. God protected them by giving them that occultation. They would go on to live their lives after having spent over three hundred years asleep in that cave.

> They remained in the Cave for three hundred years, and added nine more [to that number]. Say, 'God knows best how long they remained. To Him belongs the Unseen of the heavens and the earth. How well does He see! How well does He hear! They have no guardian besides Him, and none shares with Him in His judgement.'[11]

If occultation was utilized for ordinary people in the past, it can be understood that it was also used for God's vicegerents and the saviors of humanity. Several prophets of God went through similar experiences and faced occultation as part of their mission and role as vicegerents of God on Earth.

---

* A parallel to the story of the Companions of the Cave is recorded in Christian tradition as the story of the Seven Sleepers.

JOSEPH: THE SAVIOR OF EGYPT

Prophet Joseph was the savior of the people of Egypt. He was not only a prophet to them but also an Imam. He was responsible for taking them from a state of idol worship to the enlightenment and worship of the One True God. He took his people from hunger and hardship to success and salvation. When Joseph was born, his brothers were gravely envious of him. Joseph enjoyed a special place in their father's heart. Joseph was the son of Prophet Jacob, also known as Israel.* Because Jacob realized his son Joseph's ability and potential, he gave him special attention.

The more Jacob adored his son, the more Joseph's life was threatened by his brothers. Even though he instructed his sons to take care of their younger brother, Jacob could sense that harm would come to Joseph sooner than later. In a plot to rid themselves of Joseph and all their father's attention he took away from them, the brothers planned to throw him down a well. Unbeknownst to his brothers, God would protect Joseph by veiling the fact that he survived the fall. A caravan would pass by and find Joseph and take him as a slave. They did not know who Joseph truly was. They just saw a young boy at the bottom of a well. In fact, no one would know who he was. That would remain until the circumstances changed many years later. At that time, society would be ready for him to reveal his identity and lead them in his role as their prophet and Imam.

> These are the signs of the Manifest Book. Indeed We have sent it down as an Arabic Quran so that you may exercise your reason. We will recount to you the best of narratives in what We have revealed to you of this Quran, and indeed prior to it you were among those who are unaware [of it].
> When Joseph said to his father, 'Father! I saw eleven planets, and the sun and the moon: I saw them prostrating themselves before me,' he said, 'My son, do not recount your dream to your brothers,

---

* Banu Isra'il, or the Children of Israel, is seen numerous times in the Holy Quran. It is a reference to the descendants of Jacob.

lest they should devise schemes against you. Satan is indeed man's manifest enemy. That is how your Lord will choose you, and teach you the interpretation of dreams, and complete His blessing upon you and upon the house of Jacob, just as He completed it earlier for your fathers, Abraham and Isaac. Your Lord is indeed all-knowing and all-wise.' In Joseph and his brothers there are certainly signs for the seekers. When they said, 'Surely Joseph and his brother are dearer to our father than [the rest of] us, though we are a hardy band. Our father is indeed in manifest error.' 'Kill Joseph or cast him away into some [distant] land, so that your father's attention may be exclusively towards you, and thereafter you may become a virtuous lot.' One of them said, 'Do not kill Joseph, but cast him into the recess of a well so that some caravan may pick him up, if you are to do [anything].'[12]

Some narrations say that the brother referenced in the verses above was Levi.[*] He contributed to and prepared for the occultation, by protecting his brother Joseph in suggesting that they not kill him but throw him down a well instead. In this manner, he stayed amongst his brothers undetected of his desire to keep Joseph safe.

They said, 'Father! Why is it that you do not trust us with Joseph? We are indeed his well-wishers. Let him go with us tomorrow so that he may eat lots of fruits and play, and we will indeed take [good] care of him.' He said, 'It really upsets me that you should take him away, and I fear the wolf may eat him while you are oblivious of him.' They said, 'Should the wolf eat him while we are a hardy band, then we will indeed be losers!' So when they took him away and conspired to put him into the recess of a well, We revealed to him, '[A day will come when] you will surely inform them about this affair of theirs while they are not aware [of your identity].' In the evening, they came weeping to their father. They

---

[*] Al-Majlisi, *Bihar al-Anwar*, 12:218. Interestingly, narrations state that the prophets of the People of Israel were from the lineage of Levi. See: Majlisi, *Bihar al-Anwar*, 12:252.

said, 'Father! We had gone racing and left Joseph with our things, whereat the wolf ate him. But you will not believe us even if we spoke truly.' And they produced sham blood on his shirt. He said, 'No, your souls have made a matter seem decorous to you. Yet patience is graceful, and God is my resort against what you allege.' There came a caravan, and they sent their water-drawer, who let down his bucket. 'Good news!' he said. 'This is a young boy!' So they hid him as [a piece of] merchandise, and God knew best what they were doing. And they sold him for a cheap price, a few dirhams, for they set small store by him. The man from Egypt who had bought him said to his wife, 'Give him an honorable place [in the household]. Maybe he will be useful to us, or we may adopt him as a son.' Thus We established Joseph in the land and that We might teach him the interpretation of dreams. God has [full] command of His affairs, but most people do not know. When he came of age, We gave him judgement and [sacred] knowledge, and thus do We reward the virtuous.[13]

MOSES AND JESUS IN THE HOLY QURAN

The next prime example of occultation was embodied in the prophetic experience of Prophet Moses. He was the savior of the people of Israel.

These are the signs of the Manifest Book. We relate to you truly some of the account of Moses and Pharaoh for a people who have faith. Indeed Pharaoh tyrannized over the land, reducing its people to factions, abasing one group of them, slaughtering their sons, and sparing their women. Indeed, He was one of the agents of corruption.[14]

The Pharaoh and his people wanted to kill this promised person. For the Pharaoh, Moses was a direct threat to their rule and way of life. Thus, he instituted a policy that would prevent the rise of this potential savior and relieve himself of the threat of change and reform.

> And We desired to show favor to those who were abased in the
> land, and to make them imams, and to make them the heirs, and to
> establish them in the land, and to show Pharaoh and Haman and
> their hosts from them that of which they were apprehensive.[15]

They feared the idea of Moses and the promise of God. Though they would
try to fight it, the promise of God would nonetheless be fulfilled through
Moses. God discusses how the savior of the Israelites would be right under
the Pharaoh's nose but protected by God without them even knowing who
he was or what he would become.

> We revealed to Moses' mother, [saying], 'Nurse him; then, when
> you fear for him, cast him into the river, and do not fear or grieve,
> for We will restore him to you and make him one of the apostles.'
> Then Pharaoh's kinsmen picked him up that he might be an enemy
> and a cause of grief to them. Indeed, Pharaoh and Haman and their
> hosts were iniquitous. Pharaoh's wife said [to him], '[This infant
> will be] a [source of] comfort to me and to you. Do not kill him.
> Maybe he will benefit us, or we will adopt him as a son.' But they
> were not aware. She said to his sister, 'Follow him.' So she watched
> him from a distance, while they were not aware. Since before We
> had forbidden him to be suckled by any nurse. So she said, 'Shall I
> show you a household that will take care of him for you and they
> will be his well-wishers?' That is how We restored him to his
> mother so that she might be comforted and not grieve, and that she
> might know that God's promise is true, but most of them do not
> know.[16]

God puts the chosen ones who are threatened, in occultation as a protection
for them from external threats.

Prophet Jesus is yet another central example of occultation described in the
Holy Quran. Through his preaching, he was becoming a threat to the Roman political and social establishment that existed, and the status quo did
not wish for him to continue his work. His life was under threat from too
many directions. Note that the responsibility and mission of Jesus was

beyond leading Christianity; rather, Jesus would carry out the role of savior to humanity for the end of times.

Islam holds Jesus in this esteem and his destiny lies alongside the Awaited Mahdi to bring salvation to mankind and lead humanity into the light. Thus, when the life of Prophet Jesus was threatened, God had him enter a state of occultation. He raised him up, beyond the reach of any man, and protected him.

> And for their saying, 'We killed the Messiah, Jesus son of Mary, the apostle of God'—though they did not kill him nor did they crucify him, but so it was made to appear to them. Indeed those who differ concerning him are surely in doubt about him: they do not have any knowledge of that beyond following conjectures, and certainly, they did not kill him. Indeed, God raised him up toward Himself, and God is all-mighty, all-wise.[17]

Because of His love for Jesus and His plan for him to save humanity at the end of times, God protected Jesus and raised him to Himself. It is understood in Islamic doctrine on the end of times that Jesus will return with Imam al-Mahdi.[18]

IMAM MAHDI AND THE TWO OCCULTATIONS

The Abbasids knew that the anticipated savior of the Shi'a would be the Twelfth Imam; a son of Imam Hasan al-'Askari. Under the reign of the Abbasid Caliph al-Mu'tamid, the authorities placed Imam al-'Askari under house arrest so that any child born could be detected and killed immediately. However, the Imam's wife's pregnancy was miraculously hidden, and the twelfth Imam was protected. It was in *Sirdab al-Ghaybah* (the basement of the Imam's home) that the young Imam was able to escape from harm's way and continue his occultation. The beginning of his minor occultation, *al-ghaybat al-sughra*, commenced when he officially became the active Imam at his father's death in 874 AD. Imam al-Mahdi was only about five years old. Nonetheless, the Imam had been in occultation, his identity concealed from the world, since even before his birth. The authors will discuss the idea of concealing identity as a form of occultation below, along with the other form of occultation, which is isolation from the rest of creation.

The whole concept of occultation is a not a strange one in Shi'a belief. It happened throughout history. It was a common method used by God for his vicegerents to protect them and help them implement their purpose and mission. As the Imams became restricted from the believers due to house arrests and persecution imposed by the Abbasid authorities, the Imams emphasized the use of their representatives even more. Imam al-Mahdi's occultation started with assigning representatives.

Looking at the Holy Quran, there are two primary types of occultation. The first is one of isolation. The individual in occultation cannot access the outside world, nor can he be accessed by the outside world. The second type of occultation is one that allows for interaction. In fact, the person in occultation is fully involved in their surroundings and engaged with the people around them. However, their identity is concealed from everyone except for a few trusted individuals. Overall, the world would go on not knowing his identity. Thus, this type of occultation is one of identity rather than of the actual person. In the previous chapter, the authors discussed the prophetic examples found in the Holy Quran regarding occultation. The primary example was the son of Mary, Prophet Jesus.

> When God said, 'O Jesus, I shall take you[r soul], and I shall raise
> you up toward Myself, and I shall clear you of [the calumnies of]
> the faithless, and I shall set those who follow you above the faithless
> until the Day of Resurrection. Then to Me will be your return,
> whereat I will judge between you concerning that about which you
> used to differ.[19] And for their saying, 'We killed the Messiah, Jesus
> son of Mary, the apostle of God'—though they did not kill him nor
> did they crucify him, but so it was made to appear to them. Indeed
> those who differ concerning him are surely in doubt about him:

they do not have any knowledge of that beyond following conjectures, and certainly, they did not kill him.[20]

Based on the Quran, Muslims belief is that Jesus is in this occultation of isolation. He was raised to God and saved from those oppressing him. He remains alive and well, ready to be the savior of humanity alongside the awaited Imam al-Mahdi. The second example mentioned was the Companions of the Cave, *Ashab al-Kahf.* "They remained in the Cave for three hundred years, and added nine more [to that number]."[21]

As discussed previously, the former type of occultation is different in that it involves individuals who are directly interacting and living with the rest of the world; however, their identity is unknown to those they are interacting with. Prophet Moses was one of the prominent examples of this form of occultation. After describing the series of events that illustrate the occultation of Moses in the Holy Quran God says, "When he came of age and became fully matured, We gave him judgment and knowledge, and thus do We reward the virtuous."[22]

The Pharaoh took him and raised him, not knowing who he was. No one, apart from his mother and sister, knew the identity of that baby. When Moses was of age and ready to practice his authority as a prophet, messenger, and imam of the time, God would allow for his identity to be known to the world. Thus, his occultation ended with the revealing of his identity.

> [One day] he entered the city at a time when its people were not
> likely to take notice. He found there two men fighting, this one
> from among his followers, and that one from his enemies. The one
> who was from his followers sought his help against him who was
> from his enemies. So, Moses hit him with his fist, whereupon he
> expired. He said, 'This is of Satan's doing. Indeed, he is clearly a
> misguiding enemy.'[23] There came a man from the city outskirts,
> hurrying. He said, 'Moses! The elite are indeed conspiring to kill
> you. So, leave. I am indeed your well-wisher.'[24]

With this incident, Moses would continue his occultation. Note that the use of "followers" translated from "Shiʿa" in the Holy Quran here, indicates his role as an Imam with followers. Some of his followers recognized him and knew who he was. Again, this type of occultation is a concealment of identity rather than isolation of the person. A few trusted individuals, like the man from the outskirts of the city that advised Moses to leave, interacted with the Prophet knowing who he was.

Prophet Joseph was another prime example of occultation of identity. His life was in eminent danger while he was amongst his brothers. God thus chose that his life and identity be hidden from them. His identity was also hidden from the people of Egypt, where he was able to fulfil his role as a prophet and an Imam after working within their system for many years and gaining their trust.

So, what type of occultation does Shiʿa doctrine presume Imam al-Mahdi to be in? Is he in isolation from society and the world at large? Or is he in engagement with it? Does he interact with people and they may not even realize it, merely because his identity is concealed?

If the reader recalls, the authors discussed the purpose of mankind in the first chapter of this book. "When your Lord said to the angels, 'Indeed I am going to set a vicegerent on the earth.'"[25] The prophets of God that went into occultation, like Moses and Joseph, did so for their safety. God protected them by concealing their identity and shielding them from those who wished them harm, from a young age. Their examples even by the mere comparison of age and circumstance are almost identical to that of Imam al-Mahdi. They were not raised and isolated like Prophet Jesus, because their role and mission had not yet been fulfilled.

In the same light, Imam al-Mahdi's role of being the last Imam and vicegerent of God on Earth has yet to be fulfilled. And thus, he remains amongst society concealed in his identity until the circumstances permit for him to reveal himself. Like the prophets who went through similar occultations, he is active in those preparations that will bring the world closer to a state of readiness to accept his proper arrival. Like his forefathers – the Imams and the Prophets – he will continue to work and fulfill his God-given role, no matter the circumstance.

This role of Imamah is believed to be ordained for those from the lineage of Prophet Abraham, a promise made by God to Abraham himself. When God raised Abraham to the status of *Imam*, he made a request of his Lord. He asked that this status continue with his descendants.

> When his Lord tested Abraham with certain words and he fulfilled them, He said, 'I am making you the Imam of mankind.' Said he, 'And from among my descendants?' He said, 'My pledge does not extend to the unjust.'[26]

God accepted Abraham's request with a condition. The Imamah would continue through his lineage, except for those who are unjust. Shiʿa doctrine maintains that this condition illustrates that God's designation of authority inherently is found through the lineages of the His most virtuous servants. However, it is not just because of one's lineage that the role is ordained but rather it is coupled with piety and virtue. The status of Imamah requires the virtue, knowledge, and implementation of godly principles in manifestation of God's will on Earth. That was manifested by all those who were ordained with the role of Imamah.

> Do they envy those people for what God has given them out of His bounty? We have certainly given the progeny of Abraham the Book and wisdom, and We have given them a great sovereignty.[27]

THE VIRTUOUS SERVANT AND PATIENCE

Within the doctrine of occultation, is an understanding of those who are designated by God's will and the things that they do. Shiʿa Muslims often reflect on their "readiness" for the Imam. That readiness is connected to how patient individuals are with the trials and tribulations they endure. There is a great parallel illustrated in the Quran with the example of Khidr, *al-ʿAbd al-Salih* or the Virtuous Servant, in his exchange with one of God's greatest prophets – Moses. "[There] they found one of Our servants whom We had granted a mercy from Ourselves, and taught him a knowledge from Our own."[28]

Scholars of Quranic exegesis point out that the word "servant" in the Holy Quran is used to describe individuals at the status of Prophethood or Imamah. Though scholars maintain that they do not know for certain whether Khidr was a prophet, an imam, or simply an extremely virtuous man, it is likely he was one of the former because of the use of the word "servant" to describe him.

> Moses said to him, 'May I follow you for the purpose that you teach me some of the probity you have been taught?' He said, 'Indeed you cannot have patience with me! And how can you have patience about something you do not comprehend?' He said, 'You will find me, God willing, to be patient, and I will not disobey you in any matter.' He said, 'If you follow me, do not question me concerning anything until I myself first mention it for you.'[29]

This verse is sometimes pointed to draw a parallel with regards to Shiʿa Muslims relationship with Imam al-Mahdi. Khidr warns Moses that he will not have patience or be able to tolerate what he witnesses if he followed Khidr. Moses, however, was a prophet. So, what about the ordinary individual?

> So they went on and when they boarded the boat, he made a hole in it. He said, 'Did you make a hole in it to drown its people? You have certainly done a monstrous thing!' He said, 'Did I not say that you cannot have patience with me?' He said, 'Do not take me to task for my forgetting, and do not be hard upon me.' So they went on until they came upon a boy, whereat he slew him. He said, 'Did you slay an innocent soul, without [his having slain] anyone? You have certainly done a dire thing!' He said, 'Did I not tell you that you cannot have patience with me?' He said, 'If I question you about anything after this, do not keep me in your company. You already have enough excuse on my part.' So they went on until they

came to the people of a town. They asked its people for food, but they refused to extend them any hospitality. There they found a wall which was about to collapse, so he erected it. He said, 'Had you wished, you could have taken a wage for it.' He said, 'This is where you and I shall part. I will inform you about the interpretation of that over which you could not maintain patience. As for the boat, it belonged to some poor people who work on the sea. I wanted to make it defective, for behind them was a king seizing every ship usurpingly. As for the boy, his parents were faithful [persons], and We feared he would overwhelm them with rebellion and unfaith. So We desired that their Lord should give them in exchange one better than him in respect of purity and closer in mercy. As for the wall, it belonged to two boy orphans in the city. Under it there was a treasure belonging to them. Their father had been a virtuous man. So your Lord desired that they should come of age and take out their treasure—as a mercy from your Lord. I did not do that out of my own accord. This is the interpretation of that over which you could not maintain patience.'[30]

The story of Khidr is an example of the practice of occultation by a designee of God carrying out responsibilities that may not be understood by people, perhaps even some of the other vicegerents of God. It serves as a parallel and reminder for the Shiʿa who are faithful about the role of the Imam and how one is to interact and engage with him, when the Imam's occultation ends and he is seen by the world again.

CHAPTER 12

IMPACTING THE OCCULTATION

Indeed, God does not change a people's lot, unless they change what is in their souls.

The Holy Quran, 13:11.

MOSES AND THE PROPHETIC PROJECT

The prophets dedicated their lives working on their godly projects. They had a vision of how humanity would pursue its excellence. They had a mission to move their people in that direction. When some of the prophets experienced occultation, for various reasons according to each context and time, their work towards their goals did not cease. It continued through and through, even if it was not directly seen in the public eye. Much of the time, God's work goes unseen.

The Prophet or the Imam continues on with their work but it is undetected by those that pose a threat to the life or wellbeing of God's vicegerent. Therefore, it should be clear that Shiʿa doctrine holds that it is not that the Imam is returning, as if he were somewhere else and is now coming back. Rather, it is a reference to the Imam revealing or unveiling his identity because his occultation is merely a concealment of his identity for the purpose of protecting himself, as ordained by God, just as it was ordained for Moses and Joseph.

The Imam operates much like how they lived and engaged with the peoples of their time, though many of those people did not know who they were. An important practical question arises for the Shiʿa faithful waiting for the appearance of their Imam: What sort of impact do people have on the prophet or Imam's occultation? Does the way a community works, deals, or lives impact the occultation of the prophet or the Imam? To answer these questions, the authors go back to the story of Moses.

> He rose at dawn in the city, fearful and vigilant, when behold, the one who had sought his help the day before, shouted for his help [once again]. Moses said to him, 'You are indeed clearly perverse!'[1]

The man that Moses had helped was inadvertently exposing the prophet's identity. Moses came to his aid previously, but now his act of calling on to him again was putting Moses at risk and endangering his own wellbeing. The occultation Moses took on was to save his life from the wrath of Pharaoh and continue with his prophetic mission. This follower, however, was now undoing that by revealing his identity as he called on to him for help once again.

> But when he wanted to strike him who was an enemy of both of them, he said, 'Moses, do you want to kill me, just like the one you killed yesterday? You only want to be a tyrant in the land, and you do not desire to be one who brings about reform.'[2]

And thus, the prophet's identity was revealed. His enemy knew him by name and Moses was no longer safe. His wellbeing was once again endangered, and this time by the act of one of his followers who had merely called on to him for help. That call at that moment, however, was to the detriment of Moses.

> There came a man from the city outskirts, hurrying. He said, 'Moses! The elite are indeed conspiring to kill you. So leave. I am indeed your well-wisher.' So he left the city, fearful and vigilant. He said, 'My Lord! Deliver me from the wrongdoing lot.'[3]

The man here from the "city outskirts" was also a follower of Moses. He delivered him from harm, advised him to escape the city and truly helped him. Though one man had put his life in danger, yet another would be there to his aid and help Moses carry on his mission by protecting his life.

And when he turned his face toward Midian, he said, 'Maybe my Lord will show me the right way.' When he arrived at the well of Midian, he found there a throng of people watering [their flocks], and he found, besides them, two women holding back [their flock]. He said, 'What is your business?' They said, 'We do not water [our flock] until the shepherds have driven out [their flocks], and our father is an aged man.' So he watered [their flock] for them. Then he withdrew toward the shade and said, 'My Lord! I am indeed in need of any good You may send down to me!' Then one of the two women approached him, walking bashfully. She said, 'Indeed my father invites you to pay you the wages for watering [our flock] for us.' So when he came to him and recounted the story to him, he said, 'Do not be afraid. You have been delivered from the wrongdoing lot.' One of the two women said, 'Father, hire him. Indeed the best you can hire is a powerful and trustworthy man.' He said, 'Indeed I desire to marry you to one of these two daughters of mine, on condition that you hire yourself to me for eight years. And if you complete ten, that will be up to you, and I do not want to be hard on you. God willing, you will find me to a righteous person.' He said, 'This will be [by consent] between you and me. Whichever of the two terms I complete, there shall be no imposition upon me, and God is witness over what we say.'[4]

All in all, the prophetic mission was seemingly delayed for almost ten years by the mere act of a single person. Nonetheless, in those ten years Moses would carry on his mission, albeit in different ways of guidance and exemplary ethics. After that time had passed, he would return and engage with the Pharaoh in his role as the messenger and prophet of God. "Certainly We sent Moses with Our signs and a manifest authority to Pharaoh, Haman and Korah, but they said, 'A magician and a mendacious liar.'"[5]

That was the response when Moses had announced his message to the Pharaoh and his elites. They accused him of horrid things and wished death upon him. They were threatened by him and what he brought forth of potential influence, leadership, and hope for the masses of people the Pharaoh had suppressed. Impatient with tolerating the presence of Moses as a threat to his dominion and rule, Pharaoh ordered that Moses be killed. One of his ministers, however, would speak to the Pharaoh and convince him to act otherwise.

> A man of faith from Pharaoh's clan, who concealed his faith, 'Will you kill a man for saying, "My Lord is God," while he has already brought you manifest proofs from your Lord? Should he be lying, his falsehood will be to his own detriment; but if he is truthful, there shall visit you some of what he promises you. Indeed, God does not guide someone who is a transgressor and liar. O my people! Today sovereignty belongs to you, and you are dominant in the land. But who will save us from God's punishment should it overtake us?' Pharaoh said, 'I just point out to you what I see [to be advisable for you], and I guide you only to the way of rectitude.' He who had faith said, 'O my people! Indeed, I fear for you [a day] like the day of the [heathen] factions; like the case of the people of Noah, of Ad and Thamud, and those who came after them, and God does not desire any wrong for [His] servants. O my people! I fear for you a day of mutual distress calls, a day when you will turn back [to flee], not having anyone to protect you from God, and whomever God leads astray has no guide.[6]

God refers to that minister as "A man of faith." He was a follower of Moses, who concealed his identity to protect himself and Moses alike. The minister worked within the Pharaoh's administration, gained his trust, and had his ear for pertinent matters affecting the state. During his occultation, Moses had prepared this man who happened to also be a relative of the Pharaoh. He concealed his faith to serve that very faith without being detected. This individual, and the role he played, saved Moses from being put to death by the Pharaoh. Thus, even during his occultation Moses had key people that were helping him and following his instructions.

Some may wonder if the occultation is a contradiction to the prophet's mission. It may seem at times that the occultation halts the work of the prophet or pauses the continuation of his divine project. Though the occultation may limit the outward or apparent involvement of God's vicegerent in public affairs, it does not stop him from his work. In Shiʿa doctrine, the vicegerent of God does not cease to carry out his mission during his occultation. He is working, he is moving, he is active. The distinction here is that he is not seen or identified for who he is by the public. His role is still fulfilled, and his responsibilities are still met; it is simply in more implicit terms and in a way that can be executed without the detection of those who wish to threaten his life.

The nature of the occultation is also seen as an opportunity for the prophet or Imam to lay the foundation for his reappearance in the public domain while he is safe from the hands of tyrants and oppressors that wish him harm. This is an essential understanding of the nature of the occultation that the authors discussed in the previous chapter. Without keeping this premise in mind, the occultation can be misunderstood to be a vague and ambiguous cloud of mystery surrounding the real role that is played by the vicegerent of God and how others affect the state of occultation as well.

PEOPLE'S IMPACT ON JOSEPH'S MOVEMENT

Like the story of Moses, the series of events that took place in Joseph's life are quite telling of the nature of occultation and how people impacted it. The acts of certain individuals here played a major role in delaying, hastening, or saving the life and mission of Joseph. Take the example of Zulaykhah when she attempted to force herself onto Joseph and seduce him.

> When he came of age, We gave him judgement and [sacred] knowledge, and thus do We reward the virtuous. The woman in whose house he was, solicited him. She closed the doors and said, 'Come!' He said, 'God forbid! Indeed, He is my Lord; He has given me a good abode. Indeed, the wrongdoers are not felicitous.' She certainly made for him; and he would have made for her [too] had

he not beheld the proof of his Lord. So it was, that We might turn away from him all evil and indecency. He was indeed one of Our dedicated servants.[7]

In that situation, Joseph's state of mind was clear. To stray from his path was not an option. He would rather be thrown in prison instead of fall to the whims of lust and desire. So, he did not let Zulaykhah seduce him and instead continued to push her away. Trying to pull him towards her as he attempted to escape, she tore his shirt from behind. Joseph said,

> My Lord! The prison is dearer to me than to what they invite me. If You do not turn away their schemes from me, I will incline towards them and become one of the senseless.[8]

When the case was presented before Zulaykhah's husband, *ʿAziz* or Potiphar as mentioned in the Hebrew Bible, he chose to sentence Joseph to prison. It was clear that Zulaykhah's actions led to Joseph's imprisonment, even though the evidence would show that he was not the aggressor. If he were the true aggressor in the situation, the tear marks shown on his shirt would have been on the front of his shirt. Instead, they appeared on his back indicating that he was indeed trying to escape from Zulaykhah's plot to seduce him.

Nonetheless, Joseph's state in prison became, in a sense, another occultation. Indeed, his imprisonment had an impact on his prophetic mission and work. Again, though it changed his situation or trajectory, it did not stop him from executing his role as the vicegerent of God. Instead, he carried it out in other means and continued to prepare the grounds for his return. Wherever he was, he was a source of guidance and inspiration to those around him, even in the dark corners of a prison dungeon.

> O my prison mates! Are different masters better, or God, the One, the All-paramount? You do not worship besides Him but [mere] names that you and your fathers have coined, for which Allah has not sent down any authority. Sovereignty belongs only to God. He

has commanded you to worship none except Him. That is the upright religion, but most people do not know.[9]

In speaking to them about God, Joseph renewed their contemplation over their lives and state of being. He encouraged their reflection on belief, culture, and custom. Why do they do what they do or believe what they believe? In this reflection, his prison mates acknowledged that Joseph was different. He was not any ordinary person. There was something special about him, his personality, and his knowledge. So, they began asking him more questions. The conversation continued further. At one point, they inquired about their fate. What came after their time in this dungeon? Would they ever leave? Was there something beyond the darkness for them?

> O my prison mates! As for one of you, he will serve wine to his master, and as for the other, he will be crucified, and vultures will eat from his head. The matter about which you inquire has been decided.[10]

When the one prison mate was released to become a servant in the high chancellor's court, Joseph told him to mention him to his master and the favor he had with him. His prison mate promised that he would, and he eventually did, but it took him a few years to do so. The man had forgotten to mention Joseph at the onset of his release, which caused further delay to Joseph's own release from prison. Thus, Joseph spent a few more years in the dungeon due to his former prison mate's forgetfulness.

In looking at the examples of ordinary individuals who had a practical impact on the movement and occultation of God's prophets like Joseph and Moses, the reader can tie it back to how Shi'a Muslims view their own individual acts and behavior to affect the occultation of the Imam. Individual decisions and actions have an impact on the occultation of God's living vicegerent, just like the actions of those in history had on God's prophets.

The role that individuals wish to play during the occultation is to be determined by each individual and community. It would naturally follow that the role to be played would be to practice the directives of one's faith and be the best possible human being one can be. Of course, on a sociological level there is a great deal of diversity and roles are not reserved to piety and virtue in ethics. There are virtuous engineers, doctors, lawyers, statesmen, teachers, nurses, artists, writers, researchers, and the list goes on. But even within each of those titles, there is a sort of engagement that is key to the individual's impact in the community and perhaps on the occultation and the equilibrium of peace and harmony in the world.

It must come with the acknowledgement, first and foremost, that individual decisions have an impact – just like Joseph's prison mate had on him and Pharaoh's minister had on Moses. With the simple realization that an individual's decisions carry tremendous weight can be all the difference. Thus, when Shiʿa Muslims ask themselves the question about awaiting their Imam passively or actively, and in what role should they serve, they are encouraged to approach it with this understanding in mind. A person's passiveness can have an impact and so can their activeness. For whichever approach is taken, time is still of the essence even though the exact duration of time itself may not be discerned.

THE DURATION OF OCCULTATION

Along with identifying the role individuals can play during the occultation, and the sort of impact people have on it, there is often the question raised regarding the occultation's actual duration. How long will the occultation be? Is the time of the occultation a fixed time? When will the Imam reappear or end his occultation? God speaks to the Holy Prophet in the Quran, "They say, 'Why has not some sign been sent down to him from his Lord?' Say, '[The knowledge of] the Unseen belongs only to God. So, wait. I too am waiting along with you.'"[11]

The Shiʿa corpus of hadith speaks to the "unseen" mentioned in the verse above. It is said to be a reference to the Twelfth Imam. In one narration, a companion asked Imam al-Sadiq about the following verses.

> This is the Book, there is no doubt in it, a guidance to the
> Godwary, who believe in the Unseen, maintain the prayer, and
> spend out of what We have provided for them.[12]

The Imam replied,

> The Unseen is the Absent Proof [i.e. Imam Mahdi during his
> occultation]. The evidence of this [meaning] is the word of God:
> They say, 'Why has not some sign been sent down to him from his
> Lord?' Say, '[The knowledge of] the Unseen belongs only to God.
> So wait. I too am waiting along with you.'[13]

The matter of time is clear in Shi'a doctrine. Only God has the knowledge of it. Even the Imam himself does not know the exact time of *al-Faraj** – the relief. This is indicated in the verse above, as God tells the Holy Prophet to say, "So wait. I too am waiting along with you."

The Prophet and the Imams, with respect to the time of the occultation and the relief, are in the same situation as the rest of mankind – the knowledge of it is with God alone. Al-Fadl ibn Yasar asked Imam al-Baqir about the relief after the occultation and when it would be. "Is there a time for this matter?" he asked. The Imam responded, "Those who associate time for this matter are liars."[14]

Even an association of a designated time for this issue would fall under the classification of mistruth according to the Imams. Imam al-Baqir expounded on this idea in a conversation with his close companion Abu Basir. Abu Basir narrated that Imam al-Baqir said, "The *Waqqatun* [those who associate time] are liars. We are a Household that does not give a specific time [for this matter]. God has determined to disprove the times given by the *Waqqatun*."[15]

Abu Hamza al-Thumali, also narrates some details on the matter of time and occultation. Abu Hamza reports that Imam al-Baqir said,

---

* Al-Faraj, or the relief, is the term that refers to the end of the occultation and the reappearance of the Imam.

Surely, God, the Most Blessed and High, has appointed the time of
this matter in the 70th [year after hijrah]. When Husayn was killed,
God's wrath intensified, and he delayed it until the 140th [year
after hijrah]. We told you of this and you spread the word and
lifted the veil of secrecy. Since then God has not given us a date and
'God effaces and confirms whatever He wishes and with Him is the
Mother Book.'[16] *

Merely looking at this narration on the surface suggests two essential
things. One, there is no longer a set time for the time of the occultation and
the relief that will come thereafter. That decree is from God and the
knowledge of its time is with Him alone. Two, as discussed previously, individual and community decisions and actions have a direct impact on the
state of the occultation. The tragedy of Karbala, where the progeny and
companions of the Prophet were massacred, delayed the original time further. Then, the fact that some of the followers of the Imams themselves di-
vulged the secrets they taught them delayed the matter even further. This
narration shows how relevant people's actions are on the occultation, both
as individuals and as a collective community, in Shi'a thought and belief.

---

* God says in the Holy Quran that He 'effaces and confirms whatever He wishes.' Thus, He allows for human freewill
to change the outcome of events. A more detailed perspective on this can be found in the books of theology and
philosophy.

CONCLUSION

Be the straight line and all the crooked lines will be revealed.

Grand Ayatollah Fayyad

Though the world has been plagued by hate, terrorism, and extremism; it is also filled with individuals that are working for peace, justice, and coexistence for all on the highest levels of leadership. Pope Francis is certainly recognized as one of those leaders. Hence, his meeting with Ayatollah Sistani is no accident. The historic meeting of March 6, 2021 will certainly be a meeting of the minds working for the salvation of humanity's soul. The Pope may wish to have the Grand Ayatollah as a partner and an ally. The champion of Christian and minority rights in Iraq, Ayatollah Sistani has stopped at nothing short of calling his own followers to put the needs of these minorities before their own. The Shiʿa school of thought, which the Grand Ayatollah represents, manifests the principles of coexistence, tolerance, and the sovereignty of people – principles advocated for by the Pope and the Vatican.

The meeting with Grand Ayatollah Sistani manifests the reality of religion, as one that rejects violence and the subjugation of any people, regardless of creed or background. Religion continues to be relevant to the everyday lives of people around the world. It is a force of good and the religious leaders representing their respective faiths have a tremendous role in promoting tolerance, coexistence, and dialogue. The meeting between these two towering figures speaks volumes to not only their followers but is a testament to all people of the world.

The virtuous community, as some Shiʿa scholars have called it, awaiting the vicegerents of God is not an isolated one. Just like the individuals and communities that aided Joseph and Moses in their missions and shortened the occultation, it can be said that integration and proactive engagement is a key component to today's success for virtuous community development.

In one's engagement within society, the individual can have a direct effect on that divine leadership that he or she aspires to follow. Scores of examples are found in the Holy Quran, and in history generally, that show people's tangible effect on the occultation of God's prophets.

Even today, in the era of occultation with Imam al-Mahdi, people's actions influence the Imam's state. People have a real practical impact on the current climate the world is in.

> Indeed, God does not change a people's lot, unless they change
> what is in their souls.[1]

God says that he will not change the state of a community until they change what is within themselves. Everyone has an impact on the condition of the community. With each individual decision comes a consequence and an effect that goes beyond one's self, so much so that it can affect even the vicegerent of God.

It is said that humanity needs to go through all the different iterations of governance and society to understand what it needs. Humanity will mature and realize the faults in its movements and be able to recognize what principles will advance it as a species on all levels, rather than merely in one area over another. Through reflection on the human condition, humanity will come closer to both the realization and commitment to such principles. When humanity does this, it will then be ready for Imam al-Mahdi and Jesus the son of Mary.

The idea of a virtuous community is real. It is one that all the prophets since Adam worked for. Today, the role of the virtuous community is unique. It waits to know that it is accountable for its decisions and that it is connected through its activities in one way or another. The degrees of separation between human beings are limited.

Joseph could have been released from prison much sooner if it were not for the forgetfulness of his freed prison mate. Moses could have been executed if it were not for the faithful minister in the Pharaoh's cabinet who concealed his faith and earned the trust of the monarch. Those individuals directly impacted the life and occultation of God's vicegerents. The virtuous community today has a similar impact on the vicegerents they await.

This realization may bring an individual closer to being an active part of that virtuous community. Because with acknowledgment of responsibility, comes accountability and commitment to the principles therein. The virtuous community becomes stronger as each person works toward acknowledgement, both individually and collectively.

A virtuous community does not compel anyone against their will. It does not wish to force anyone into salvation. It does not desire indoctrination. Instead, it asks for liberation, freedom, and choice. The true community awaiting God's vicegerents, simply wishes to preserve its principles so that it may help its community and humanity overall reach its potential.

In that pursuit, Shi'a Muslims wish to practice their faith and preserve these principles just like every group and community should be respected in their practice and faith. The Shi'a desire to protect their existence and wellbeing as a community because they know they can contribute to the advancement of humanity. In that light, it is better for people to see action rather than merely hearing a message, as actions speak much louder than words.

As Grand Ayatollah Shaykh Ishaq al-Fayyad, one of the great scholars of the Holy City of Najaf, advised, "Be the straight line, and all the other crooked lines will be revealed." One does not need to preach, but simply act.

We pray that we can act consistently and virtuously. In exhibiting a commitment to coexistence, tolerance, and peace, we pray that humanity comes closer together in pursuit of its highest ideals. Through this promise and spirit of action, we can uplift ourselves and humanity and bring us all closer to light.

ENDNOTES

PREFACE

1 Oliver, "Shiʿa shrine blasts spark reprisal attacks", *The Guardian*.
2 Tornielli, "Pope Francis' ecumenism – Vatican Insider", *Vatican Insider*.
3 "Pope Francis 'a friend of the Islamic community", *Buenos Aires Herald*.

CHAPTER 1: SAVING THE CRADLE OF CIVILIZATION

1 Crawford, *Sumer and the Sumerians*; Bocquet-Appel, "When the World's Population Took Off: The Springboard of the Neolithic Demographic Transition", *Science* 333 (6042), 560–561.
2 "Biography of the Grand Ayatollah", *The Official Website of the Office of His Eminence Al-Sayyid Ali Al-Husseini Al-Sistani*.
3 Oliver, "Shiʿa shrine blasts spark reprisal attacks", *The Guardian*.
4 "Statement of the Office of His Eminence regarding Muslim Unity and Rejection of Sectarianism", *The Official Website of the Office of His Eminence Al-Sayyid Ali Al-Husseini Al-Sistani*.
5 "Advice and Guidance to the Fighters on the Battlefields – Archive", *The Official Website of the Office of His Eminence Al-Sayyid Ali Al-Husseini Al-Sistani*.
6 Ibid.
7 Ibid.
8 "The Grand Ayatollah", YouTube.

CHAPTER 2: THE HISTORIC MEETING OF THE POPE AND THE AYATOLLAH

1   Rubin and Ambrogetti, *Pope Francis – Conversations with Jorge Bergoglio*, 45–46.

2   Brady and Cunningham, "St. Francis of Assisi", *Encyclopædia Britannica*.

3   Bethune, "Pope Francis: How the first New World pontiff could save the church", *Maclean's*.

4   "Pope Francis wants 'poor Church for the poor'", *BBC News*.

5   Uebbing, "Pope Francis' personality begins to change routines", *Catholic News Agency*.

6   Speciale, "Pope washes feet of two girls, two Muslims at youth prison", *The Washington Post*.

7   "Chaldean prelate invites pope to visit Iraq", *catholicculture.org*.

8   Bruni, "Declaration of the Director of the Holy See Press Office, Matteo Bruni."

9   Watkins, "Pope Francis to Visit Iraq, First Apostolic Journey in 15 Months," *Vatican News*.

10 Ibid. "The Polish Pope [Pope St. John II] had planned to travel to Iraq at the end of 1999. That trip never took place because Saddam Hussein decided to postpone it, after months of negotiations."

11 Brockhaus, "Pope Francis Lends Support to Committee on Abu Dhabi Declaration," *Catholic News Agency*.

12 Altieri, "Pope Francis Releases Encyclical Letter Fratelli Tutti," *Catholic Herald*.

13 See: Guizot, *The History of Civilization in Europe*, 204, 205.

14 "Statement of the Office of His Eminence regarding Muslim Unity and Rejection of Sectarianism", *The Official Website of the Office of His Eminence Al-Sayyid Ali Al-Husseini Al-Sistani*.

15 Sallum, *al-Masihiyun fi'l-Iraq al-Tarikh al-Shamil wa'l-Tahaddiyat al-Rahinah*.

16 "Pope's visit to Iraq will send message of coexistence, says Iraqi president", *The Middle East Eye*.

17 The Holy Quran, 49:13.

18 The Holy Quran, 3:103.

CHAPTER 3: THE VICEGERENTS OF GOD AND HUMAN PURPOSE

1   Arastu, *God's Emissaries*, 17-21. God's Emissaries is an excellent resource for an in-depth study on Earth's early inhabitants, the creation of Adam, and the angels' inquiry with God, in addition to the historical narrative of the prophets from a Shi'i perspective.

2   The Holy Quran, 2:30.

3   The Holy Quran, 2:31 – 32.

4   The Holy Quran, 2:31 – 32.

5   The Holy Quran, 2:33.

6   The Holy Quran, 95:4 – 6.

7   The Holy Quran, 51:56.

8   Tabataba'i, *A Shi'ite Anthology*.

9   The Holy Quran, 1:6. The first chapter of the Quran, titled "Al-Fatihah" translated as "The Opener" or "The Key", hold a great deal of significance in Muslim piety. It is recited in every unit of ritual prayers. Seven verses in total, it is often the first chapter that Muslims learn as a central prayer to the lordship and mercy of God.

10   The Holy Quran, 2:213.

11   The Holy Quran, 6:71.

12   The Holy Quran, 33:4.

13   Al-Subhani, *al-Ilahiyyat*, 1:732.

14   The Holy Quran, 40:60.

15   See: al-Samawi, *Ask Those Who Know,* Chapter 8: Concerning the two Sahihs of al-Bukhari and Muslim.

16   The Holy Quran, 6:124.

17   The Holy Quran, 3:179.

18   Tabataba'i, *al-Mizan*, exegesis of verse 2:213.

19   The Holy Quran, 62:2.

20   The Holy Quran, 2:286.

21   The Holy Quran, 21:107.

22   The Holy Quran, 5:3.

23   The Holy Quran, 13:7.

24   Tabataba'i, *Shi'ite Islam*, 192.

25   Donaldson, *The Shi'ite Religion*, 66–78.

26   Ayoub, *Redemptive Suffering in Islam*, 55.

27   Al-Bukhari, *Jami' al-Sahih*, 6:3.

28   Al-Nisaburi, *al-Mustadrak*, 3:109.

29   Al-Khabbaz, *The Mahdi*, 23.

CHAPTER 4: THE SOURCES OF DIVINE GUIDANCE

1   The Holy Quran, 2:30.

2   Al-Hakeem, *al-Jama'at al-Salihah*, 1:43-58.

3   The Holy Quran, 15:9.

4   Al-Radi, *Nahj al-Balaghah*, Short Saying 169. Another translation of this has appeared as, "For the man who has eyes the dawn has already appeared."

5   The Holy Quran, 4:165.

6   Tabataba'i, *Tafsir al-Mizan*, exegesis of verses 3:7-9.

7   The Holy Quran, 3:7.

8   Al-Thahabi, *Tathkirat al-Huffaz*, 1:1-5.

9   Ibid.

10   Al-Shaybani, *Musnad Ahmad*, Tr. 6221.

11   Al-Mufid, *al-Irshad*, 91.

12   Al-Tabarsi, *al-Ihtijaj*, 56.

13   The Holy Quran, 5:67.

14   Vaglieri, "Ghadīr Khumm," *Encyclopedia of Islam*.

15   Al-Nasa'i, *al-Khasa'is*, 96.

16   Al-Shaybani, *Fada'il al-Sahabah*, 2:597.

17   Al-Mufid, *al-Irshad*, 85-87; al-Tabari, *Tarikh al-Tabari*, 1577-81.

18   Al-Mufid, *al-Irshad*, 46 – 48.

19   Mavani, *Religious Authority and Political Thought in Twelver Shi'ism*.

20   The Holy Quran, 53:3 – 4.

21   The Holy Quran, 56:77 – 80.

22   See: Tabataba'i, *Tafsir al-Mizan*, exegesis of verses 56:77 – 80.

23   The Holy Quran, 33:33.

24   The Holy Quran, 3:61.

25   Tabataba'i, *Tafsir al-Mizan*, exegesis of verses 3:61-63.

26   The Holy Quran, 21:107.

27   The Holy Quran, 53:3

28   The Holy Quran, 53:4

29   Al-Nisaburi, *Al-Mustadrak*, 3:134.

30   Al-Majlisi, *Bihar al-Anwar*, 38:38. This narration is also reported with a version that states, "…it [the truth] turns wherever he [Ali] turns."

31   Al-Hindi, *Kanz al-'Ummal*, 6:392.

32   Al-Majlisi, *Mir'at Al-'Uqul*, 289.

33   The Holy Quran, 5:55.

34   Steigerwald, "Twelver Shī'ī Ta'wīl", *The Blackwell Companion to the Qur'ān*, 373 – 385.

35   Al-Hasakani, *Shawahid al-Tanzil*, 1:164. Shah-Kazemi, "Light upon Light? The Qur'an and the Gospel of John", *Interreligious Hermeneutics*, 2:116–148; Shomali, "Imamate and Wilayah, Pt. IV", *Message of Thaqalayn*, 13:1.

36   Al-Qanduzi, *Yanabi' al-Mawaddah*, 3:503.

37   Al-Qanduzi, *Yanabi' al-Mawaddah*, 3:506.

38 Ibid 3:504.

CHAPTER 5: FAITH & WORKS

1 The Holy Quran, 62:2.

2 Al-Kulayni, *Al-Kafi*, 2:24, H. 2.

3 Al-Saduq, *'Uyun Akhbar al-Rida*, 1:260.

4 Al-Kulayni, *al-Kafi*, 2:26-27

5 The Holy Quran, 49:14.

6 The Holy Quran, 6:160.

7 Al-Kulayni, *al-Kafi*, 2:26-27, H.5.

8 Al-Kulayni, *al-Kafi*, 2:38, H.6.

9 Al-Kulayni, *al-Kafi*, 2:38, H.7.

10 Al-Kulayni, *al-Kafi*, 2:18-19; al-'Amili, *Wasa'il al-Shi'ah*, 1:7, H.2.

11 The Holy Quran, 42:23.

12 Al-Kulayni, *al-Kafi*, 2:46; al-Majlisi, *Bihar al-Anwar*, 27:82.

13 Al-Majlisi, *Bihar al-Anwar*, 67:306; al-Harrani, *Tuhaf al-'Uqul*, 104.

14 Al-Shafi'i, *Diwan Al-Shafi'i*, 87.

15 Al-'Amili, *Wasa'il al-Shi'ah*, 11:141, H. 6.

16 Al-Amudi, *Ghurar al-Hikam*, No. 6244. Citing: The Holy Quran, 42:23.

17 The Holy Quran, 61:2 – 3.

18 Al-Hakeem, *Marjaeya: A Candid Conversation*, 17.

19 Sunni sources: Al-Bayhaqi, *al-Sunan al-Kubra*, vol. 4, Book 11, Ch. 6, Nu. 7904; al-Tabari, *Tafsir al-Tabari*, 3:187; al-Razi, *al-Tafsir al-Kabir*, 5:251; Ibn al-Jawzi, *al-Mawdu'at*, 2:187. Shi'a sources: al-Kulayni, *al-Kafi*, Book 14 (the Book of Fasting); al-Saduq, *Man La Yahdaruh al-Faqih*, 2:182; Al-'Amili, *Wasa'il al-Shi'a*, 10:19; al-Majlisi, *Bihar al-Anwar*, vol. 93, ch. 48.

20 Al-Hakeem, *al-Jama'at al-Salihah*, 1:146-150.

21 Al-Hakeem, *The Shi'a*, 61-62.

22 See: Al-Hakeem, *Understanding Karbala*; al-Hakeem and Albodairi, *The Saga: the Battle of Karbala*.

23 Al-Hakeem, *The Shi'a*, 140.

24 The Holy Quran, 22:32.

25 Ibid, 2:156.

26 The Holy Quran, 97:1-5.

27 Al-'Amili, *Wasa'il al-Shi'a*, 8:89.

28 Esposito, "Mosque", The Oxford Dictionary of Islam.

29 Al-Bukhari, *Sahih al-Bukhari*, 439; al-Nisaburi, *Sahih Muslim*, 533.

CHAPTER 6: THE HERITAGE OF RELIGIOUS EDUCATION

1   The Holy Quran, 96:1-5.

2   Al-Tabrisi, *Mishkat al-Anwar*, 346, H. 713.

3   Armstrong, *Islam: A Short History*, 13.

4   Al-ʿAmili, *Wasaʾil Al-Shiʿa*, 27:26.

5   Al-Kulayni, *Al-Kafi*, 1:30.

6   Al-Hakeem, *Creed*, 39; citing: Al-Saduq, *al-Amali*, 438.

7   Al-ʿAmili, *Wasaʾil Al-Shiʿa*, 18:14.

8   Al-Kulayni, *Al-Kafi*, 1:41.

9   Al-Hakeem, *al-Jamaʿat al-Salihah*, 1:123-25.

10   Al-ʿAyashi, *Tafseer Al-ʿAyashi*, 1:30.

11   Al-Hakeem, *Creed*, 9–16.

12   Al-Majlisi, *Bihar al-Anwar*, 2:303.

13   Al-Hakeem, *Creed*, 9–16.

14   Al-Hindi, *Kanz Al-ʿUmmal*, 1:186.

15   The Holy Quran, 53:3 – 4.

16   Al-Majlisi, *Bihar al-Anwar*, 2:242, H. 38.

17   Ibid.

18   Al-Kulayni, *al-Kafi*, 1:239, H. 1; al-Saffar, *Basaʾir al-Darajat*, 143 and 151-152.

19   Al-Hakeem, *al-Jamaʿat al-Salihah*, 1:127-29.

20   Al-Majlisi, Bihar al-Anwar 2:184.

21   Al-Kashshi, *Ikhtiyar Maʿrifat al-Rijal*, 1:61.

22   Stapleton, Azo, and Husayn, "Chemistry in Iraq and Persia in the Tenth Century A.D.", *Memoirs of the Asiatic Society of Bengal*, VIII (6): 317–418.

23   Al-Hakeem, *al-Jamaʿat al-Salihah*, 1:132.

24   Al-Hakeem, *al-Jamaʿat al-Salihah*, 1:133-34.

25   Al-Nuri, *Mustadrak Al-Wasaʾil*, 13:48.

26   Al-Radi, *Nahj al-Balaghah*, Letter 47.

27   Al-Radi, *Nahj al-Balaghah*, Letter 53.

CHAPTER 7: RELIGIOUS INSTITUTIONS

1   Al-Hakeem, *al-Jamaʿat al-Salihah*, 1:137-38.

2   Taylor, "Jaʿfar al-Sādiq, Spiritual Forebear of the Sufis," *Islamic Culture* 40/2, April 1966, 97–113.

3   Jestice, *Holy People of the World*, 1:415; Adamec, *Historical Dictionary of Islam*, 12; *Abd-Allah*, Mālik and Medina, 44.

4   For more information on the movement of the seminary over the centuries, see: Al-Hakeem, *The Shiʿa*, 112-28.

5   Al-Hakeem, *al-Jamaʿat al-Salihah*, 1:137-38.

6   Campo, *Encyclopedia of Islam*, 386, 652, 677.

7   Al-Hakeem, *al-Jamaʿat al-Salihah*, 1:141.

8   Al-Rayshahri, *Mizan al-Hikmah*, 6:457.

9   Al-Kulayni, *al-Kafi*, 1:32.

10   Al-Hakeem, *Understanding Karbala*, 165-175.

11   Ibid, 178-186.

12   Ibid, 189-192.

13   Taylor, "Jaʿfar al-Sādiq, Spiritual Forebear of the Sufis," *Islamic Culture* 40/2, April 1966, 97–113.

14   See: Tabatabaʾi, *Shiʿite Islam*.

15   Al-Hakeem, *Marjaeya: A Candid Conversation*, 7-16.

16   Al-Qummi, *Kamal al-Din*, 484.

17   See Ayatollah Sayyid Muhammad Saʿid Al-Hakeem's book, *Marjaeya: A Candid Conversation*, for discussion on relieving one's burden before God and further detail on the topic of *taqlid*, 7-23.

18   Al-Hakeem, *Marjaeya: A Candid Conversation*, 25-44; al-Hakeem, *al-Jamaʿat al-Salihah*, 1:67-8.

19   Al-ʿAmili, *Wasaʾil al-Shiʿa*, 18:19.

20   Al-ʿAmili, *Wasaʾil al-Shiʿa*, 18:101.

21   Al-Kulayni, *al-Kafi*, 1:407.

22   Al-Kulayni, *al-Kafi*, 1:183-184.

23   Al-Hakeem, *al-Jamaʿat al-Salihah*, 1:222-226.

24   Al-Hakeem, *al-Jamaʿat al-Salihah*, 1:139-40.

25   Al-ʿAmili, *Wasaʾil al-Shiʿa*, 18:104. Citing: The Holy Quran, 56:10. In another tradition by Abu ʿAbbas Al-Fadl ibn Abdulmalik, he narrates from Imam al-Sadiq, "The most beloved people to me, whether alive or dead, are four: Burayd ibn Muʿawiyah al-ʿUjali, Zurarah, Muhammad ibn Muslim, and al-Ahwal [also known as Muʾmin al-Taq]. These are the most beloved to me living or dead."

26   Al-ʿAmili, *Wasaʾil al-Shiʿa*, 18:105.

27   Al-ʿAmili, *Wasaʾil al-Shiʿa*, 18:108.

28   Al-ʿAmili, *Wasaʾil al-Shiʿa*, 18:106.

29   Al-Hakeem, *al-Jamaʿat al-Salihah*, 1:227-32.

30   Ibid, 232.

31   Al-Hakeem, *Marjaeya: A Candid Conversation*, 90-2.

32   The Holy Quran, 8:41.

[33] See Ayatollah Sayyid Muhammad Saʿid Al-Hakeem's book, *Marjaeya: A Candid Conversation*, Chapter: The Marjaeya and Colonialism, for a more detailed discussion on the stances of the Marjiʿiyyah throughout history with external pressures from forces such as the Ottoman Empire and colonial powers.

CHAPTER 8: IDENTITY

[1] Al-Hakeem, *al-Jamaʿat al-Salihah*, 1:239-50.

[2] Ibid, 241.

[3] The Holy Quran, 21:107.

[4] Al-Amudi, *Ghurar al-Hikam*, 403, H. 8048.

[5] Al-Hakeem, *al-Jamaʿat al-Salihah*, 1:239-40.

[6] See: al-Hakeem, *Fi Rihab Al-ʿAqidah*.

[7] Al-Radi, *Nahj al-Balaghah*, Letter 53.

[8] The Holy Quran, 37:83.

[9] The Holy Quran, 28:15.

[10] Al-Qummi, *Tafsir al-Qummi*, 2:223.

[11] Al-ʿAyyashi, *Tafsir al-ʿAyyashi*, 2:243.

[12] Al-Majlisi, *Bihar al-Anwar*, 68:156-57.

[13] Al-Nisaburi, *Sahih Muslim*, 15:173-175.

[14] Al-Kulayni, *Al-Kafi*.

[15] Al-Tusi, *al-Amali*, 190-191.

[16] For a detailed discussion on ʿUthman's caliphate, the disenfranchisement of minorities and non-Arabs during his reign, and the rise of the Umayyads thereafter, see: Chamseddine, *Hussain's Revolution*, 29-44.

[17] Al-Tusi, *al-Amali*, 353.

[18] Al-Saduq, *al-Amali*, 66.

[19] The Holy Quran, 4:69.

[20] Al-Majlisi, *Bihar al-Anwar*, 27:123-125. Citing: The Holy Quran, 39:9

[21] The Holy Quran, 10:62.

[22] Al-ʿAyyashi, *Tafsir al-ʿAyyashi*, 2:124.

[23] The Holy Quran, 70:22 – 23.

[24] The Holy Quran, 23:9.

[25] The Holy Quran, 56:27.

[26] Al-Astrabadi, *Taʾwil al-Ayat*, 2:724.

[27] Al-Saduq, *Sifat al-Shiʿa*, 2; Al-Majlisi, *Bihar al-Anwar*, 68:167.

[28] The Holy Quran, 3:68.

[29] Al-Hakeem, *Fi Rihab Al-ʿAqidah*, 119-120. Citing: al-Kulayni, *al-Kafi*, Chapter: al-Hub fi Allah wa'l-Bughd fi Allah, Hadith 6.

[30]   Al-Majlisi, *Bihar Al-Anwar*, 65:55.

[31]   Al-Qummi, *Tafsir al-Qummi*, 1:105.

[32]   Al-Saduq, *al-Amali*, 416.

[33]   Al-Majlisi, *Bihar al-Anwar*, 65:17. See also: al-Hindi, *Kanz al-'Ummal*, 12:49.

[34]   The Holy Quran, 56:10 – 12.

[35]   Al-Mufid, *al-Amali*, 298; Al-Tusi, *al-Amali*, 72.

[36]   Al-Himyari, *Qurb al-Isnad*, 101-102.

[37]   Al-Hakeem, *al-Jama'at al-Salihah*, 1:65.

[38]   Al-Radi, *Nahj al-Balaghah*, Letter 53.

CHAPTER 9: COMMUNITY RELATIONS

[1]   The Holy Quran, 30:21. This verse is often recited at the wedding ceremonies (as well as on the invitation cards to guests) of Muslims, celebrating their newlyweds' marriage and the beginning of their new lives together.

[2]   The Holy Quran, 49:13.

[3]   Al-'Amili, *Wasa'il al-Shi'a*, 8:399.

[4]   See: Cacioppo and Patrick, *Loneliness: Human nature and the need for social connection*.

[5]   Al-'Amili, *Wasa'il al-Shi'a*, 8:567.

[6]   The Holy Quran, 57:27.

[7]   Al-Hakeem, *al-Jama'at al-Salihah*, 1:263-8.

[8]   Al-'Amili, *Wasa'il al-Shi'a*, 8:542.

[9]   Al-'Amili, *Wasa'il al-Shi'a*, 11:108.

[10]   Al-'Amili, *Wasa'il al-Shi'a*, 11:559.

[11]   Al-'Amili, *Wasa'il al-Shi'a*, 11:595.

[12]   Al-Kulayni, *al-Kafi*, 2:362; Al-Saduq, *al-Amali*, 380.

[13]   Al-'Amili, *Wasa'il al-Shi'a*, 8:458.

[14]   Al-'Amili, *Wasa'il al-Shi'a*, 8:426.

[15]   Al-'Amili, *Wasa'il al-Shi'a*, 8:426.

[16]   Abbas, *The Prophet's Heir*, 183. Citing: Chittick, *Sufism: A Short Introduction*, 84.

[17]   Al-'Amili, *Wasa'il al-Shi'a*, 11:559.

[18]   Al-'Amili, *Wasa'il al-Shi'a*, 11:434.

[19]   The Holy Quran, 4:36.

[20]   Imam Ali al-Sajjad, *The Treatise on Rights*, Right #22.

[21]   Al-Kulayni, *Al-Kafi*, 2:130. A man came to the Prophet and said, "O, prophet of God! I am young and vigorous, and ready for action and service. I wish to go to the battle-front, but my mother does not let me leave her and go to war." The Prophet replied, "Go and stay with your mother. I swear to the God Who chose me as prophet that the

spiritual reward which you receive for serving her even one night and making her happy with your presence, is greater than a one-year long holy war."

22   Al-Nisaburi, *Sahih Muslim*, H. 1974.

23   Imam Ali al-Sajjad, *The Treatise on Rights*, Right #23.

24   Imam Ali al-Sajjad, *The Treatise on Rights*, Right #24.

25   Al-Kulayni, *al-Kafi*, 2:347-348.

26   Imam Ali al-Sajjad, *The Treatise on Rights*, Right #25.

27   Al-ʿAmili, *Wasaʾil al-Shiʿa*, 8:404.

28   Al-Tabari, *Dalaʾil al-Imamah*, 56.

29   Imam Ali al-Sajjad, *The Treatise on Rights*, Right #31.

30   Imam Ali al-Sajjad, *The Treatise on Rights*, Right #32.

31   Imam Ali al-Sajjad, *The Treatise on Rights*, Right #33.

32   Al-ʿAmili, *Wasaʾil al-Shiʿa*, 8:551.

33   Imam Ali al-Sajjad, *The Treatise on Rights*, Right #16; al-ʿAmili, *Wasaʾil al-Shiʿah*, 11:134.

34   The Holy Quran, 13:11.

CHAPTER 10: INTEGRATION & COEXISTENCE

1   Sayyid Ali al-Hakeem in an interview with the authors, February 2021. Quoting Sayyid Ali al-Hakeem: "We are advocates of a homeland; we are not advocates of power. If the current political system requires the Shiʿi to govern, then he shall govern; but if the current political system requires someone else to govern, then they will govern. The Shiʿa only expect to be treated, and for everyone else to be treated, as citizens of nations. Religion, creed, or ethnicity should never be a qualifier for special treatment…"

2   An-Naʾim, *What Is an American Muslim?*, 1.

3   Ibid, 50-61.

4   See: Du Bois, *The Souls of Black Folk*. W. E. B.

5   Al-Kulayni, *al-Kafi*, 2:635.

6   Ibid, 2:643.

7   Al-Hakeem, *al-Jamaʿat al-Salihah*, 1:322.

8   The Holy Quran, 49:13.

9   Al-Radi, *Nahj al-Balaghah*, Hadith 438.

10   An-Naʾim, *What Is an American Muslim?*, 48.

11   Basu, "After 9/11, turbans made Sikhs targets," *CNN.com*.

12   Al-ʿAmili, *Wasaʾil al-Shiʿa*, 11:75.

13   Al-ʿAmili, *Wasaʾil al-Shiʿa*, 11:75-76.

14   The Holy Quran, 28:21 – 22.

15   Ibn Ishaq, *Sirat Rasul Allah*, 114.

16   See: Razwy, *A Restatement of the History of Islam & Muslims*.

17   Al-ʿAmili, *Wasaʾil al-Shiʿa*, 11:76.

18   Al-ʿAmili, *Wasaʾil al-Shiʿa*, 11:49.

19   Al-Muʿtazili, *Sharh Nahj al-Balaghah*, 7:37.

20   Al-Radi, *Nahj al-Balaghah*, Sermon 11.

21   The Holy Quran, 21:107.

22   Al-ʿAmili, *Wasaʾil al-Shiʿa*, 8:398.

23   Al-Tusi, *al-Amali*, 440; Narrated by the companion Sulayman ibn Mahran.

24   The Holy Quran, 33:21.

25   The Holy Quran, 68:1 – 7.

26   Covey, *The 7 Habits*, "Habit 5: Seek First to Understand, Then to Be Understood® Leadership." "Most people do not listen with the intent to understand; they listen with the intent to reply."

27   For more detailed accounts of Shiʿa persecution in history, see: Al-Hakeem, *The Shiʿa*, 139-154.

28   Ibn Saʿd, *al-Tabaqat*, 3:189; Kohlberg, "Some Imami-Shiʿi Views on Taqiyya," *Journal of the American Oriental Society*, 95 (3): 395–402.

29   The Holy Quran, 16:106.

30   Al-Kulayni, *Al-Kafi*, 2:219.

31   Al-ʿAmili, *Wasaʾil al-Shiʿa*, 11:461.

32   Al-Kulayni, *Al-Kafi*, 2:219.

33   Al-Hakeem, al-Jamaʿat al-Salihah, 1:330-2.

34   Al-ʿAmili, *Wasaʾil al-Shiʿa*, 11:450-451.

35   Al-Kulayni, *al-Kafi*, 2:213.

36   Al-ʿAmili, *Wasaʾil al-Shiʿa*, 15:246.

37   Al-Hakeem, *al-Jamaʿat al-Salihah*, 1:63.

38   Al-Majlisi, *Bihar Al-Anwar*, 12:292.

39   Al-Majlisi, *Bihar al-Anwar*, 72:370-9.

40   Al-ʿAmili, *Wasaʾil al-Shiʿa*, 6:131.

41   Al-ʿAmili, *Wasaʾil al-Shiʿa*, 11:203.

42   Mentioned in the following Sunni sources: Al-Nasaʾi, *al-Sunan al-Kubra*, 96, No. 79; al-Bukhari, *al-Tarikh al-Kabir*, 3:96; al-Nisaburi, *Sahih Muslim*, no. 2408; al-Shaybani, *Musnad Ahmad*, 3:17; Ibn Abu 'Asim, *Kitab al-Sunnah*, 629, no. 1551, 630, no. 1555, 629, no. 1551; al-Yaʿqubi, *Tarikh al-Yaʿqubi*, 2:112; Ibn Taymiyyah, *Minhaj al-Sunnah*, 4:85; Ibn Kathir, *al-Bidayah wa'l-Nihayah*, 5:209, 6:199, quoting al-Nasaʾi, and stating that his narration on Ghadir Khum is *sahih* (i.e. authentic).

43   Abbas, *The Prophet's Heir*, 118, 99.

44   Al-Muʿtazili, *Sharh Nahj al-Balaghah*, 20:326.

45   Al-Radi, *Nahj al-Balaghah*, Sermon No. 73.

46   Abdulbar, *al-Isti'ab*, 1103.

47   See: Al Yasin, *Sulh Al-Hasan*. Also see: Al-Hakeem, *Understanding Karbala*.

48   The Holy Quran, 5:32.

49   See: Al-Hakeem, *Understanding Karbala*.

50   See: "Advice from His Eminence Sayyid Ali Al-Sistani to the Believing Youth," *Official Website of Grand Ayatollah Sayyid Ali Al-Sistani*.

51   Al-Naraqi, al-Khaza'in, 1:487, 528.

CHAPTER 11: THE DOCTRINE OF OCCULTATION

1   The Holy Quran, 21:105.

2   The Holy Quran, 24:55.

3   The Holy Quran, 5:3.

4   The Holy Quran, 2:256.

5   Al-Radi, *Nahj al-Balaghah*, Sermon 73.

6   See: Al-Sanad, *Imam al-Mahdi Fil Quran al-Karim*.

7   The Holy Quran, 12:3.

8   The Holy Quran, 12:111.

9   See: Al-Sanad, *Imam al-Mahdi Fil Quran al-Karim*.

10   The Holy Quran, 18:9 – 11.

11   The Holy Quran, 18:25 – 26.

12   The Holy Quran, 12:1 – 10.

13   The Holy Quran, 12:11 – 22.

14   The Holy Quran, 28:2 – 4.

15   The Holy Quran, 28:5 – 6.

16   The Holy Quran, 7 – 13.

17   The Holy Quran, 4:157 – 158.

18   See: Rizvi, *Muhammad is the Last Prophet*.

19   The Holy Quran, 3:55.

20   The Holy Quran, 4:157.

21   The Holy Quran, 18:25.

22   The Holy Quran, 28:14.

23   The Holy Quran, 28:15.

24   The Holy Quran, 28:20.

25   The Holy Quran, 2:30.

26   The Holy Quran, 2:124.

27   The Holy Quran, 4:54.

28   The Holy Quran, 18:65.

29   The Holy Quran, 18:66 – 70.

30   The Holy Quran, 18:71 – 82.

CHAPTER 12: IMPACTING THE OCCULTATION

1   The Holy Quran, 28:18.

2   The Holy Quran, 28:19.

3   The Holy Quran, 28:20-21.

4   The Holy Quran, 28:22 – 28.

5   The Holy Quran, 40:23-24.

6   The Holy Quran, 40:28 – 33.

7   The Holy Quran, 12:22 – 24.

8   The Holy Quran, 12:33.

9   The Holy Quran, 12:39 – 40.

10   The Holy Quran, 12:41.

11   The Holy Quran, 10:20.

12   The Holy Quran, 2:2-3.

13   Al-Saduq, *Kamal al-Din*, 340.

14   Al-Kulayni, *al-Kafi*, 1:368.

15   Al-Nuʿmani, *al-Ghaybah*, 304-05.

16   Al-Kulayni, *al-Kafi*, 1:368. Citing: The Holy Quran, 13:39.

CONCLUSION

1   The Holy Quran, 13:11.

SELECT BIBLIOGRAPHY

The Holy Quran. ʿAli Quli Qaraʾi (translator). Tahrike Tarsile Qurʾan, 2015.

Abbas, Hassan. *The Prophet's Heir*. Yale University Press, 2021.

Abd-Allah, Umar F. *Mālik and Medina: Islamic Legal Reasoning in the Formative Period*. Leiden: Brill, 2013.

Abdulbar, Yusuf. *Al-Istiʿab*. Beirut: Dar al-Jil, 1992 CE.

Adamec, Ludwig W. *Historical Dictionary of Islam*.

Al Yasin, Shaykh Radi. *Sulh al-Hasan*. Qum: Ansariyan Publications, 1998.

Al-ʿAmili, Muhammad ibn al-Hasan. *Wasaʾil al-Shiʿa*.

Al-Amudi, Abu al-Fath. *Ghurar al-Hikam wa Durar al-Kalim*.

Al-Astrabadi, Ali. *Taʾwil al-Ayat*. Qum: Madrasat al-Imam al-Mahdi, 1407 AH.

Al-ʿAyyashi, Muhammad ibn Masʿud. *Tafsir al-ʿAyyashi*.

Al-Barqi, Ahmad ibn Muhammad. *Al-Mahasin*.

Al-Bayhaqi, Abu Bakr. Al-Sunnan al-Kubra.

Al-Bukhari, Muhammad ibn Ismael. *Al-Tarikh al-Kabir*.

Al-Bukhari, Muhammad ibn Ismael. *Jami' al-Sahih*. L'Iden: E. J. Brill, 1868-1908.

Al-Bukhari, Muhammad ibn Ismael. *Sahih al-Bukhari*.

Al-Hakeem, Ayatollah Sayyid Muhammad Baqir. *Dawr Ahl al-Bayt Fi Binaʾ al-Jamaʿat al-Salihah*. Najaf: Muʾassasat Turath al-Shahid al-Hakeem, 2007 (5th ed).

Al-Hakeem, Ayatollah Sayyid Muhammad Saʿid. *Fi Rihab al-ʿAqidah*. 9th ed. The Holy City of Najaf: Dar al-Hilal, 2012.

Al-Hakeem, Ayatollah Sayyid Muhammad Saʿid. *Marjaeya: A Candid Conversation*. The Mainstay Foundation, 2018.

Al-Hakeem, Ayatollah Sayyid Muhammad Saʿid. *Understanding Karbala (Arabic: Faji'at al-Taff)*. Abridged and Adapted. The Mainstay Foundation, 2017.

Al-Hakeem, Riyadh. *The Shiʿa: Identity. Persecution. Horizons*. The Mainstay Foundation, 2015.

Al-Hakeem, Sayyid Ali. *Creed: God and His Ambassadors*. The Mainstay Foundation, 2015.

Al-Hakeem, Sayyid Hassan, and Mohamed Ali Albodairi. *The Saga: the Battle of Karbala*. The Mainstay Foundation, 2018.

Al-Hakeem, Sayyid Riyad. *The Shiʿa: Identity, Persecution, Horizons*. The Mainstay Foundation, 2015.

Al-Harrani, Ibn Shuʿbah. *Tuhaf al-ʿUqul*. Qum: Jamaʿat al-Mudarrisin, 1404 AH (2ⁿᵈ ed).

Al-Hasakani, ʿUbaydullah ibn ʿAbdullah. *Shawahid al-Tanzil*. Beirut: al-Aʿlami.

Al-Himyari, ʿAbdullah ibn Jaʿfar. *Qurb al-Isnad*.

Al-Hindi, Ali ibn Husamuldin. *Kanz Al-ʿUmmal*.

Al-Kashani, Muhammad ibn Murtada. *Maʿadin al-Hikmah*.

Al-Kashshi, Muhammad ibn al-Hasan. *Ikhtiyar Maʿrifat al-Rijal*.

Al-Khabbaz, Sayyid Muneer. *The Mahdi: Understanding the Awaited One*. The Mainstay Foundation, 2018.

Al-Kulayni, Muhammad ibn Yaʿqub. *Al-Kafi*.

Al-Majlisi, Muhammad Baqir. *Bihar al-Anwar*. Beirut: Dar Ihyaʾ al-Turath, 1983 CE.

Al-Majlisi, Muhammad Baqir. *Mirʾat Al-ʿUqul*.

Al-Mubarakpuri, Safi-ur-Rahman. *The Sealed Nectar* (Ar-Raheeq Al-Makhtum). Darussalam, 2002.

Al-Mufid, Muhammad ibn Muhammad. *Al-Amali*.

Al-Mufid, Muhammad ibn Muhammad. *Kitab al-Irshad*. I. K. A. Howard (translator). Elmhurst: Tahrike Tarsile Qurʾan, 1981.

Al-Muʿtazili, Ibn Abu al-Hadid. *Sharh Nahj al-Balaghah*.

Al-Naraqi, Ahmad ibn Muhammad Mahdi. *Al-Khazaʾin*.

Al-Nasaʾi, Ahmad ibn Ali. *Al-Sunan al-Kubra*.

Al-Nisaburi, Muhammad ibn ʿAbdullah. *Al-Mustadrak*. Beirut: Dar Al-Kutub Al-ʿIlmiyyah.

Al-Nisaburi, Muslim ibn al-Hajjaj. *Sahih Muslim*. Beirut: 1981 CE.

Al-Nasaʾi, Ahmad ibn Shuʿayb. *Al-Khasaʾis*. Kuwait: Al-Muʿalla.

Al-Nuʿmani, Muhammad ibn Ibrahim. *Al-Ghaybah*. Dar al-Jawadayn, 2011 CE.

Al-Nuri, Husayn. *Mustadrak Al-Wasaʾil*. Muʾassasat Aal al-Bayt.

Al-Qanduzi, Sulayman ibn Ibrahim. *Yanabiʿ al-Mawaddah*. Beirut: al-Aʿlami.

Al-Qummi, Ali ibn Ibrahim. *Tafsir al-Qummi*.

Al-Qummi, Shaykh ʿAbbas. *Selections from Mafatih Al-Jinan: Duʿaas and Ziyarahs*. Era of Appearance Foundation, 2008.

Al-Radi, Muhammad ibn al-Husayn. *Nahj Al-Balaghah*.

Al-Rayshahri, Muhammad. *Mizan al-Hikmah*.

Al-Razi, Abu al-Futuh. *Tafsir rawh al-Jinan wa Ruh al-Janan*.

Al-Razi, Fakhr al-Din. *Al-Tafsir al-Kabir*.

Al-Sabzawari Sayyid Abdula'la. *Sharh al-Asmaa'*. Al-Balagh, 2006

Al-Saduq, Muhammad ibn Ali. *Al-Amali*.

Al-Saduq, Muhammad ibn Ali. *Kamal al-Din*. Beirut: al-A'lami, 1991 CE.

Al-Saduq, Muhammad ibn Ali. *Man La Yahdaruh al-Faqih*.

Al-Saduq, Muhammad ibn Ali. *Sifat al-Shi'a*.

Al-Saduq, Muhammad ibn Ali. *'Uyun Akhbar al-Rida*.

Al-Saffar, Muhammad ibn al-Hasan. *Basa'ir al-Darajat*.

Al-Sanad, Ayatollah Shaykh Muhammad. *Imam al-Mahdi Fil Quran al-Karim*. The Holy City of
        Najaf, n.d.

Al-Shafi'i, Muhammad ibn Idriss. *Diwan Al-Shafi'i*. Damascus: Dar al-Qalam, 1999 CE.

Al-Shaybani, Ahmad ibn Hanbal. *Fada'il al-Sahabah*. Dar al-'Ilm, 1983 C.

Al-Shaybani, Ahmad ibn Hanbal. *Musnad Ahmad*.

Al-Sistani, Grand Ayatollah Sayyid Ali. "Advice from His Eminence Sayyid Ali al-Sistani to the
        Believing Youth." Sistani.org. Accessed February 23, 2021. https://www.sis-
        tani.org/english/archive/25240/.

Al-Sistani, Grand Ayatollah Sayyid Ali. *A Code of Practice for Muslims in the West*. 2017.

Al-Subhani, Ayatollah Ja'far. *Al-Ilahiyyat*. Beirut: Dar al-Islamiyyah (3rd ed).

Al-Tabari, Muhammad ibn Ayyub. *Tuhfat al-Ghara'ib*.

Al-Tabari, Muhammad ibn Jarir. *Dala'il al-Imamah*. Beirut: al-A'lami, 1988.

Al-Tabari, Muhammad ibn Jarir. *Tafsir al-Tabari*.

Al-Tabarsi, Ahmad ibn Ali. *Al-Ihtijaj*. Mashhad: Nashr al-Murtaza.

Al-Tabrisi, Ali. *Mishkat al-Anwar*.

Al-Thahabi, Muhammad ibn Ahmad. *Tathkirat al-Huffaz*. Dar al-Ma'arif, 1374 AH.

Altieri, Christopher. "Pope Francis Releases Encyclical Letter Fratelli Tutti." *Catholic Herald*. De-
        cember 2, 2020. https://catholicherald.co.uk/pope-francis-releases-encyclical-letter-
        fratelli-tutti/.

Al-Tusi, Muhammad ibn al-Hasan. *Al-Amali*.

Al-Ya'qubi, Ahmad ibn Ishaq. *Tarikh al-Ya'qubi*.

An-Na'im, 'Abdullahi Ahmed. *What Is an American Muslim? Embracing Faith and Citizenship*.
        New York: Oxford University Press, 2014.

Arastu, Rizwan. *God's Emissaries*. Imam Mahdi Association of Marjaeya, 2014.

Armstrong, Karen. *Islam: A Short History*. Random House Publishing Group, 2007.

Ayoub, Mahmoud. *Redemptive Suffering in Islam: A Study of the Devotional Aspects of Twelver
        Shi'ism*. The Hague: Mouton, 1978.

Bahr al-'Ulum, Muhammad Sadiq. *Al-Imam al-Sistani*. Beirut: Daar al-Mahajjah al-Bayda', 2009.

Bahr al-'Ulum, Muhammad Sadiq. *Al-Najaf al-Ashraf Bayn al-Marji'iyyah wa'l-Siyasah*. Beirut:
        Dar al-Zahra', 2009.

Basu, Moni. "After 9/11, turbans made Sikhs targets." *CNN.com*. 15 September 2016, http://www.cnn.com/2016/09/15/us/sikh-hate-crime-victims/.

Bethune, Brian. "Pope Francis: How the first New World pontiff could save the church." *Maclean's*. 26 March 2013. Retrieved 22 February 2021.

Bocquet-Appel, Jean-Pierre. "When the World's Population Took Off: The Springboard of the Neolithic Demographic Transition". *Science* 333 (6042). July 29, 2011.

Brady, Ignatius Charles and Lawrence Cunningham. "St. Francis of Assisi". *Encyclopædia Britannica*. 29 September 2020. Retrieved 21 February 2021.

Brockhaus, Hannah. "Pope Francis Lends Support to Committee on Abu Dhabi Declaration." *Catholic News Agency*. May 14, 2020. https://www.catholicnewsagency.com/news/pope-francis-lends-support-to-committee-on-abu-dhabi-declaration-20817.

Bruni, Matteo. "Declaration of the Director of the Holy See Press Office, Matteo Bruni." Declaration of the Director of the Holy See Press Office, Matteo Bruni (Holy See Press Office, July 12, 2020). https://press.vatican.va/.

Cacioppo, J. T. and W. Patrick. *Loneliness: Human nature and the need for social connection*. W W Norton & Co, 2008.

Campo, Juan E. *Encyclopedia of Islam* (Encyclopedia of World Religions). New York: Facts on File, 2009.

Chamseddine, Muhammad Mahdi. *Hussain's Revolution*. The Mainstay Foundation, 2016.

Chittick, William C. *Sufism: A Short Introduction*. Lahore: Suhail Academy, 2005.

Covey, Stephen R. *The 7 Habits of Highly Effective People*. Provo, UT: Franklin Covey, 1998.

Crawford, Harriet E. W. *Sumer and the Sumerians*. Cambridge University Press, 2004 (2nd ed.).;

Donaldson, Dwight M. *The Shi'ite Religion: A History of Islam in Persia and Irak*. Burleigh Press, 1933.

Du Bois, W. E. B. *The Souls of Black Folk*. Chicago: A. C. McClurg & Co., 1903.

Guizot, Francois. *The History of Civilization in Europe*. William Hazlitt (translator). Indiana: Liberty Fund, 1997.

Ibn Abu 'Asim, Ahmad ibn 'Amr. *Kitab al-Sunnah*.

Ibn al-Jawzi, Abdul Rahman. *Al-Mawdu'at*.

Ibn al-Mashhadi, Muhammad ibn Ja'far. *Al-Mazar*.

Ibn Ishaq, Muhammad. *Sirat Rasul Allah*. Guillaume, A. (translator). Oxford University Press, 1955.

Ibn Kathir, Ishmael ibn 'Amr. *Al-Bidayah wa'l-Nihayah*.

Ibn Sa'd, Muhammad. *Kitab al-Tabaqat al-Kabir*. Bewley, A. (translator). London: Ta-Ha Publishers, 2013.

Ibn Tawus, Ali ibn Musa. *Misbah al-Za'ir*.

Ibn Taymiyyah, Ahmad ibn Abdulhalim. *Minhaj al-Sunnah*.

Imam Ali al-Sajjad. The Treatise on Rights.

Jestice, Phyllis G. *Holy People of the World: A Cross-cultural Encyclopedia.*

John L. Esposito, ed. "Mosque." *The Oxford Dictionary of Islam.* Oxford University Press, 2014.

Kohlberg, Etan. *"Some Imami-Shiʿi Views on Taqiyya."* Journal of the American Oriental Society 95(3), 1975.

Lebling, Robert. *Legends of the Fire Spirits: Jinn and Genies from Arabia to Zanzibar.* I.B.Tauris. 30 July 2010.

Mavani, Hamid. "Religious Authority and Political Thought in Twelver Shiʿism: From Ali to Post-Khomeini." *Routledge Studies in Political Islam.* Abingdon: Routledge, 2013.

Oliver, Mark. "Shiʿa shrine blasts spark reprisal attacks". *The Guardian.* February 23, 2006. Retrieved April 22, 2010.

Razwy, Sayyid Ali Asghar. *A Restatement of the History of Islam & Muslims.* United Kingdom: World Federation of K. S. I. Muslim Communities, 2017.

Razwy, Sayyid Ali Asghar. *A Restatement of the History of Islam & Muslims.* United Kingdom: World Federation of K. S. I. Muslim Communities, 2017.

Rizvi, Sayyid Muhammad. *Khums: an Islamic Tax.* Qum: Ansariyan Publications, 1992.

Rizvi, Sayyid Muhammad. *Khums: an Islamic Tax.* Qum: Ansariyan Publications, 1992.

Rizvi, Sayyid Saʿeed Akhtar. *Muhammad is the Last Prophet.* Bilal Muslim Mission of Tanzania, 2015.

Rubin, Sergio and Francesca Ambrogetti. *Pope Francis – Conversations with Jorge Bergoglio.* Berkley, 2014.

Salloum, Saʿad. *Al--Masihiyun fi'l-Iraq al-Tarikh al-Shamil wa'l-Tahaddiyat al-Rahinah* (Arabic: The Christians of Iraq: A Comprehensive History and the Challenges of Today). *Masarat lil-Tanmiya al-Thaqafiya w al-ʿIlamiya.*

Sayyid, Kamāl and Jasim Alyawy. *Malik al-Ashtar.* Qum: Ansariyan Foundation, 1996.

Shah-Kazemi, Reza. "Light upon Light? The Qurʾan and the Gospel of John." *Interreligious Hermeneutics, Interreligious Dialogue Series vol. 2.* Eugene: Wipf & Stock Publishers, 2010.

Shomali, Mohammad Ali. "Imamate and Wilayah, Pt. IV." Message of Thaqalayn, vol. 13, no. 1. London, 2004.

Speciale, Alessandro. "Pope washes feet of two girls, two Muslims at youth prison." *The Washington Post (On Faith).* 29 March 2013. Retrieved 23 February 2021.

Stapleton, Henry E., R.F. Azo, and Hidayat Husayn. "Chemistry in Iraq and Persia in the Tenth Century AD." *Memoirs of the Asiatic Society of Bengal,* 1927.

Steigerwald, Diana (2008), "Twelver Shīʿī Taʾwīl." *The Blackwell Companion to the Qurʾān, Blackwell Companions to Religion.* Oxford: Blackwell Publishing, 2008.

Tabatabaʾi, Sayyid Mohammad Husayn. A Shiʿite Anthology. William C. Chittick (translator). SUNY press, 1981.

Tabataba'i, Sayyid Mohammad Husayn. *Shi'ite Islam*. Seyyed Hossein Nasr (translator). SUNY press, 1977.

Tabataba'i, Sayyid Muhammad Husayn. *Tafsir al-Mizan*.

Taylor, John B. "Ja'far al-Sādiq, Spiritual Forebear of the Sufis." *Islamic Culture* 40/2, April 1966.

Uebbing, David. "Pope Francis' personality begins to change routines". *Catholic News Agency*. Retrieved 24 February 2021.

Vaglieri, Laura Veccia. "Ghadīr Khumm". *Encyclopedia of Islam*. Brill Online, 2012 (2nd ed).

Watkins, Devin. "Pope Francis to Visit Iraq, First Apostolic Journey in 15 Months." *Vatican News*. December 7, 2020. https://www.vaticannews.va/en/pope/news/2020-12/pope-francis-apostolic-journey-iraq-march-2021.html.

Ysuf, Imtiyaz. "Laylat al-Qadr." *The Oxford Encyclopedia of the Islamic World*.

"Chaldean prelate invites pope to visit Iraq." *catholicculture.org*. 22 March 2013. Retrieved 19 February 2021.

"Pope Francis wants 'poor Church for the poor'". *BBC News*. 16 March 2013. Retrieved 16 March 2013.

"Biography of the Grand Ayatollah." *The Official Website of the Office of His Eminence Al-Sayyid Ali Al-Husseini Al-Sistani*. Accessed February 26, 2021. https://www.sistani.org/english/data/2/.

"Pope's visit to Iraq will send message of coexistence, says Iraqi president." *The Middle East Eye*. https://www.middleeasteye.net/news/iraq-pope-francis-visit-message-coexistence-president

"Statement of the Office of His Eminence regarding Muslim Unity and Rejection of Sectarianism", *The Official Website of the Office of His Eminence Al-Sayyid Ali Al-Husseini Al-Sistani*. https://www.sistani.org/arabic/statement/1504/

"The Grand Ayatollah." YouTube. "Ahlulbayt: Documentaries." Directed by Amir Taki, 2016. https://www.youtube.com/watch?v=qbzBJIWNorc&t=2569s.

"The Official Website of the Office of His Eminence Al-Sayyid Ali Al-Husseini Al-Sistani," Advice and Guidance to the Fighters on the Battlefields - Archive, accessed February 26, 2021, https://www.sistani.org/english/archive/25036/.

.

Printed in Great Britain
by Amazon